Contemporary American Fiction

ONE WEEK LOAN

Edinburgh Critical Guides to Literature
Series Editors: Martin Halliwell, University of Leicester and Andy
Mousley, De Montfort University

Published Titles:
Gothic Literature, Andrew Smith
Canadian Literature, Faye Hammill
Women's Poetry, Jo Gill
Contemporary American Drama, Annette J. Saddik
Shakespeare, Gabriel Egan
Asian American Literature, Bella Adams
Children's Literature, M. O. Grenby
Contemporary British Fiction, Nick Bentley
Renaissance Literature, Siobhan Keenan
Scottish Literature, Gerard Carruthers
Contemporary American Fiction, David Brauner

Forthcoming Titles in the Series:
Restoration and Eighteenth-Century Literature, Hamish Mathison
Victorian Literature, David Amigoni
Crime Fiction, Stacy Gillis
Modern American Literature, Catherine Morley
Modernist Literature, Rachel Potter
Medieval Literature, Pamela King
African American Literature, Jennifer Terry
Contemporary British Drama, David Lane
Contemporary Poetry, Nerys Williams
Postcolonial Literature, Dave Gunning

Contemporary American Fiction

David Brauner

Edinburgh University Press

This book is dedicated to Henry Tang, who first got me reading
contemporary American fiction

© David Brauner, 2010

Edinburgh University Press Ltd
22 George Square, Edinburgh

www.euppublishing.com

Typeset in 11.5/13 Monotype Ehrhardt
by Servis Filmsetting Ltd, Stockport, Cheshire and
printed and bound in Great Britain by
CPI Antony Rowe, Chippenham and Eastbourne

A CIP record for this book is available from the British Library

ISBN 978 0 7486 2267 2 (hardback)
ISBN 978 0 7486 2268 9 (paperback)

Contents

Series Preface

The study of English literature in the early twenty-first century is host to an exhilarating range of critical approaches, theories and historical perspectives. 'English' ranges from traditional modes of study such as Shakespeare and Romanticism to popular interest in national and area literatures such as the United States, Ireland and the Caribbean. The subject also spans a diverse array of genres from tragedy to cyberpunk, incorporates such hybrid fields of study as Asian American literature, Black British literature, creative writing and literary adaptations, and remains eclectic in its methodology.

Such diversity is cause for both celebration and consternation. English is varied enough to promise enrichment and enjoyment for all kinds of readers and to challenge preconceptions about what the study of literature might involve. But how are readers to navigate their way through such literary and cultural diversity? And how are students to make sense of the various literary categories and periodisations, such as modernism and the Renaissance, or the proliferating theories of literature, from feminism and marxism to queer theory and eco-criticism? The Edinburgh Critical Guides to Literature series reflects the challenges and pluralities of English today, but at the same time it offers readers clear and accessible routes through the texts, contexts, genres, historical periods and debates within the subject.

Martin Halliwell and Andy Mousley

Acknowledgements

I am grateful to the editors of this series, particularly Professor Martin Halliwell, for commissioning me to write this volume in the first place and for their scrupulous and sensitive scrutiny of the manuscript. I have also greatly appreciated the care and efficiency with which Eliza Wright and Jackie Jones at Edinburgh University Press have handled the publication process. Heartfelt thanks go to the friends and colleagues with whom I have shared countless stimulating discussions over the years that have contributed indirectly to the writing of this book: Bryan Cheyette, Martin Halliwell (again), Alison Kelly, Christine MacLeod, Catherine Morley, Derek Parker Royal, Debra Shostak and Aliki Varvogli. I also owe a debt to the students who have taken my 'Contemporary American Fiction' and 'Fiction and Ethnicity' modules at the University of Reading, whose stimulating discussion of and questions about some of the texts included in this study have fed into my work. Finally, I was greatly aided in the completion of this book by an RETF award from the University of Reading that gave me a term's leave, by the careful copy-editing of Ruth Willats, and, above all, by the intellectual and moral support of my wife, Anne Button. I am wholly responsible for any weaknesses in this book, but I must share credit for its strengths with her.

The author gratefully acknowledges permission to reproduce in altered form portions of '"Speak Again": The Politics of Rewriting in Jane Smiley's *A Thousand Acres*', published in *Modern Language Review* 96 (2001), pp. 654–66.

Chronology

Date	Historical Events	Significant Publications in American fiction
1980	Ronald Reagan elected President; John Lennon assassinated by Mark Chapman in New York.	Marilynne Robinson, *Housekeeping;* Jane Smiley, *Barn Blind*; Carol Shields, *Happenstance*; John Kennedy Toole, *A Confederacy of Dunces.*
1981	John Hinckley attempts to assassinate Ronald Reagan; first cases of AIDS diagnosed; first space shuttle, *Columbia*, launched.	David Bradley, *The Chaneysville Incident*; Raymond Carver, *What We Talk About When We Talk About Love*; Philip Roth, *Zuckerman Unbound*; John Updike, *Rabbit is Rich.*
1982	Vietnam Veterans Memorial opens in Washington, DC.	Don DeLillo, *The Names*; Charles Johnson, *Oxherding Tale*; Bernard Malamud, *God's Grace*; Gloria Naylor, *The Women of Brewster Place*; Alice Walker, *The Color Purple.*

Date	Historical Events	Significant Publications in American fiction
1983	Ronald Reagan announces 'Star Wars' missile defence system; US invades Grenada.	Kathy Acker, *Great Expectations*; Joan Didion, *Salvador*; Rebecca Goldstein, *The Mind–Body Problem*; William Kennedy, *Ironweed*; Philip Roth, *The Anatomy Lesson.*
1984	Ronald Reagan re-elected in record Republican landslide.	Saul Bellow, *Him With His Foot in His Mouth and Other Stories*; Sandra Cisneros, *The House on Mango Street*; Louise Erdrich, *Love Medicine*; William Gibson, *Neuromancer*; Joseph Heller, *God Knows*; Jay McInerney, *Bright Lights, Big City*; John Updike, *The Witches of Eastwick.*
1985	World Wide Web launched; Microsoft Windows launched; Live Aid concert in Philadelphia.	Paul Auster, *City of Glass*; Cormac McCarthy, *Blood Meridian*; Don DeLillo, *White Noise*; E. L. Doctorow, *World's Fair*; Bret Easton Ellis, *Less Than Zero*; Mary Gordon, *Men and Angels*; Bobbie Ann Mason, *In Country*; Richard Powers, *Three Farmers on Their Way to a Dance*; Anne Tyler, *The Accidental Tourist*; Helena Maria Viramontes, *The Moths, and Other Stories.*

Date	Historical Events	Significant Publications in American fiction
1986	*Challenger* space shuttle explodes.	Richard Ford, *The Sportswriter*; Tama Janowitz, *Slaves of New York*; David Leavitt, *The Lost Language of Cranes*; Philip Roth, *The Counterlife*; Art Spiegelman, *Maus*.
1987	'Black Monday' stock market crash; Tower Commission Report published on Iran–Contra scandal.	Paul Auster, *The New York Trilogy*; Stephen King, *Misery*; Toni Morrison, *Beloved*; Cynthia Ozick, *The Messiah of Stockholm*; Carol Shields, *Swann*; Tom Wolfe, *The Bonfire of the Vanities*.
1988	George H. W. Bush elected President; Pan Am flight from London to New York explodes over Scottish town of Lockerbie.	Dorothy Allison, *Trash*; Nicholson Baker, *The Mezzanine*; Raymond Carver, *Where I'm Calling From*; Don DeLillo, *Libra*; Alison Lurie, *The Truth About Lorin Jones*; Bharati Mukherjee, *The Middleman and Other Stories*; Anne Tyler, *Breathing Lessons*.
1989	*Exxon Valdez* oil tanker runs aground in Alaska, spilling 240,000 gallons of oil.	Saul Bellow, *The Bellarosa Connection*; Maxine Hong Kingston, *Tripmaster Monkey: His Fake Book*; Bharati Mukherjee, *Jasmine*; Joyce Carol Oates, *American Appetites*; Cynthia Ozick, *The Shawl*; Amy Tan, *The Joy Luck Club*; Tobias Wolff, *This Boy's Life*.

Date	Historical Events	Significant Publications in American fiction
1990	First Gulf War begins after Iraq invades Kuwait; Senate votes narrowly in favour of appointing Clarence Thomas to Supreme Court after allegations of sexual impropriety from his former employee, Anita Hill, leave the Judiciary Committee split on whether to approve his nomination.	Charles Johnson, *Middle Passage*; Joyce Carol Oates, *Because it is Bitter, and Because it is My Heart*; Tim O'Brien, *The Things They Carried*; Philip Roth, *Deception*; Thomas Pynchon, *Vineland*; John Updike, *Rabbit at Rest*.
1991	Gulf War ends; Iraqi forces defeated; Oakland, CA firestorm kills twenty-five people.	Douglas Coupland, *Generation X*; Don DeLillo, *Mao II*; Bret Easton Ellis, *American Psycho*; Gish Jen, *Typical American*; Norman Mailer, *Harlot's Ghost*; Emily Prager, *Eve's Tattoo*; Richard Powers, *The Gold Bug Variations*; Anne Tyler, *Saint Maybe*.
1992	Bill Clinton elected President; riots in Los Angeles following the acquittal of four LAPD policemen who had been caught on film beating Rodney King, an African-American man.	Cormac McCarthy, *All the Pretty Horses*; Tama Janowitz, *The Male Cross-Dresser Support Group*; Denis Johnson, *Jesus' Son*; Jay McInerney, *Brightness Falls*; Toni Morrison, *Jazz*; Gloria Naylor, *Bailey's Cafe*; Donna Tart, *The Secret History*.

Date	Historical Events	Significant Publications in American fiction
1994	Inception of North American Free Trade Agreement.	Scott Bradfield, *What's Wrong With America*; Bernard Malamud, *Complete Stories*; Rick Moody, *The Ice Storm*; Lorrie Moore, *Who Will Run the Frog Hospital?*; Grace Paley, *Collected Stories*.
1995	Oklahoma City bombing kills 168 people; O. J. Simpson trial – Simpson acquitted of the murders of his ex-wife, Nicole Simpson, and her friend, Ronald Goldman.	Po Bronson, *Bombadiers*; Michael Chabon, *Wonder Boys*; Richard Ford, *Independence Day*; Rebecca Goldstein, *Mazel*; Chang-rae Lee, *Native Speaker*; Richard Powers, *Galatea 2.2*; Philip Roth, *Sabbath's Theater*.
1996	Bill Clinton re-elected President; TWA flight from New York to Rome explodes near Long Island, killing 230 people.	Gish Jen, *Mona in the Promised Land*; Jane Hamilton, *A Map of the World*; Steven Millhauser, *Martin Dressler: The Tale of an American Dreamer*; Joyce Carol Oates, *We Were the Mulvaneys*; Chuck Palahniuk, *Fight Club*; Annie Proulx, *Accordion Crimes*; David Foster Wallace, *Infinite Jest*.
1997	Civil court orders O. J. Simpson to pay $33.5 million in damages to relatives of Nicole Simpson and Ronald Goldman.	Don DeLillo, *Underworld*; Deborah Eisenberg, *The Work (So Far) of Deborah Eisenberg*; Charles Frazier, *Cold Mountain*; David Mamet, *The Old Religion*; Cynthia Ozick, *The Puttermesser Papers*; Thomas Pynchon, *Mason and*

Date	Historical Events	Significant Publications in American fiction
		Dixon; Philip Roth, *American Pastoral*; Carol Shields, *Larry's Party*.
1998	US embassy bombings in Tanzania and Kenya kill 224 people.	Michael Cunnigham, *The Hours*; Barbara Kingsolver, *The Poisonwood Bible*; Cormac McCarthy, *Cities of the Plain*; Toni Morrison, *Paradise*; Danzy Senna, *From Caucasia with Love*; John Edgar Wideman, *Two Cities*; Tom Wolfe, *A Man in Full*.
1999	Unsuccessful attempt to impeach Clinton; Columbine Masssacre – two students embark on a shooting spree at Columbine High School, Colorado, killing fifteen people, including themselves.	Allegra Goodman, *Kaaterskill Falls*; Jhumpa Lahiri, *Interpreter of Maladies*; Annie Proulx, *Close Range*; Jane Smiley, *The All-True Travels and Adventures of Lidie Newton*.
2000	George W. Bush elected President in controversial circumstances, the outcome hinging on a small number of votes in Florida.	Michael Chabon, *The Amazing Adventures of Kavalier and Clay*; Mark Danielewski, *House of Leaves*; Andre Dubus, *House of Sand and Fog*; Dave Eggers, *A Heartbreaking Work of Staggering Genius*; Jonathan Lethem, *Motherless Brooklyn*; Philip Roth, *The Human Stain*; Colson Whitehead, *The Intuitionist*.

Date	Historical Events	Significant Publications in American fiction
2001	9/11 – terrorist attacks on the World Trade Center and Pentagon; the twin towers are destroyed, with the loss of 2,752 people; US forces invade Afghanistan; National Book Festival established by Laura Bush.	Percival Everett, *Erasure*; Don DeLillo, *The Body Artist*; Jonathan Franzen, *The Corrections*.
2002	Department of Homeland Security created; 'Washington sniper' murders: John Allen Muhammad and his accomplice, Lee Boyd Malvo, shoot ten people in the Washington, DC area.	Paul Auster, *The Book of Illusions*; Jeffrey Eugenides, *Middlesex*; Jonathan Safran Foer, *Everything is Illuminated*; Carol Shields, *Unless*.
2003	US forces invade Iraq; *Columbia* space shuttle disintegrates on re-entry into earth's atmosphere.	Siri Hustvedt, *What I Loved*; Edward P. Jones, *The Known World*; Richard Powers, *The Time of Our Singing*.
2004	George W. Bush re-elected President.	Gish Jen, *The Love Wife*; Marilynne Robinson, *Gilead*; Philip Roth, *The Plot Against America*.
2005	'Hurricane Katrina' devastates New Orleans, killing 1,836 people.	Michael Cunningham, *Specimen Days*; Bret Easton Ellis, *Lunar Park*; Jonathan Safran Foer, *Incredibly Loud and Extremely Close*; Nicole Krauss, *The History of Love*; Benjamin Kunkel, *Indecision*.

Date	Historical Events	Significant Publications in American fiction
2006	Capitol Hill Massacre – a gunman kills seven people, including himself, at a party in Seattle; Saddam Hussein sentenced to death and executed by Iraqi court.	Dave Eggers, *What is the What*; Deborah Eisenberg, *Twilight of the Superheroes*; Amy Hempel, *The Collected Stories*; Richard Powers, *The Echo Maker*; Philip Roth, *Everyman*; John Updike, *Terrorist*.
2007	Virginia Tech Massacre – a student embarks on shooting spree at Virginia Polytechnic Institute and State University, killing thirty-three people, including himself.	Michael Chabon, *The Yiddish Policemen's Union*; Don DeLillo, *Falling Man*; Allegra Goodman, *Intuition*; Denis Johnson, *Tree of Smoke*; Philip Roth, *Exit Ghost*; Jane Smiley, *Ten Days in the Hills*.
2008	Barack Obama is elected President; stock market crashes, precipitating global financial crisis and subsequent recession.	Jhumpa Lahiri, *Unaccustomed Earth*; Steven Millhauser, *Dangerous Laughter: Thirteen Stories*; Lorrie Moore, *The Collected Stories*; Toni Morrison, *A Mercy*; Marilynne Robinson, *Home*.

Introduction

At first sight, the title of this book may seem self-explanatory, but in fact all three key terms – 'contemporary', 'American' and 'fiction' – have been keenly contested in academic discourse of the final decade of the twentieth and the first decade of the twenty-first centuries. It seems sensible, then, to begin by clarifying the parameters within which I deploy them in the context of this study, before going on to provide a brief description of the way in which the book is organised and what it sets out to achieve.

CONTEMPORARY

The word contemporary describes something that is in a sense logically impossible, since, in the time it takes to describe, define or otherwise fix that which is current, it has already been superseded. Put another way, 'contemporary' signifies both a period of history and that which has not yet been historicised. Understood pragmatically, as opposed to literally, 'contemporary' is often used as a synonym for 'modern'. In academic discourse, however, because of the proliferation of terms connected with 'modern', such as 'modernism' and 'postmodernism', 'modernity' and 'postmodernity', each with its own set of ideological and historical associations, 'contemporary' can be a useful, if necessarily vague, way of referring to material produced in the recent past without becoming implicated in abstruse debates about whether we are now in a modern, post-modern or indeed post-postmodern era. Having said that, the term 'contemporary' has itself been subjected to critical scrutiny as part of a more general project to re-evaluate the concepts of 'periodisa-tion' and 'temporality', with some theorists counter-intuitively constructing what they call a 'post-contemporary' discursive space, exemplified by the titles published in the Duke University Press 'Post-Contemporary Interventions' series.[1]

Related to, but in a sense also separate from, these semantic and philosophical considerations are two practical questions that always attend criticism of contemporary literature. How recent does the literature have to be to qualify as contemporary? And how do you keep your work up to date when new developments are taking place even as you write? For the purposes of this book, I have extended the term far enough back to include fiction pub-lished in the mid-1980s and as far forward as 2005.[2] My hope in confining myself to this twenty-year span is to expose readers to a reasonable chronological range, ensuring that the *Zeitgeist* of the earliest work is not too remote from that of the present (whilst at the same time not wishing to understate the changes that have taken place) and also that sufficient time has elapsed between the publication of the most recent work and my own consideration of it to allow a retrospective consideration of its significance.

In adopting this strategy I have deliberately rejected a tempt-ing and perhaps more obvious scheme: namely, to consider only fiction published after 9/11. It has now become a critical com-monplace that the events of that day precipitated a paradigm shift in American consciousness and culture. Yet the very abbreviation by which the terrorist attacks on the World Trade Center and Pentagon has come to be known (with the month preceding the day, inverting the order in which much of the rest of the world refers to dates) exposes the limitations of this alleged shift in the American worldview. In fact, while 9/11 was certainly a water-shed event for the United States and indeed for the rest of the world, whether it has encouraged the US to engage more with the outside world or to conceive of itself in a more global context is highly debatable. Although American foreign policy has become more interventionist, leading to the prolonged deployment of large numbers of troops in Iraq and Afghanistan, the main consequence of 9/11 for domestic policy has been the creation of the Homeland Security Agency, which has made it more difficult for many foreign nationals to enter the US and, as its name suggests, turned the focus very much on the idea of America as a discrete entity. Moreover, the emergence, during the 2008 presidential campaign, of the fact that the Republican vice-presidential candidate, Sarah Palin, had only recently acquired a passport and had never travelled abroad was a timely reminder of the continuing insularity and parochialism of much of Middle America. Policy statements made by Barack Obama during his electoral campaign and the early months of his presidency suggest that the US may well be entering a new period of engagement with global politics, but it is too early to say if or how this will affect the considerable constituency to which Palin appealed.

In terms of contemporary American fiction too, it seems that there is much more continuity than disjunction between the work published in the years immediately preceding and succeeding 9/11. There have been relatively few American fictions engaging explicitly with 9/11, and of those that have done so, most have concentrated on the American experience. Those novels, such as John Updike's *Terrorist* (2006) and Don DeLillo's *Falling Man* (2007), that have attempted to inhabit the minds of the perpetrators of terrorism have received harsh criticism for the alleged shortcomings of their portrayals. More generally, I can see little evidence of a radical shift in the kind of fiction that most American authors are producing in the post-9/11 period, so that taking 9/11 as the starting point of a new contemporary or post-contemporary era seems at best premature, at worst a kind of literary-critical opportunism.

AMERICAN

In general usage, the meaning of 'American' is straightforward – it is an adjective describing something pertaining to a particular nation: the United States. What constitutes American literature, however, has become a vexed question on a number levels. There is profound disagreement among scholars about the historical, geographical, linguistic and ethnic parameters within which American literature should be situated. Should the canon begin with pre-colonial Native American oral narratives and songs, with the first colonial writing or with the Declaration of Independence? Should the work of expatriate authors who become citizens of other countries, such as T. S. Eliot, the American-born modernist poet who became a pillar of the English establishment, be included? What about writers who are born abroad but settle in the US? Does it matter if they become naturalised citizens, such as the Indian-born American author Bharati Mukherjee, or simply remain residents, such as the New York-based Australian novelist Peter Carey? Does it make any difference if, like the Nobel Prize-winning author of Yiddish fiction, Isaac Bashevis Singer, they continue to write in their native language, or if, like Vladimir Nabokov, who began his career publishing in his mother tongue of Russian but later wrote in English, they adopt the official language of the US? And what implications does the fact that over 12 per cent of Americans now speak Spanish as their first language have for the notion that American literature is Anglophone?

In the last thirty years or so there has been much heated debate about these and other issues. In particular, the traditional domination of the American canon by Caucasian men has been challenged by two complementary, yet also contradictory, movements: multiculturalism and globalisation. As David Hollinger has pointed out, the first of these has been spectacularly successful in establishing a consensus that 'the United States ought to sustain rather than diminish a great variety of distinctive cultures carried by ethno-racial groups'.[3] What Hollinger calls the 'sheer triumph' of this 'doctrine' is most visible in the increased representation on college courses and in popular textbooks, reference works and anthologies, of African-American, Asian-American, Latin-American and Native American authors, many of them women.[4] This increased recognition of ethnic diversity within American literature has resulted in the old monolithic model of a unified national literature being displaced by a more pluralistic one in which the macro-narrative of American literary history is fragmented into a series of micro-narratives. At the same time, however, there has been a concerted effort to push the boundaries of American literary identity outwards to incorporate it into a larger, transnational conception of literary history. Just as multiculturalism challenged the hegemony of Dead White European Males (DWEMS), so a key objective of many advocates of transnationalism has been to overturn the ideas of American exceptionalism and Manifest Destiny. In this respect the projects are compatible, with both rejecting parochialism in favour of a cosmopolitan view of American culture. Indeed, as Hollinger suggests, 'particularization is sometimes actually facilitated by the strategies of globalization' (2005, p. 146). On the other hand, from Paul Gilroy's seminal repositioning of African-American culture in the transnational context of a 'black Atlantic' to Paul Giles' recasting of the American canon as the product of a 'transatlantic imaginary', to John Muthyala's advocacy of a 'transgeographical perspective from which to study the literary and cultural histories of the Americas', transnationalist criticism in practice has tended to neglect or understate the particularity of different American literatures, preferring to absorb them into new transatlantic, global and post-national grand narratives.[5]

These studies, and many others, have certainly helped to counter what was once a prevailing insularity in American Studies, but, if anything, the pendulum has now swung the other way. 'Transatlantic Studies', as it is now known, is the new orthodoxy, as is evidenced not just by the proliferation of individual studies to adopt this approach but also by the establishment of academic journals such as the *Journal for Transatlantic Studies* (2002), which treats 'the transatlantic region as an area with a distinct character and a rich history', and *Comparative American Studies* (2003), whose mission is to 'reposition discussions about American culture within an international, comparative framework' as a response to 'this time of increasing globalization'.[6] There are now Masters degrees in Transatlantic Studies, book series such as Edinburgh University Press's 'Studies in Transatlantic Literatures' and Routledge's 'Transnational Perspectives on American Literature', and even an entry in HarperCollins' *Encyclopedia of American Literature*, posted on a site sponsored by the US government, on the 'Globalization of American Literature'.[7]

In some respects, this enthusiasm for contextualising American literature in international and global terms can be seen as part of a trend in English Studies – an American version of postcolonialism in which, as the title of Judie Newman's book puts it, *Fictions of America* are read as *Narratives of Global Empire*,[8] or indeed as part of a larger cultural and political movement in which the map of America is both literally and figuratively redrawn, so that, in Hollinger's words, the 'prophets of "postnationality" explain that the boundary between the United States and Mexico is an imperialist fiction' (2005, p. 2). Whatever the relative virtues of this vision of 'postnationality' and of the 'transnational', 'transatlantic' and 'global' versions of American identity, the fact remains that there is in contemporary American fiction a conspicuous and tenacious preoccupation with national identity, not least in the fiction written by the very authors most often appropriated by the architects of transnational and global superstructures.[9]

While there is certainly an international reach to some recent American fiction, in terms of themes and settings it would be misleading to suggest that contemporary American fiction in general is now predominantly transnational rather than national. On the contrary, one of the things that continues to distinguish American fiction from, say, British fiction is its explicit investment in, and analysis of, national identity. The number of novels by the writers featured in this study that include in their titles some form of the word 'America' is instructive: Don DeLillo's first novel was *Americana* (1971), Gish Jen's *Typical American* (1991); *American Pastoral* (1997) was the first of Philip Roth's so-called 'American Trilogy' and, long before that, he had the *chutzpah* to publish a book called *The Great American Novel* (1973); and then, of course, there is Bret Easton Ellis's *American Psycho* (1991), which I discuss in Chapter 1. There are several others that cite specific American locales – for example, Paul Auster's *New York Trilogy* (1987) and *Brooklyn Follies* (2005) and Annie Proulx's three volumes of 'Wyoming Stories', *Close Range* (1998), *Bad Dirt* (2005) and *Fine Just the Way It Is* (2008). Finally, several of the texts that I discuss invoke the semi-mythical status of the American landscape: Jane Smiley's *A Thousand Acres*, Gish Jen's *Mona in the Promised Land*, Charles Frazier's *Cold Mountain*, Annie Proulx's 'Brokeback Mountain' and Cormac McCarthy's *No Country for Old Men*.

The emergence over the past three decades of Native American, Latin-American and Asian-American authors, and the persistent prominence of African-American and Jewish-American authors, has certainly produced an unprecedented diversity in contemporary American fiction. Diversity does not necessarily mean transnationality, however. Nomenclature is in this sense revealing: the labels used to identify these various identities are all hyphenated, suggesting that in each case the author's background becomes incorporated into a hybridised form of Americanness, rather than displacing or effacing it. Writers such as Sherman Alexie, Sandra Cisneros and Bharati Mukherjee are arguably just as interested in defining Americanness as were Nathaniel Hawthorne, Herman Melville and Mark Twain. Three decades after Roth parodied it, the quest to write the great *American* novel – a book that would attain the status of a national epic – is alive and well, as Catherine Morley's *The Quest for Epic in Contemporary American Fiction* (2009) eloquently demonstrates. For the purposes of this book, I have chosen to interpret 'American' flexibly enough to accommodate Carol Shields, a writer who spent her formative years in America but later relocated to Canada and became a Canadian citizen, as well as Auster and Roth, who spent some years living in Europe, and Gish Jen, a second-generation Chinese-American.

FICTION

In common usage, fiction is defined negatively as that which is not factual. In the literary context, it is often used lazily as a synonym for novels, but in fact the novel is simply one of several forms that fiction can take. Conventionally, fiction in literature is understood to be a non-factual, sustained prose narrative. Depending on its length, a work of fiction may be a short story, a novella or a novel. At what point a short story becomes a novella, or a novella a novel, is a moot point. Most of the fictions I discuss in this book are quite clearly novels though their length varies considerably, from the 304 pages of Jen's *Mona in the Promised Land* to the 631 pages of Powers' *The Time of Our Singing*. There are two exceptions, however: Auster's *City of Glass*, which might be called either a novella or a short novel; and Proulx's 'Brokeback Mountain', which is a short story. All of the texts I deal with are prose works, but this is not always the case with fiction. For example, the increasing academic attention being given to contemporary American graphic novels, which rely on pictures as well as words to convey their narratives, raises questions about the traditional criteria for fiction, as does the occasional appearance of novels-in-verse, such as Nabokov's *Pale Fire* (1962) and Brad Leithauser's *Darlington's Fall: A Novel in Verse* (2002), and epistolary novels, such as John Barth's *LETTERS* (1979) and Alice Walker's *The Color Purple* (1983).[10]

Most problematic of all is the third criterion cited above: the non-factual nature of fiction. Libraries, bookshops and many other institutions have historically relied on the distinction between fiction and non-fiction to help them organise their collections of books. Yet in practice the boundary separating them is often blurred. In Chapter 10 of Auster's *City of Glass* there is a long set-piece in which a character named Paul Auster discusses his theory that, in Cervantes' *Don Quixote* (1605–15), which is often credited as the first great novel, the protagonist is in fact the author of his own narrative. During the course of Auster's conversation with the protagonist of *City of Glass*, Daniel Quinn, whose initials are the same as Cervantes' hero, the two men remark on the pains that Cervantes takes to present his novel as a factual account of real events and as 'an attack on the dangers of the make-believe'.[11] They do not mention that this strategy takes a further twist in the second volume of the novel, published ten years after the first, in which Don Quixote and his companion, Sancho Panza, repeatedly encounter characters who know of them because they have read Cervantes' book. At the close of Roth's *The Human Stain* there is a similar meta-fictional moment when Nathan Zuckerman, the narrator, is engaged in conversation with Les Farley, whom he believes is responsible for killing the novel's protagonist, Coleman Silk, and his lover, Farley's ex-wife, Faunia. Zuckerman tells Farley that he is a writer who writes 'about people like you' and that the book he is currently working on is called *The Human Stain*.[12]

No one would argue that these books are anything other than fiction, but the introduction of the author of *City of Glass* and the title of *The Human Stain* into their respective narratives raises troubling questions for readers. Is the Auster who talks to Quinn about *Don Quixote* the same Auster who wrote the scene between the two? In the most literal sense obviously not, since Quinn only exists within the pages of the novella, whereas Auster inhabits the real world. Yet Auster, like Cervantes, goes to great lengths to maintain the pretence, giving his fictional Auster a wife and son with the same names as his real-life family. Is *The Human Stain* mentioned by Zuckerman the same book as the one in which he appears? Again, this is logically impossible, since we know that the actual author of the novel is Philip Roth, the real-life writer, rather than Zuckerman, a fictional creation. However, those familiar with Zuckerman's history as Roth's alter ego (one who advises Roth not to publish his autobiography, *The Facts* (1988), in a letter appended to the end of that ostensibly non-fictional book), or with those books in which Roth appears as a character in his own fiction, such as *Deception* (1990), *Operation Shylock* (1993) and *The Plot Against America* (2004), will recognise that this episode is part of an ongoing project to complicate the relationship between what Roth calls the 'written' and 'unwritten' worlds.[13]

Roth discovered early in his career that readers often assume that fiction is thinly veiled autobiography, when the bestselling novelist Jacqueline Susann told Johnny Carson that she would like to meet the author of *Portnoy's Complaint* (1969), Roth's infamous novel about a compulsive onanist, but not to shake his hand.[14] In a more serious vein, the reception of Bret Easton Ellis's *American Psycho* (1991), published three years after Salman Rushdie's *The Satanic Verses* (1988), reinforced the fact that the generic conventions of fiction provide no protection against those who want to hold the author responsible for the sins of his characters. Described by Tammy Bruce, head of the National Organization of Women, as 'a how-to manual for the torture and dismemberment of women', *American Psycho* was widely interpreted as evidence that Ellis himself was a psychopathic misogynist, just as *The Satanic Verses* was regarded by many Muslims as evidence that its author was an apostate determined to desecrate the name of the Prophet.[15]

Finally, several of the fictions that I discuss here borrow from or imitate other, non-fictional genres. Misleading though the title of Carol Shields' *The Stone Diaries* (1994) is (it contains no diary entries), it does include some of the apparatus of an autobiography (family portraits, a family tree and chapters titled according to different phases of its subject's life), as well as an entirely epistolary chapter; *City of Glass* contains a number of lengthy digressions, including a whole chapter devoted to summarising the arguments of a (fictional) academic book and several historical anecdotes and mini-essays; *American Psycho* contains several essays on pop bands and singers; and *Cold Mountain* features long extracts from *Travels through North and South Carolina etc.* (1791) by the eighteenth-century American naturalist William Bartram. These examples demonstrate vividly just how heterogeneous and flexible are the forms that fiction takes.

STRUCTURE AND OBJECTIVES

I have divided this book into four thematically organised chapters. In Chapter 1 I discuss the use of irony and paradox in Don DeLillo's *White Noise*, Paul Auster's *City of Glass* and Bret Easton Ellis's *American Psycho*. Chapter 2 focuses on the ways in which gender and sexuality are mediated through leitmotifs of secrecy, silence and 'alternate histories' (a phrase Shields uses to describe a mode of storytelling that privileges everyday events rather than the traditional landmarks of history) in Jane Smiley's *A Thousand Acres*, Carol Shields' *The Stone Diaries* and Jeffrey Eugenides' *Middlesex*. Chapter 3 looks at the representation of race and ethnicity in Gish Jen's *Mona in the Promised Land*, Philip Roth's *The Human Stain* and Richard Powers' *The Time of Our Singing*. In Chapter 4 I compare three Western fictions – Charles Frazier's *Cold Mountain*, Annie Proulx's 'Brokeback Mountain' and Cormac McCarthy's *No Country for Old Men* – with their cinematic adaptations, directed by Anthony Minghella, Ang Lee and Ethan and Joel Coen, respectively, focusing on the generic differences between the two media.

Each chapter serves a dual purpose: to offer detailed readings of each text which are intended to be accessible and helpful to students and at the same time relevant to teachers and researchers;

but also to say something of more general interest about the ideas with which these texts engage. I have deliberately avoided the use of theoretical jargon while still intervening in some of the debates with which theory has been most concerned over the twenty years or so from the publication of the earliest fiction discussed in this book to the latest. In particular, my choice and treatment of the four main topics of the book – irony and paradox, gender and sexuality, race and ethnicity, and the relationship between what are sometimes (tendentiously) called literary and visual texts – is intended to counter what I would call the 'post-mania' of much recent academic discourse. I have argued above that the 'post-national' approach to American Studies is distorting the field; more tendentious, however, is the increasing use in the media and in certain schools of theoretical writing of labels such as 'post-ironic', 'post-gender', 'post-feminism', 'post-ethnicity' and 'post-race'.

In an article published in 2003, the journalist Zoe Williams noted that 'post-ironic' had become a 'very modish' term, used 'to suggest one of three things: i) that irony has ended; ii) that postmodernism and irony are interchangeable, and can be conflated into one handy word; or iii) that we are more ironic than we used to be, and therefore need to add a prefix suggesting even greater ironic distance than irony on its own can supply'. Williams then adds, quite rightly, 'None of these things is true'.[16] In an influential essay published ten years before Williams' article, the American author David Foster Wallace lamented what he saw as the jaded orthodoxies of postmodern irony in contemporary American fiction. In what has since been taken as a manifesto for a 'new sincerity' in American letters, Wallace predicted that

> The next real literary 'rebels' in this country might well emerge as some weird bunch of 'anti-rebels', born oglers who dare to back away from ironic watching, who have the childish gall actually to endorse single-entendre values. Who treat old untrendy human troubles and emotions in U.S. life with reverence and conviction.[17]

Wallace's paradoxical suggestion that the dominance of irony requires a rebellion from writers who will be 'anti-rebels' in their rejection of irony is itself arguably ironic, given the knowing arch-ness of his own fiction. It is also misleading in that, like much criticism of American fiction over the past thirty years, it greatly exaggerates the influence of postmodernism. Even in its 1970s and 1980s heyday, postmodernist fiction remained a minority faction in American fiction. Realism has in fact always been the dominant mode in terms of the production and reception of American fiction: the 'anti-rebels' whom Wallace calls for already existed and con-tinue to flourish. In this context, it makes no sense to speak of a 'post-ironic' era.

If Wallace's diagnosis of the condition of contemporary American fiction is as much a symptom of the disparity between high and low culture as an attempt to destabilise those categories, then much recent work on gender identity demonstrates even more forcibly the gulf between lived experience and academic theory. It is difficult to overstate the influence of Judith Butler in this field. In *Bodies That Matter: On the Discursive Limits of 'Sex'* (1994), *Gender Trouble: Feminism and the Subversion of Identity* (1999), 'The End of Sexual Difference' (2001) and *Undoing Gender* (2004), Butler has revolutionised thinking and writing about sexual and gender identity and the relationship between the two.[18] In par-ticular, she has insisted that gender is the product of discursive 'performativity' rather than of biological difference – a notion that has become widely accepted within academic discourse but that, as Debra Shostak argues in 'Theory Uncompromised by Practicality: Hybridity in Jeffrey Eugenides' *Middlesex*', tends to reinstate the very 'prevailing social norms' that she wants to resist.[19]

If undoing gender remains a possibility only in the abstract realm of theory, equally removed from reality is the popular notion that we are living in, or moving into, a 'post-feminist' era, as the fundamental aims of feminism – equal rights, equal pay, equal opportunities – have quite clearly not yet been achieved in the US, or indeed elsewhere in the world. Statistics from the 2003 US Census revealed that 'Women make only 75.5 cents for every dollar that men earn' and that 'Between 2002 and 2003, median annual earnings for full-time year-round women workers shrank by 0.6 percent, to $30,724, while men's earnings remained unchanged, at $40,668'.[20] Yet the American media constantly represent feminism as at best redundant and outmoded, at worst pernicious and dangerous.[21] Many of my students seem to regard feminism as either irrelevant to them or a stigma to be shunned.

If post-feminism is largely the creation of right-wing commentators and broadcasters, the terms 'post-ethnic' and 'post-racial' are, conversely, most often deployed in the service of progressive politics. In his seminal book *Postethnic America: Beyond Multiculturalism* (1995), Hollinger is careful to emphasise that 'the project of postethnicity differs decisively from many "posts" of our time' in that it is not intended as a repudiation of the project of multiculturalism, which promoted the idea of ethnicity as valuable difference, but rather a way of 'building upon it and critically redefining its contributions' (p. 5). He also concedes that America 'may now be squandering an opportunity to create for itself a *post*ethnic future in which affiliation on the basis of shared descent would be more voluntary than prescribed' (p. 19). In spite of these qualifications, and his persuasive argument that 'defenders of cultural diversity need to take a step beyond multiculturalism, toward a perspective I call "postethnic" . . . [that] favors voluntary over involuntary affiliations . . . and promotes solidarities of wide scope that incorporate people with different ethnic and racial backgrounds' (p. 3), Hollinger's term been glibly reproduced and conflated with 'post-racial', especially in the wake of Obama's election victory, both by liberals envisaging an end to racism and by neoconservatives keen to discredit affirmative action.

As I was writing this, it was being widely reported that the eminent African-American literary critic Henry Louis Gates had been arrested by police in Cambridge, Massachusetts. Returning home after making a documentary in China, Gates apparently found that his front door was jammed and so gained access at the back, turning off the alarm and then forcing open the front door. At this point he was confronted by a police officer who had been called by a passerby who had observed Gates acting suspiciously. An argument ensued and Gates was arrested and charged with disorder offences, in spite of having produced evidence that he was the homeowner. Obama himself condemned the 'stupid' conduct of the police and the charges were dropped. Whatever the facts of the case (the nature of the exchange between the police officer and

Gates is, not surprisingly, hotly contested), it is hard not to conclude that Gates would not have been arrested had he been white and that the charges against him were only dropped because of his high profile. Of course, this incident is in itself trivial compared to the appalling social problems faced by the black urban underclass found in many major American cities. Nonetheless, the media treatment of the case and, in particular, of Obama's intervention, has provided ample proof, if proof were needed, that the euphoric declarations of a post-race America that greeted Obama's election were ridiculously premature and that prophesies of a post-ethnic future for America are likely to remain the stuff of utopian idealism.

In the first three chapters, then, I make a case for the continued usefulness of terms such as irony, gender, feminism, race and ethnicity. This is not to say that such terms are unproblematic (it is difficult to use 'race' in particular without becoming implicated in racism), but rather that to consign them to history through the simple expedient of attaching the prefix 'post-' to them is to ignore the reality of contemporary American fiction and of contemporary America. In Chapter 4, too, I try to provide a corrective to what I see as a misguided attempt to discard useful terminology that has taken hold in the field of what is known as 'adaptation theory'. In analysing the relationship between three contemporary American fictions and their film adaptations, I argue that, whatever the respective merits of book and film, it is legitimate to talk of the former as the original and to discuss the relationship between the two in terms of the fidelity of the latter to the former. This may seem an uncontroversial position to adopt, but it puts me at odds with many current film theorists, for whom the terms 'original' and 'fidelity' signify an investment in an old-fashioned generic hierarchy that places literature above film. Finally, in the Conclusion, I discuss the problems of determining canonicity in contemporary American fiction.

Overall, then, this book aims to explore a range of contemporary American fictions (by established and lesser-known authors) that, while necessarily far from comprehensive, should give readers a reasonable sense of both the diversity of contemporary American fiction and the affinities that exist between many of its authors.

There is no single overarching thesis here, but I do argue that much contemporary American fiction is characterised by a paradox; that in the very process of challenging conventional ideas of irony, gender, race and nationality, it reinstates the centrality of these terms. In this sense, contemporary American fiction might be said to be both radical and conservative, both innovative and conventional, both experimental and traditional.

NOTES

1. In Scott McLemee's review of one of the books published in this series, Clint Burnham's *The Jamesonian Unconscious: The Aesthetics of Marxist Theory* (1995), he observes that 'THE TERM "POST-CONTEMPORARY"' (capitalisation in original) is puzzling. During a somewhat protracted attempt to find out what it meant, I received a long answer-machine message from an editor at Duke University Press. He said, among other things, that 'post-contemporary interpretation seeks to place the present within a historical narrative, while recognizing that the contemporary is always already disappearing. Yet the present is, so to speak, always before us'. Scott McLemee, 'Jameson and Son', *Lingua Franca* (July/August 1995), http://www.mclemee.com/id37.html.

2. In the Chronology, I start at 1980 and end at 2008 in order to give readers a sense of what immediately preceded and succeeded the period covered by the fiction that I discuss.

3. David A. Hollinger, *Postethnic America: Beyond Multiculturalism*, rev. edn. (New York: Basic Books, 2005), p. 101. All subsequent references in the text are to this edition.

4. A fine example of this shift is to be found in a comparison of the contents of the most recent edition of the *Heath Anthology of American Literature*, ed. Paul Lauter et al. (New York: Houghton Mifflin, 2008) with that of the first edition of the *Norton Anthology of Literature*, ed. Ronald S. Gottesman et al. (New York: Norton, 1979).

5. Paul Gilroy, *The Black Atlantic: Modernity and Double Consciousness* (London: Verso, 1993); Paul Giles, *Virtual*

Americas: Transnational Fictions and the Transatlantic Imaginary (Durham, NC: Duke University Press, 2002); John Muthyala, *Reworlding America: Myth, History and Narrative* (Athens, OH: Ohio University Press, 2006).

6. http://www.dundee.ac.uk/iteas/journal.htm; http://www.the asa.net/journals/name/comparative_american_studies_an_in ternational_ journal/.

7. http://www.georgeperkins.net/the-harpercollins-reader-s-encyclopedia-of-american-literature/.

8. Judie Newman, *Fictions of America: Narratives of Global Empire* (London: Routledge, 2009).

9. Bharati Mukherjee, for example, who is the central figure in Newman's book, famously advertised her 'Americanness' by posing for a photo-shoot wrapped in the Stars and Stripes and is no less interested in, if perhaps more critical of, American identity in her fiction.

10. Nabokov's novel is in fact a 999-line poem, written by John Shade, a fictional American poet, and an elaborate critical apparatus by a fictional editor and friend of the poet, Charles Kinbote, while Alice Walker's consists of a series of letters and interspersed diary entries.

11. Paul Auster, *New York Trilogy* (London: Faber and Faber, 1988), p. 98.

12. Philip Roth, *The Human Stain* (London: Jonathan Cape, 2000), p. 356.

13. Philip Roth, *Reading Myself and Others* (New York: Vintage, 2001), xiii.

14. Ibid., 'Imagining Jews', pp. 252–3.

15. Tammy Bruce is quoted in James Annesley, *Blank Fictions: Culture, Consumption and Contemporary American Narrative* (London: Pluto Press, 2008), p. 11.

16. Zoe Williams, 'The Final Irony', *The Guardian* ('Weekend'), 28 June 2003, p. 28.

17. David Foster Wallace, 'E unibus pluram: television and U.S. fiction', *The Review of Contemporary Fiction* (Summer 1993), p. 37 (1–39). http://findarticles.com/p/articles/mi_hb3544/is_n2_v13/ai_n28624826/.

18. Judith Butler, *Bodies That Matter: On the Discursive Limits of 'Sex'* (New York: Routledge, 1994); *Gender Trouble: Feminism and the Subversion of Identity* (New York: Routledge, 1999); 'The End of Sexual Difference' (2001), in *Feminist Consequences: Theory for the New Century*, ed. Elisabeth Bronfen and Misha Kavka (New York: Columbia University Press, 2001), pp. 414–34; and *Undoing Gender* (New York: Routledge, 2004).

19. See Debra Shostak, 'Theory Uncompromised by Practicality: Hybridity in Jeffrey Eugenides' *Middlesex*', *Contemporary Literature* 49:3 (Fall 2008), pp. 383–412.

20. 'Gender Wage Gap Widening, Census Data Shows', *About. com: U.S. Government Info*, http://usgovinfo.about.com/od/censusandstatistics/a/paygapgrows.htm.

21. See Martha Fineman and Martha T. McCluskey (eds.), *Feminism, Media and the Law* (Oxford: Oxford University Press, 1997) for an excellent collection of articles on this subject.

'The space reserved for irony': Irony and Paradox in Don DeLillo's *White Noise*, Paul Auster's *City of Glass* and Bret Easton Ellis's *American Psycho*

Irony is one of the buzzwords of our time. It is used as a catch-all which encompasses bad manners (as in the sarcastic response to an innocent question – 'How was your day?' 'Just great'), bad luck (as in the chorus of Alanis Morissette's song 'Ironic' (1995), which begins 'It's like rain on your wedding day') and bad taste (as in Jeff Koon's ghastly sculpture of Michael Jackson with his chimpanzee, Bubbles). Irony relies on a shared sense of normative values, a consensus about what is socially acceptable. As such, it is essentially a moral concept, yet paradoxically, it can also provide an alibi against accusations of immorality. In other words, irony can be used to bypass or circumvent the strait and narrow path of conventional morality. Under the cover of irony, you can get away with saying and writing things that might otherwise get you into all sorts of trouble – think of Sacha Baron Cohen in his guise as Borat encouraging the audience in a Texas bar to sing along to his rendition of 'Throw the Jew Down the Well', or Chris Rock complaining about 'niggas' in his stand-up routines. This also has an aesthetic dimension: bad writing can become good writing if refracted through the prism of irony; and finally, irony can become cannibalistic, so that one ironic reading both cancels out another and at the same time confirms it. It is this process – which I call the ironic paradox – that I want to trace through a reading of three canonical yet controversial novels: Don DeLillo's *White Noise* (1985), Paul Auster's *City of Glass* (1985) and Bret Easton Ellis's *American Psycho* (1991). I argue that these three works simultaneously invite and resist ironic readings and that, in different ways, their authors rely on paradox as both a rhetorical strategy and an organising principle to construct and deconstruct this ironic framework.

All three fictions exhibit the self-reflexivity, tonal ambiguity, generic hybridity and intertextuality that characterise postmodernist fiction, yet they also invoke the conventions of the classic realist novel. They allude to various kinds of popular genre fiction, notably the campus novel, the detective novel and the Gothic horror novel, while at the same time situating themselves in the canonical tradition of American literature. On the one hand, DeLillo, Auster and Ellis encourage their readers to collaborate with them in the construction of meaning; on the other, they frustrate, alienate and antagonise them by withholding meaning. It is in the tension between these conflicting impulses that the ironic paradox functions.

Finally, I reflect on the ways in which these novels, written towards the end of the twentieth century, exhibit a millenarian fascination with ideas of apocalypse and eschatology, and can be read, their radical form notwithstanding, as essentially conservative moral critiques of the state of the American nation in the 1980s and 1990s. It is arguably this aspect of the novels that has led, in spite of initial critical indifference and hostility, to their gradual incorporation in the canon of contemporary American fiction and to their current status as modern classics, widely taught and studied in campuses across the US, the UK and elsewhere.

DON DELILLO, *WHITE NOISE*

Published in 1984, *White Noise* is DeLillo's eighth novel and probably (with *Underworld*, published in 2000) his best known. It won the National Book Award in 1985 and has since become a staple of academic books and college courses on postmodernism, even though formally it is rather traditional. It is a novel that is preoccupied with grand universal themes – love, death, the nature of reality – but also very much of its time (dated, for example, by its references to the mid-1980s fad for generic foods and by its topical satire at the expense of cultural studies, here called 'American environments').[1] It is a novel that parodies academic discourse and critiques the cultural relativism that seeks to dispense with the distinction between high and low culture (what DeLillo refers to as 'an Aristotelianism of bubble gum wrappers and detergent jingles', p. 9); but it is also a novel that revels in the world of mass media and marketing and even locates spiritual meaning in the most apparently soulless of cultural contexts. It is, in short, a novel of paradoxes in which the phenomena that define (post)modern life – capitalism, consumerism, technology – are represented with an irony that is itself ironised.

Primarily given over to a Whitmanian catalogue of the various items that undergraduates bring with them to campus, the novel's opening paragraph appears to be part of a third-person narrative. It is only in the second paragraph that it becomes clear that *White Noise* has a first-person narrator:

> I've witnessed this spectacle every September for twenty-one years. It is a brilliant event, invariably. The students greet each other with comic cries and gestures of sodden [*sic*] collapse. Their summer has been bloated with criminal pleasures, as always. The parents stand sun-dazed near their automobiles, seeing images of themselves in every direction. The conscientious suntans. The well-made faces and wry looks. They feel a sense of renewal, of communal recognition. The women crisp and alert, in diet and trim, knowing people's names. Their husbands content to measure out the time, distant but ungrudging, accomplished in parenthood, something about them suggesting massive insurance coverage. This assembly of station wagons, as much as anything they might do in the course of the year, more than formal liturgies or laws, tells the parents they are a collection of the like-minded and the spiritually akin, a people, a nation. (pp. 3–4)

The tone of the narrator Jack Gladney, a college professor who has made his name by founding the new discipline of 'Hitler Studies', is characteristically ambiguous. There seems at first to be a note of lofty irony in the phrases 'spectacle' and 'brilliant event'; like the observer in Philip Larkin's 'Show Saturday', Gladney appears wryly amused at the antics of the crowd.[2] Like Larkin's poetic persona, however, Gladney's satirical gaze is complicated by a sympathetic acknowledgement of the valuable social and spiritual function that the annual advent of the new term performs. On the one hand, Gladney uses terse, verbless sentences to emphasise the generic appearance of the parents, with their 'conscientious suntans' and 'well-made faces' – both phrases literally nonsensical but brilliantly suggestive of what Gladney elsewhere sardonically diagnoses as the widespread delusion in American culture that 'it is possible to ward off death by following rules of good grooming' (p. 7). On the other hand, there is a certain indulgent affection in his description. Like the fathers of the students, Gladney himself is 'ungrudging'; in common with them, he feels 'a sense of renewal', so that what might have seemed like expressions of weary tedium earlier in the passage ('invariably', 'as always') become signs of a reassuring predictability. Or rather, both meanings are held in suspense. Similarly, the final lines of the paragraph can be read ironically: on one level the use of sacred diction ('formal liturgies or laws', 'spiritually akin, a people, a nation') highlights the incongruity between religious rituals and the essentially inconsequential routines enacted by this secular congregation. Then again, Gladney's use of the verb 'witness' (with its religious connotations) in the opening line suggests that such gatherings are a modern, civic equivalent of church services, and that the parents are indeed 'like-minded' in ways profounder than their choice of 'automobiles' (a curiously old-fashioned locution, perhaps bespeaking a sense of national identity founded on a shared sense of history).

Certainly, both strands of meaning in this passage – the ironic commentary on the homogeneity and conservatism of the students and their parents *and* the recognition of the quasi-religious resonance of their assembly – are reinforced by the revelation, two paragraphs later, that this campus is part of an institution, College-on-the-Hill, a name that is anonymously generic but alludes to the

New Testament 'city on a hill' invoked by Christ (Matthew 5.14), which became such a central trope for the early American settlers. They are also symptomatic of the way in which irony tends, paradoxically, to be ironically subverted throughout *White Noise*. DeLillo's novel is punctuated by a series of set-pieces involving Jack shopping: with his family, and with his friend and colleague, the doyen of 'Elvis Studies', Murray Jay Siskind; in supermarkets and in shopping malls. On many of these occasions, shopping turns out to be neither simply shopping nor the retail therapy that has become a familiar concept for twenty-first-century readers, but something more closely resembling a mystical or religious experience. When Jack checks the balance of his account at an ATM and finds that it 'roughly corresponded to my estimate', he feels, mysteriously, that '[t]he system had blessed my life', that 'something of deep personal value, but not money, not that at all, had been authenticated and confirmed' (p. 46). Instead of receiving a benediction from a priest, God's representative on earth, obscured behind a screen in a confessional, Gladney derives existential affirmation from information displayed on a screen that metonymically represents an invisible, omnipresent and omnipotent 'system'. In isolation, this episode might seem symptomatic of Jack's technophobia; he feels '[w]aves of relief and gratitude' when the computer confirms his expectations because he fears that it may, at any time, arbitrarily and suddenly withdraw its 'support and approval' (p. 46). In this light, Jack resembles a naive child for whom all technology seems the product of magic rather than physical laws and mathematical logic; or one of Thomas Pynchon's paranoid protagonists, forever trying in vain to decipher the code of some obscure, indefinable, amorphous system.[3] The fact that Jack cannot name the 'something of personal value' that he believes has been 'authenticated' does little to dispel the impression that he has ironically mistaken the rational order of the banking system for a numinous entity that confers or withholds spiritual, rather than financial, credit. However, one has only to recognise that every banknote in circulation has no intrinsic value, invoking instead a promise 'to pay the bearer on demand the sum of' its denomination (on UK paper currency), or to remember what happens when public confidence in the financial system founders, whether in Germany in the

1930s, Zimbabwe in the early 2000s or Iceland in 2008, to realise that the banking system relies as much on faith as on reason. Moreover, each time Jack spends money, he experiences a similar epiphany. Walking home from the supermarket, he compares his family's load with Murray's 'single lightweight bag of white items', concluding that 'in the mass and variety of our purchases, in the sheer plenitude those crowded bags suggested . . . the security and contentment these products brought to some snug home in our souls . . . we had achieved a fullness of being' (p. 20) inaccessible to the likes of Murray. Just as the numbers on the ATM screen supply Jack with spiritual sustenance, so the items from the supermarket provide metaphysical, as well as physical, nourishment for the Gladneys, making their 'souls' feel 'snug' and their very selves replete with a 'fullness of being'. Again, it is difficult to know how to read this passage. Is Jack simply dignifying, through extravagant rhetoric, a feeling of smug superiority engendered by the conspicuousness of his consumption compared to Murray's meagre rations? Or is DeLillo seriously suggesting that shopping is a means of communing with a higher order of things, of transmuting base products into something of loftier value – literal consumption replacing the symbolic consumption of the Eucharist wafer and wine? The most extended allegorical passage of this sort, which occurs when the Gladneys visit a shopping mall, seems to support the latter reading:

> People swarmed through the boutiques and gourmet shops. Organ music rose from the great court . . . My family gloried in the event. I was one of them, shopping, at last . . . I kept seeing myself unexpectedly in some reflecting surface . . . I filled myself out, found new aspects of myself, located a person I'd forgotten existed. Brightness settled around me . . . Our images appeared on mirrored columns, in glassware and chrome, on TV monitors in security rooms . . . Voices rose ten stories from the gardens and promenades, a roar that echoed and swirled through the vast gallery, mixing with noises from the tiers, with shuffling feet and chiming bells, the hum of escalators, the sound of people eating, the human buzz of some vivid and happy transaction. (p. 84)

Although the closing metaphor of this passage couches the activities of the shoppers in commercial terms (the word 'transaction' being used most frequently to describe the process by which money is exchanged for goods) and seems to allude to the scientific term that lends the novel its title (the various noises of the mall combining to create a white noise that seems not only to suppress but also to express the shoppers' feelings), the dominant metaphor of this episode figures the shopping mall as a sort of cathedral to which shoppers flock not simply in order to acquire material possessions but to share in a communal experience. The people swarming through the shops resemble pilgrims arriving at a shrine or church congregants assembling for a service, the organ music rising through the Great Court providing a suitably ecumenical accompaniment. Just as Jack had relished the other occasion on which large numbers of people gathered for a common purpose (the arrival of the College-on-the-Hill students and their families), so here he is exhilarated by the sense of being part of a larger community. In fact, these episodes are implicitly connected – to each other, and to the other, somewhat less benign, public occurrence that takes place later in the novel – by the word 'event'. Jack calls the arrival of the students a 'brilliant event'; here he notes that his family 'gloried in the event' and later he will find himself exposed to an unspecified atmospheric contamination referred to euphemistically as 'The Airborne Toxic Event'. Although he initially appears to exclude himself from his family's euphoria, he subsequently undergoes a conversion, literally seeing the light (reflected, together with their own images, in the shiny surfaces that are so ubiquitous in the mall) and experiencing an existential expansiveness ('I filled myself out') that is expressed in terms that echo those he used at the supermarket (when he felt a 'fullness of being'). Jack's visit to the mall not only creates a bond of intimacy with his family ('I was one of them', Jack comments) and seems to fulfil a long-cherished hope ('at last'), it also engenders a sense of well-being so profound that Jack begins literally to glow with pride, a 'brightness' settling on him like a halo. When the voices rise ten storeys, they seem like a hallelujah chorus, acclaiming Jack's apotheosis.

On the other hand, this sustained religious metaphor can be read ironically. If shopping has become a religion, it is one based on narcissism (emphasised by the way in which the Gladneys encounter images of themselves everywhere they look, another echo of the gathering of student families at the start of the novel, when the parents keep 'seeing images of themselves in every direction') and materialism (symbolised by the excesses of the mall, which may have superficial architectural affinities with a vast, vaulted temple for the worship of God, but is devoted to Mammon). Once again, DeLillo's tone is delicately poised between satire and encomium: Jack's revelling in the sensual details of the mall is also DeLillo's, but his unreliability as a narrator makes his revelation that he 'found new aspects of [him]self' difficult to take at face value.

Paradoxically, Jack is profoundly moved by the most superficial things – the proliferation of surfaces in the mall (mirrors, TV monitors, chrome-plated products and features) gives him a feeling of depth. Something similar occurs later in the novel. As Jack watches his children, reflecting that they 'were like figures in an ad for the Rosicrucians' (in itself a contradiction, since the Rosicrucians are a secretive sect who do not openly acknowledge their existence, let alone advertise it), he hears his daughter, Steffie, muttering in her sleep:

> [T]wo clearly audible words, familiar and elusive at the same time, words that seemed to have a ritual meaning, part of a verbal spell or ecstatic chant.
> *Toyota Celica.*
> . . . The utterance was beautiful and mysterious, gold-shot with looming wonder. It was like the name of an ancient power in the sky, tablet-carved in cuneiform . . . it struck me with the impact of a moment of splendid transcendence.
> (p. 155)

Even before he has identified them (they are paradoxically both 'familiar and elusive'), Jack is convinced that Steffie's words have a mystical significance. When they are revealed – italicised and set apart as a self-contained paragraph (devoid of speech marks) for maximum visual impact – they seem at first to be the punch-line to a joke of which Jack is the butt. In other words, his romantic conviction that his daughter is unconsciously reciting an old incantation or ceremonial verse seems to be ironically undermined by the disclosure that she is in fact naming the make and model of a popular car. However, far from being deflated by the bathetic content of Steffie's dream, Jack is inspired by it to new heights of lyricism. He imbues Steffie's unconscious parroting of a banal brand name with Delphic wisdom, interpreting it as the enigmatic testament to a pagan deity.

What we have here is an ironic paradox. Jack's initial, instinctive recognition that Steffie's words connect her – and himself as their auditor – to the ancient tradition of seeing dreams as visionary and prophetic is rendered ironic by the realisation that she is simply reciting the name of a product from a car commercial, but then this irony is both reinforced and subverted by Jack's insistence that behind this apparently trivial manifestation of the pervasiveness of advertising lies a revelation of cosmic magnitude. Either Jack is so deluded that he ignores the empirical evidence altogether, or he sees something that isn't readily apparent, something that transforms transparent vacuity into transcendent meaning. Like the swelling sound that circulates through the mall, Steffie's sleep-talking is part of the white noise generated by modern life, at once audible, because it consists of sound-waves that cover a wide frequency range, and inaudible, because its familiarity makes it inconspicuous, but also resonant of a pre-modern existence, an ancient era of wonder and mystery.

This is why the novel is called *White Noise*. Usually white noise is, by definition, something that is constantly there in the background, a hum that we don't notice. In DeLillo's novel, however, it is a palpable presence – a phenomenon that at times threatens to displace those things (plot, characterisation, themes) that we expect to find in prose fiction. It manifests itself not just in the set-pieces discussed above, but microcosmically, in the form of televisions as ubiquitous and invasive as the surveillance screens of Big Brother in George Orwell's *1984*. It is no coincidence that, at the climax of the narrative, when Jack confronts Willie Mink, the man whom he blames for his wife's addiction to a drug that is supposed to alleviate the fear of death, the television set looms large, virtually eclipsing the two antagonists:

As the TV picture jumped, wobbled, caught itself in snarls, Mink appeared to grow more vivid. The precise nature of events. Things in their actual state. Eventually he worked himself out of the deep fold, rising nicely, sharply outlined against the busy air. White noise everywhere. 'Containing iron, niacin and riboflavin.' (p. 310)

The way in which Mink comes into sharper focus just as the television reception loses its integrity suggests that there is an inverse correlation between the two images: when the TV picture is clear, Mink himself is blurry, and vice versa. Paradoxically, however, the terms Jack uses to describe this process foreground the television and render ironic Mink's apparent emergence from its dominion. Because of the vague nature of the characteristically verb-less sentences that seem to offer clarity ('The precise nature of events. Things in their actual state'), the effort that it costs Mink to extricate himself from its field of influence ('*Eventually* he *worked* himself out of the deep fold') and the persistence of the white noise in the 'busy air', the overall impression conveyed by DeLillo's diction subverts the ostensible meaning of the passage. Moreover, the television literally has the last word, in the form of a snatch of an advertisement (presumably for a breakfast cereal) that is the last of a series of such apparent non-sequiturs that appear periodically throughout the novel.[4] Instead of a dramatic showdown between Jack and his nemesis, there is a bathetic message from a sponsor (perhaps a parody of the product placement that has become such a feature of Hollywood movies).

The ambiguous role of the television in this scene is characteristic of the novel's treatment of technology in general: it is comic in the sense that it upstages Jack and Willie with its ephemeral promotion of the nutritive value of a cereal, but also threatening in its erratic movement – 'jump[ing], wobbl[ing], ca[tching] itself in snarls' – and in the way that it fills the air with its static electricity. DeLillo has said of *White Noise* that '[i]t is a novel about fear, death and technology. A comedy of course', and indeed he exploits this tension in the novel itself.[5] All three of the main sections of the book have titles that explicitly signal its emphasis on technology and they all contain examples of technology-related catastrophes or near-catastrophes which are both ominous and absurd. Although the first section, 'Waves and Radiation', is primarily concerned with Jack's efforts to maintain his high profile at the Campus-on-the-Hill, it is punctuated by a series of episodes that suggest that technology itself has become a sort of white noise – so embedded in modern life that it is largely invisible until it begins ironically to threaten the very existence that it is designed to protect and enhance.

In the second chapter, for example, the Gladneys are eating together when a 'smoke alarm went off in the hallway upstairs, either to let us know the battery had just died or because the house was on fire' (p. 8). They ignore it, assuming, correctly, that the former is the case. Chapter 9 begins with the news that the local grade school had been evacuated earlier that week because some of the pupils and teachers had exhibited possible symptoms of having been exposed to a harmful substance on the premises:

> No one knew what was wrong. Investigators said it could be the ventilating system, the paint or varnish, the foam insulation, the electrical insulation, the cafeteria food, the rays emitted by micro-computers, the asbestos fireproofing, the adhesive on shipping containers, the fumes from the chlorinated pool, or perhaps something deeper, finer-grained, more closely woven into the basic state of things. (p. 35)

This paragraph has many of the familiar hallmarks of DeLillo's prose: the long list of items (in this case possible sources of contamination), the enigmatic reference to 'the basic state of things' (a phrase that anticipates the phrase '[t]hings in their actual state' from the episode with Mink discussed above) and the implied irony that lies behind Jack's neutral tone: namely, that if all the items mentioned are really potentially hazardous, then not just the school environment but modern life in general is fundamentally unsafe, rendering any investigation redundant. Finally, in Chapter 18, Jack and his ex-wife, Tweedy Browner, waiting at the airport to meet their daughter, witness the arrival of a group of traumatised passengers who have just disembarked from a plane that lost all power and went into a precipitous descent before its engines suddenly restarted just in time to prevent a disaster. One of the passengers, recounting the sequence of events, describes how mass panic had ensued after a voice on the intercom was overheard crying: 'We're falling out of the sky! . . . We're a silver gleaming death machine!' (p. 90) before another member of the crew restored calm by 'decid[ing] to pretend that it was not a crash but a crash landing that was seconds away' (p. 91).

Again, there is (grim) irony here, in that what is conventionally the source of reassurance (the cockpit) here becomes the instigator of terror, an irony amplified by the incongruous exuberance of his language. The other comic element here – the notion that a mere change of terminology can change the nature of the event itself (a crash becoming a 'crash landing') – anticipates the pivotal event in the second section of the novel.

The Airborne Toxic Event that gives its name to the second section occurs when an area of Blacksmith, where the Gladneys live, is evacuated after a poisonous vapour, Nyolene D, one of 'a new generation of toxic waste', escapes into the atmosphere (p. 111). When Jack stops at a petrol station to fill his car he is (possibly) exposed to the contaminated cloud passing overhead and is encouraged to consult one of a team of number-crunching, uniformed computer operators to discover the risks he has incurred. Engaging the young man in conversation, Jack learns that he is part of an organisation called SIMUVAC (short for simulated evacuation). When the man tells Jack that they are using the event as 'a model' for their simulated evacuation procedures, Jack is incredulous ('Are you saying you saw a chance to use the real event in order to rehearse the simulation?') but not indignant (he then asks, 'How's it going?' p. 139). At this point the man explains that 'we don't have our victims laid out where we'd want them if this was an actual simulation' (p. 139), a sentiment echoed by a representative of the organisation behind the SIMUVAC operation, a consultancy firm called Advanced Disaster Management, who complains that 'there is no substitute for the planned simulation' and warns his audience of volunteer helpers that if a real accident occurs, 'it is important to remember that we are not here to mend broken bones or put out real fires' (p. 206). The irony of this episode closely resembles the black humour that characterised much American fiction in the 1960s: the absurd, perverted priorities of SIMUVAC are particularly reminiscent of the twisted logic of the military authorities in Joseph Heller's *Catch-22* (1961). This unambiguous, broad-stroked satire marks a change in the novel's tone and focus from that of the first section, and there is a further, more radical shift in the third section.

If 'Waves and Radiation' made *White Noise* appear to be primarily a comic campus novel and 'The Airborne Toxic Event' a satire on the dehumanising effects of modern technology, then 'Dylarama' reads like a parody of a detective novel. It deals with Jack's discovery that Babette has become addicted to a drug, Dylar, which allegedly relieves the fear of death, and with his subsequent decision to seek revenge on the man who has been supplying her with it in return for sex. Babette refers to this man only as Mr Gray, refusing to divulge any of his distinguishing features; when Jack tries to picture him he can only come up with a man who 'was literally gray, giving off a visual buzz' (p. 214). This last phrase seems to be a synonym for white noise, sharing with it a synaesthetic quality. Although Gray promises Babette that the Dylar will inhibit that part of her brain from which her fear of death derives, it has no effect at all. For Jack he is a ghostly figure – 'hazy, unfinished' – and his 'visual buzz', like the television static that distorts the image of Willie Mink (one of Gray's agents), implicitly undermines the claims that he makes, as the following conversation between Jack and Babette makes clear:

'What if death is nothing but sound?'
'Electrical noise.'
'You hear it forever. Sound all around. How awful.'
'Uniform, white.' (p. 198)

This exchange suggests that white noise may be a metaphor for death: omnipresent and yet unremarked, familiar yet elusive, simple yet ineffable. Earlier in the novel, Jack observes that the noise of traffic is 'a remote and steady murmur . . . as of dead souls babbling at the edge of a dream' (p. 4). Elsewhere, however, he describes the hubbub in the supermarket as a 'dull and unlocatable roar, as of some form of swarming life just outside the range of human apprehension' (p. 36) and the hum of the refrigerator as an 'eerie static, insistent but near subliminal, that made me think of wintering souls, some form of dormant life approaching the threshold of perception' (p. 258). Paradoxically, then, white noise seems to symbolise both death and life, or perhaps the mysterious construct connecting the two, the soul (a word that crops up in two of the passages above): that which is felt instinctively to exist but remains forever unlocatable, 'just outside the range of human apprehension', but at the same time tantalisingly 'approaching the threshold of perception'. If this is the case, then it is appropriate that Jack's botched attempt at murder (he hunts down Gray, wounds but fails to kill Mink – who may or may not be Gray – is wounded by him, before deciding to try to rescue him) ends with both Jack and his victim being tended by nuns in a convent.

The final irony of the novel is that these women, far from offering the key to accessing the mysteries of the soul, resoundingly slam the door shut. Engaging Sister Hermann Marie, who cleans and dresses his wound, in conversation, Jack is shocked to discover that she does not believe in the traditional religious verities. He accuses her of hypocrisy, asking if her 'dedication is a pretense', but the nun performs a neat chiasmus on the phrase, countering that 'Our pretense is a dedication' (p. 319). When Jack tells her to '[a]ct like' a nun, he misses the irony, for that is precisely what Sister Hermann Marie and her fellow devotees do: just as the SIMUVAC workers are trained to respond to simulated disaster scenarios rather than actual catastrophes, so the nuns regard it as their duty not to believe in earnest but to perform effectively the role of devout believers, to *act like* nuns. In a secular society, the Sister explains to Jack, '[t]hose who have abandoned belief must still believe in us' (p. 319). Paradoxically, non-believers need to believe that believers still exist in order to feel at ease with their own scepticism.

Irony in *White Noise* is pervasive, not just as a rhetorical strategy but as a concept that is explicitly invoked. For Jack, a shared sense of irony is central to his marriage:

> Babette and I tell each other everything . . . In these night recitations we create a space between things as we felt them at the

time and as we speak them now. This is the space reserved for irony, sympathy and fond amusement, the means by which we rescue ourselves from the past. (pp. 29–30)

Placed here in apposition to 'sympathy', Jack represents irony as a benign source of mutual understanding, but this in itself is ironic, because it turns out that the confidence that Jack has in the transparency of his relationship with Babette is misplaced. By the end of the novel, Jack has discovered that Babette has become addicted to Dylar and has been sleeping with the man who supplies her with it.

Similarly, Murray Jay Siskind includes irony in a list of qualities that he takes to be symptomatic of 'a civilized world-weariness and a tragic sense of history' (p. 21) and uses the word repeatedly to represent what he sees as the injustices he suffers in his relations with women:

> I was in a situation with a woman in Detroit. She needed my semen in a divorce suit. The irony is that I love women . . . The second irony is that it's not the bodies of women that I ultimately crave but their minds . . . What fun it is to talk to an intelligent woman wearing stockings as she crosses her legs . . . The third and related irony is that it's the most complex and neurotic and difficult women that I am invariably drawn to. (p. 11)

Here each irony that Murray cites is itself implicitly ironised by the details that precede and follow it: the bald declaration that he 'love[s] women' rings hollow, following the clinical, euphemistic language he uses to describe the nature of his 'situation' with the (unnamed) woman in Detroit; the claim that he is more interested in the mind than the body of women is undermined by his confession that what he finds 'fun' about conversing with intelligent women is not listening to what they have to say but fetishising their leg wear; and finally, his alleged attraction to 'complex and neurotic and difficult women' is compromised by the very reductive terms he uses to characterise them.

It is typical of *White Noise* that Jack's sentimental advocacy of irony and Murray's self-pitying representation of himself as its victim are treated with equal scepticism. Yet scepticism is itself invariably subjected to scepticism in the novel and it is this that makes it paradoxically both the culmination of the ironic postmodernism initiated by writers like Pynchon in the 1960s and a precursor of the 'new sincerity' exemplified by writers such as Dave Eggers in the first decade of the twenty-first century.

PAUL AUSTER, *CITY OF GLASS*

City of Glass was Auster's first published work of fiction but not his first foray into writing. In fact, it could be seen as the culmination, rather than the beginning, of the early phase of his career. His first book, *The Invention of Solitude* (1982), is partly a biography of his father and partly a meta-biography, a meditation on the difficulties of writing biography, just as *City of Glass* is partly crime fiction and partly a deconstruction of the genre. For many years before the publication of these books Auster had been a translator of French poetry and a cultural critic. Many of the essays written during this period and collected in *The Art of Hunger* (1992) anticipate the concerns of *City of Glass* and the other two novellas – *Ghosts* (1986) and *The Locked Room* (1986) – with which it was collected in a single volume entitled *The New York Trilogy* in 1987. They are peppered with existential paradoxes thrown out with studied casualness, such as the claims that Ungaretti's 'work is an expression of the inexhaustible difficulty of expression itself'; that in Dupin's poetry 'the poem can be born only when all chances for its life have been destroyed'; and that in the paintings of the Canadian abstract expressionist Jean-Paul Riopelle, 'The body must empty itself of the world in order to find the world, and each thing must be made to disappear before it can be seen.'[6] At times these paradoxes are smoothly aphoristic ('Where no possibility exists, everything becomes possible again'), at times they are awkwardly self-conscious ('[John Ashbery's] pessimism about our ever really being able to know anything results, paradoxically, in a poetry that is open to everything') (pp. 75, 104). Cumulatively, they begin to seem ironic – to assume a self-parodic dimension – like the portentous pronouncements of a *faux*-philosopher who mistakes pretension for Socratic wisdom.

The titles of the three stories that comprise *The New York Trilogy* are also paradoxical: *City of Glass* suggests an expansive and solid yet also fragile construction; it invokes images of light and space, which contrast obviously with *The Locked Room*'s connotations of claustrophobic constriction. A locked room is also an ambiguous space in that, like a wall (one of Auster's favourite symbols), it can be used both to keep out unwanted intruders and keep in undesirable individuals; the locked room imprisons its occupant, but at the same time protects him from the perils of the outside world, preserving him in a state of purdah. Sandwiched between these stories is *Ghosts*, who are spirits trapped in a purgatorial afterlife yet able to move more freely than mortals, spectres who are at one and the same time invisible and palpable, impenetrable and translucent, disembodied and corporeal.

These larger paradoxes are echoed at the local level in the twists and turns of Auster's spare, elliptical prose. A perfect example of this is the opening sentence of *City of Glass*:

> It was a wrong number that started it, the telephone ringing three times in the dead of night, and the voice on the other end asking for someone he was not.[7]

On the face of it, this is the most straightforward, most undemanding and most unambiguous of sentences: its reader-friendliness even extends to the use of a formula familiar enough to warrant the term cliché: 'the dead of night'. Yet the plainness of the language disguises – or rather, precipitates – semantic confusion. When the voice asks 'for someone he was not', does this 'someone' refer to an individual who was not the individual who answered the telephone? If so, does he actually say: 'Can I speak to someone you are not?' Or does the pronoun 'he' refer to the caller himself? The phrase 'wrong number' would suggest the former, but the syntax points to the latter. The choice of the word 'for', as opposed to 'to speak to', also raises the possibility that the disembodied voice is making a profound plea for help rather than simply hoping to get hold of a particular individual. More fundamentally, what exactly is it that the wrong number started? Because this is the first sentence of the book, the pronoun 'it' has no prior referent. Some of these questions are answered as the story develops, but the fundamental paradox – that the very simplicity of the language Auster uses creates complexity and ambiguity – establishes the precarious foundations on which *City of Glass* is built.

Later, the protagonist, Daniel Quinn, having for a time impersonated the man whom the caller asked for (a man called Paul Auster, but who is a private detective rather than a novelist), decides that he wants to withdraw from the case that he had accepted in Auster's name. However, when he tries to phone his clients, Virginia Stillman and her husband, Peter, who have hired Quinn to protect Peter from the father who had held him in isolation (in a locked room) for nine years, he finds the line constantly busy. Rather than feeling frustrated at his inability to get through, Quinn takes 'comfort in the thought that whenever he dialled the number, the sound would be there for him, never swerving in its denial, negating speech and the possibility of speech, as insistent as the beating of a heart' (p. 106). The heartbeat simile associates the impossibility of verbal communication with life rather than with death, as we might expect. Quinn interprets it as evidence that 'the fates' have decreed that he 'could not yet break his connection with the case' (p. 111). Though wary of resorting to such mystical terms to explain his experiences, Quinn decides that:

[I]t came closer than any other term he could think of. Fate in the sense of what was, of what happened to be. It was something like the word 'it' in the phrase 'it is raining' or 'it is night'. What that 'it' referred to Quinn had never known. A generalized condition of things as they were, perhaps; the state of is-ness that was the ground on which the happenings of the world took place. He could not be any more definite than that. But perhaps he wasn't really searching for anything definite. (p. 111)

I shall return to Auster's invocation of the idea of 'fate' later, but for now I want to draw attention to the way in which this discussion of the meaning of two of the shortest, most common words in the English language ('it' and 'is') recalls the use of the first two words of *City of Glass* ('It was a wrong number that started it . . .'). Whereas in the first sentence of the novella these words implicitly raise questions about the capacity of language to communicate meaning, here Quinn reflects explicitly on the uncertainties that accrue even – or perhaps especially – around the simplest of words. While the busy line disables communication Quinn is content, but when he tries to re-enter language in order to rationalise and clarify his sense of what the signal signifies – fate – he finds himself thrown into confusion ('What that "it" referred to Quinn had never known') and uncertainty ('A generalized condition of things as they were, *perhaps*'). In the end, he has to retreat from the search for meaning altogether, taking refuge in the half-hearted assertion that he does not require clarity ('*perhaps* he wasn't really searching for anything definite').

Quinn's realisation that language may obstruct rather than facil- itate meaning begins when he first hears the caller, Peter Stillman's voice on the telephone: 'It [the voice] was at once mechanical and filled with feeling, hardly more than a whisper and yet perfectly audible, and so even in tone that he was unable to tell if it belonged to a man or a woman' (p. 7). The paradoxical nature of Stillman's voice – both emotionless and 'filled with feeling', both barely perceptible and 'perfectly audible', both female and male – is reinforced by his appearance:

> Everything about Peter Stillman was white . . . Against the pallor of his skin . . . the effect was almost transparent, as though one could see through to the blue veins behind the skin of his face. This blue was almost the same as the blue of his eyes: a milky blue that seemed to dissolve into a mixture of sky and clouds. Quinn could not image [*sic*] himself addressing a word to this person. It was as though Stillman's presence was a command to be silent. (p. 15)

The whiteness of Stillman's appearance alludes to Herman Melville,[8] of course (a key figure in *The New York Trilogy*), but also, perhaps less obviously, to something that Edmond Jabès, the French poet and philosopher, said to Auster in a conversation that took place between the two writers in 1978 and that was reprinted in *The Art of Hunger*: 'Our reading takes place in the very whiteness between the words, for this whiteness reminds us of the much greater space in which the word evolves' (p. 163). Like Melville's whale, Stillman's whiteness paradoxically signifies both an appalling void of meaning and the possibility of a boundless hermeneutic space, as implied in Jabès' observation about the great white spaces between words in which interpretation can roam freely. Like language itself, Stillman appears transparent, or rather, in Auster's characteristically equivocal phrase, '*almost* transparent' (just as the blue of his eyes is *almost* identical to that of his skin), and yet rather than promoting understanding, this near-transparency seems to occlude it. Whereas in the usual, figurative sense of the phrase 'seeing through' someone means that their true motives are exposed, in spite of their best efforts to conceal them, here the fact that Quinn can almost literally see through Stillman signifies not that he can read him like a book or as Jabès would have it, like the intertextual spaces of a book, but rather that he is completely illegible. As Aliki Varvogli puts it in her excellent book on Auster, *The World that is the Book* (2001): 'even though he appears to be transparent, Stillman is in fact impenetrable'.[9] The paradoxical title of the first part of Auster's first book, *The Invention of Solitude*, 'Portrait of an Invisible Man' (which refers to Auster's late father), might equally well be applied to Stillman. The more information we get about Stillman the less clearly defined he becomes. Indeed, Quinn is so confused by Stillman that he is unable even to trust the evidence of his eyes: each statement he makes about him is either qualified with the word 'almost' or couched in the conditional tense ('*as though* one could see through to the blue veins behind the skin of his face'; '*as though* Stillman's presence was a command to be silent').

In this sense, Stillman becomes a metaphor of sorts for Auster's fictional practice; an embodiment (and disembodiment) of a *modus operandi* in which concision and precision paradoxically coexist with redundancy and indeterminacy. For Auster, minimalism is not simply a stylistic preference – a rhetorical strategy – but also the product of a pragmatic economy, the expression of what, in *The Art of Hunger*, he calls 'the desire . . . to allow events to speak for themselves, to choose the exact detail that will say everything and thereby allow as much as possible to remain unsaid' (p. 49). Yet, as the paradoxical nature of this last observation suggests (how can a detail 'say everything' and at the same time leave 'as much as possible unsaid'?), less in Auster is also more. On the one hand, the diction of *City of Glass* is enticingly open-ended; it conforms to the reader-response-like model for the creation of textual meaning that Auster articulated in an interview with Joseph Mallia (reprinted in *The Art of Hunger*): 'The one thing I try to do in all my books is to leave enough room in the prose for the reader to inhabit it. Because I finally believe it is the reader who writes the book and not the writer' (p. 282). Yet on another level language in the *Trilogy* is not as accommodating as Auster's manifesto would have us believe. It is not just that Auster's prosaic, pared-down mode of expression, rather than empowering the reader, often thwarts any attempt to construct meaning; it is that the main plots of his novellas are both underdeveloped and overdetermined.

Again, there is arguably a tension between theory and practice here – that is to say, between Auster's non-fictional statements about his art and the characteristics of the art itself. In an interview with Mark Irwin in *The Art of Hunger*, Auster commented that 'If my work is about anything, I think it's about the unexpected, the idea that anything can happen' (p. 333). This might be understood as Auster defending his fiction against charges of implausibility: he is fond of saying things such as 'the world is full of strange events. Reality is a great deal more mysterious than we ever give it credit for' (p. 278) and 'truth is stranger than fiction. What I am after, I suppose, is to write fiction as strange as the world I live in' (p. 288). Certainly, many of the key events in the *Trilogy* (Quinn's descent into vagrancy in *City of Glass*, Blue's refusal simply to quit his job in *Ghosts*, Fanshawe's sudden flight in *The Locked Room*) are surprising in the sense of being apparently inexplicable. Yet this is not to say that they seem random or arbitrary. On the contrary, the *Trilogy* is often at pains to ensure that everything that happens in its pages is not only expected, but indeed seems inevitable – in other words, there should be no room for the possibility that things might have happened in any other way than in the way that they do. If the first sentence of *City of Glass* is, as we have seen, hedged about with ambiguities and paradoxes, the one thing that it insists on, somewhat portentously, is the fact that it was the wrong number (and by implication definitely not anything else) that started 'it', whatever 'it' might signify. The proleptic tone is amplified in the next sentence ('Much later . . . he would conclude that nothing was real except chance', p. 3) and is echoed in casual asides sprinkled throughout not just *City of Glass* but *Ghosts* ('Little does Blue know, of course, that the case will go on for years' (p. 136) and *The Locked Room* as well ('Even before I stepped into the apartment, I knew that Fanshawe had to be dead' (p. 201). Moreover, the idea implied by the word 'chance', that the protagonist's fortunes are determined by accident rather than design, is immediately undermined in the next sentence, in which the narrator announces that the issue of '[w]hether it might have turned out differently, or whether it was all predetermined with the first word that came from the stranger's mouth, is not the question' (p. 3).

This refusal to explore alternative explanations for the events of the book – the deliberate averting of the narrator's gaze from roads not taken, counter-lives that might have been lived – becomes something of a refrain in *The New York Trilogy* as a whole. For example, when Blue, the private investigator protagonist of *Ghosts*, struggles in vain to get to grips with one of the key texts in the traditional canon of American literature, Henry Thoreau's *Walden* (1854), the narrator comments:

> What he does not know is that were he to find the patience to read the book in the spirit in which it asks to be read, his entire life would begin to change, and little by little he would come to a full understanding of his situation . . . But lost chances are as much a part of life as chances taken, and a story cannot dwell on what might have been. (p. 163)

This is a version of the classical rhetorical trope, *occupatio*, in that by declaring that he will not 'dwell on what might have been', the narrator paradoxically draws attention to the way in which things might have been different somehow – radically different – for Blue, if only he had been a more sensitive and persistent reader. We might expect that the argument that 'lost chances' are integral to life would be a prelude to a discussion of the nature of such missed opportunities, but here Auster ironically gestures towards this opening only to shut it down. He assures us that Blue's 'entire life' would have changed had he been a different kind of reader – perhaps one attuned to Thoreau's subtle use of irony – but there is no explanation of *how* such a change would have been effected or of *why Walden* matters so much. In fact, presented as baldly as this, the idea that Thoreau's book might have saved Blue's life seems absurd – a joke, perhaps, aimed at the cult status that *Walden* attained for many countercultural Americans in the 1960s.[10]

Aliki Varvogli argues persuasively that Auster's extensive use of 'texts such as . . . *Walden* does not imply an intention to ridicule them, nor an unquestioning acceptance of them' (p. 25), but if Auster does not intend to ridicule *Walden* itself, here he does seem to be treating ironically the exaggerated reverence which it has inspired. Similarly, when Varvogli observes that 'Despite never having heard of *Walden* Blue is engaged in an ironic re-enactment of Thoreau's experiment, as well as being trapped in a book the key to which is *Walden*' (p. 43), I think her description of Blue's predicament as 'an ironic re-enactment of Thoreau's experiment' is apt, but I am sceptical of the idea that *Walden* is the key to *Ghosts*. The irony of Auster's use of Thoreau, it seems to me, lies precisely in the incongruous disparity between Blue's isolation in urban Brooklyn and Thoreau's at rural Walden Pond, and in the earnestness with which he encourages us to pursue the parallels between the two texts.

Referring to the episode in which Black tells Blue the story of how Walt Whitman's brain, having been donated by the poet to the American Anthropometric Society, ends up being 'spattered all over the place' after a lab assistant drops it, Varvogli comments: 'Blue, as usual, misses the point of this story, but its ironies are not lost on the reader' (p. 51). For me, this crystallises the problem of Auster's use of irony in the *Trilogy*, because I think the irony here, as in the earlier reference to *Walden* as the key to Blue's salvation, is not just at Blue's expense, and indeed at Whitman's, but also at the reader's. In bringing Whitman's inflated sense of his own genius literally down to earth with a bump, Auster is engaging in an act of iconoclasm with which he implicitly invites the reader to collude.

At the same time, if the puncturing of Whitman's pretensions is what Varvogli calls 'the point' of this story, it still begs the question of why Black (and Auster) tells it at this juncture. Even if it is true that most of Auster's readers will be more alert to the ironies of the Whitman anecdote than Blue is, they are likely to be as much in the dark as he is about what the larger point of the story is, if indeed there is one. Just as we are never told how *Walden* might have helped Blue to alter the course of his life, so we are never told what relevance, if any, the fate of Whitman's brain has to Blue's predicament. In this sense, the reader who complacently assumes that she or he understands more than Blue may be as much a victim of Auster's irony as a collaborator in its creation.

If there is any way of pinning down Auster's ironic perspective in the *Trilogy*, perhaps it is to be found in the encounter between Daniel Quinn, the protagonist of *City of Glass*, and Paul Auster, the man whose identity he decides to assume when he answers the telephone and hears a voice, for the third time, asking for a detective with that name. When Quinn decides to track down Auster, he discovers to his dismay that he is not a detective at all, but an author like (though of course also unlike) Quinn himself. Most of the conversation between the two men is taken up by a lengthy summary Auster provides of an essay he is writing about Cervantes' *Don Quixote*. If there is a suggestion that *Walden* is the ur-text for *Ghosts* and that *The Locked Room* is a rewriting of *Fanshawe* (after whom the subject of Auster's story is named), the obscure first novel by that other canonical nineteenth-century American writer, Nathaniel Hawthorne, then this seems to be the moment when Daniel Quinn (whose initials are the same as those of Cervantes' hero) is given to understand, by the author of the *Trilogy* itself, that the heart of his mystery lies in this famous seventeenth-century Spanish novel. Yet as soon as he has finished his disquisition on Cervantes, Auster implicitly undermines the gravity with which he has delivered his theories about the novel:

> Auster leaned back on the sofa, smiled with a certain ironic pleasure, and lit a cigarette. The man was obviously enjoying himself, but the precise nature of that pleasure eluded Quinn. It seemed to be a kind of soundless laughter, a joke

that stopped short of its punchline, a generalized mirth that had no object. (p. 120)

We are not told the source of Auster's amusement, and of course we might simply attribute it to Quinn's paranoia, but it is also possible to read this as a metaphor for the relationship between Auster and his readers – one that stands as an ironic counterpoint to the portrait of the artist that Auster depicts in the interviews I cited earlier. Auster's deliberate refusal to connect his eccentric theory about *Don Quixote* to Quinn's case, his 'ironic pleasure' in observing Quinn's discomfiture (if that is what it is), and his withdrawal into an enigmatic silence that he breaks only briefly to introduce his son, also called Daniel ('Daniel', he said to the boy, 'this is Daniel.' And then to Quinn, with that same ironic smile, 'Daniel, this is Daniel'), and to issue an invitation to dinner that Quinn declines, can be read as an analogue for the ironic detachment and puzzling reticence that the *Trilogy* itself practises.

Then again, the Auster who appears in *City of Glass*, though he shares his name with the author of the *Trilogy* and has a wife and son with the same names as those of the author, is not identical to him. If he were, he could not possibly appear in the book, appearing to know nothing of the book in which he appears. Furthermore, *City of Glass* ends with the belated revelation that the narrator of the story is a friend of Auster's, or rather a former friend, since he accuses the author of having 'behaved badly throughout' (p. 132). Needless to say, he does not explain what he means by this, but it does call into question the portrait of Auster given earlier in the story. If he appears somewhat complacent and aloof, is that because the narrator's disillusionment has coloured his representation of him? If this is the case, then the reader who has interpreted Auster's 'ironic smile' as evidence of the real author's attitude towards Quinn, and/or towards him/herself, may have fallen victim to a further irony, which paradoxically undermines that earlier reading but also reinstates it, since the real Auster ventriloquises the narrator of the story just as surely as he puts words into his namesake's mouth.

At one point the unnamed narrator of *The Locked Room* observes that 'In the end, each life is no more than the sum of contingent facts, a chronicle of chance intersections, of flukes, of random

events that divulge nothing but their c
but by insisting so conspicuously or
events in *City of Glass*, Auster r
they are the product neither of h
of cause and effect, but rather of au
use of prolepsis, *occupatio* and, above all, a
paradoxically ironising itself, Auster creates a n
lises the positions of both author and reader in way
of postmodernism, while at the same time, through its
tion of jokes, digressions and anecdotes, providing some
old-fashioned pleasures of story-telling.

BRET EASTON ELLIS, *AMERICAN PSYCHO*

Even before it was published, *American Psycho*, Bret Easton Ellis's fourth book, had become notorious for its graphic representation of the torture and mutilation of the (mostly female) victims of its serial killer protagonist, Patrick Bateman. Amid charges of misogyny, the original publishers of the novel, Simon & Schuster, dropped it, and when it did appear, under the Vintage imprint, it was greeted with widespread outrage. Roger Straus, of Farrar, Straus & Giroux, denounced it as 'the most revolting book I have ever read', the *New York Times* urged its readers not to buy it, many bookstores refused to stock it and there were organised boycotts of those that did.[11] It was banned in some countries; in others, it was sold only to those over eighteen years of age, in shrink-wrapped packaging. Ellis was already a controversial figure after the publication of his first novel, *Less Than Zero* (1985), which chronicled in explicit detail the decadent lifestyles of a group of bored Californian rich kids, but the furore over *American Psycho* was of a different order of magnitude altogether. Since its publication, however, the novel has been gradually canonised: it is now widely taught on college courses; it features in a series of guides to contemporary classics; the image used on the book's dustcover also adorns the front cover of the '1001 Books You Must Read Before You Die'; and a well-received film version was released in 2000. You can even buy an action figure of its protagonist, Patrick Bateman.

City of Glass and *White Noise*, the key question in
Psycho is: how can we tell when, or if, Ellis is being ironic?
er, the stakes are higher in this novel, because though the
ned narrator of Auster's story and Jack Gladney are both
liable as narrators as their peculiar anxieties and predilections
judice their accounts of events, their narratives contain nothing
extreme as Bateman's. In one of the few initial positive reviews
of the novel, Terence Blacker claimed that *American Psycho* had
been largely misunderstood, Ellis's intention in 'mirroring the
lethal vacuousness of his narrator' being to satirise the 'hedonistic,
coke-fuelled consumerism of the eighties'.[12] However, in an interview with Larry McCafferty the late David Foster Wallace, a contemporary of Ellis's, was scathing about the idea that 'bad writing'
can be read as 'an ingenious mimesis of a bad world'.[13] For Wallace,
the logical end of such an argument was that 'If readers believe
the world is stupid, shallow and mean, then Ellis can write a mean
shallow stupid novel that becomes a mordant deadpan commentary
on the badness of everything' (p. 132).

Like the opening of *White Noise*, *American Psycho* initially gives
the impression of being a third person narrative. Not until page 8
does the first-person pronoun appear:

> I shiver and hand her [Courtney] my black wool Giorgio
> Armani overcoat and she takes it from me, carefully airkissing
> my right cheek, then she performs the same exact movements
> on Price while taking his Armani overcoat. The new Talking
> Heads on CD plays softly in the living room.[14] (Ellis 1991:
> 8)

This passage is striking not simply by virtue of it being the first time
that the voice of the narrator and protagonist, Patrick Bateman, is
heard, but also because it raises several questions that are central
to the novel. On the face of it, this is a neutral piece of descriptive
prose, but in fact the ambiguity of the syntax mirrors the ambiguity of the situation as a whole ('exact same movements' could mean
either that precisely identical movements were performed in each
case or that the two movements were performed with equal precision). Until this point it had seemed likely that the symbolically

named Price was the protagonist of the novel, but with the appearance of the (as yet unnamed) narrator, Price is suddenly relegated to subordinate status and indeed disappears altogether for most of the rest of the novel. It is not clear whether the narrator (addressed as Bateman a few lines later) intends any satirical comment on the mores of his social world in his description of Courtney's careful air-kissing greeting, or in noting that he and Price both have Armani overcoats. Certainly, this last fact paves the way for a running joke involving the fact that the men in Bateman's circle constantly mistake, and are mistaken for, one another, the implication being that their (lack of) personalities, their clothes, and all other visual signifiers (ethnicity, age, class) are so homogeneous as to make them virtually interchangeable. But the two telling details are those at the start and end of the passage. Why does Bateman shiver? Is he cold? Perhaps, but it seems unlikely, given his general insensitivity and the fact that the venue of the party (it takes place in the apartment of Evelyn, Bateman's girlfriend) is bound to be comfortably warm. It seems more like an involuntary shudder – a premonition of the horrors to which Bateman himself will seem impervious, but which will chill most readers to the bone.

Second, the mention of the Talking Heads CD playing in the background seems calculated to remind readers of the last of the three epigraphs at the start of the novel:

And as things fell apart
Nobody paid much attention.[15]

The appositeness of this epigraph is clear enough: as the novel proceeds, Bateman commits more and more horrific murders with increasing recklessness and even attempts on several occasions to confess his crimes, only to find that he is either ignored completely or contradicted. Both Bateman and the world he inhabits appear, for much of the novel, to be disintegrating. However, references to the work of the band also recur on a number of occasions in the main text of *American Psycho*: it becomes the soundtrack not just to Evelyn's party but also to the first detailed description of Bateman's domestic routines (p. 27). These episodes both precede the revelations about what else goes on in Bateman's apartment (rape, torture, mutilation, murder), but the final mention of the band, towards the end of the novel, occurs in a context that exposes the full extent of Bateman's depravity:

> Today I was obsessed with the idea of faxing Sarah's blood I drained from her vagina over to her office in the mergers division at Chase Manhattan, and I didn't work out this morning because I'd made a necklace from the bones of some girl's vertebrae and wanted to stay home and wear it around my neck while I masturbated in the white marble tub in my bathroom, grunting and moaning like some kind of animal. Then I watched a movie about five lesbians and ten vibrators. Favorite group: Talking Heads. Drinks: J & B or Absolut on the rocks. TV show: *Late Night with David Letterman*. Soda: Diet Pepsi. Water: Evian. Sport: Baseball. (p. 380)

There are several ironies in this passage. The most glaring is that Bateman expresses self-loathing only with reference to his onanism (describing the noises he makes while masturbating – 'grunting and moaning like some kind of animal' – with distaste), while his grotesque fetishisation of his victim's body parts and bodily fluids is described with casual detachment (so habitual have Bateman's murders become that he identifies the owner of the bones from which he constructs the necklace only as 'some girl'). That his only regret is that his perverse sexual activities have prevented his customary visit to the gym draws attention to the ironic disparity between the fastidious care, indeed reverence, with which Bateman treats his own body (long passages of the novel are devoted to descriptions of the various beauty and health products that he favours) and the absolute lack of regard or scruples he demonstrates for others'. It is the final irony of the passage which primarily concerns me here, however: namely, the apparent non-sequitur that concludes the paragraph.

At the end of this blood-curdling description of Bateman's use of his victims' remains, he appends an elliptical list of some of his lifestyle preferences. Such lists have become something of a commonplace in what is sometimes called 'ladlit' (after the designation 'chicklit', signifying fiction aimed at a young female market), as exemplified by Nick Hornby's *High Fidelity* (1995), which is punctuated with its protagonist's itemised 'top tens'.[16] Whereas novels such as Hornby's represent the male mania for cataloguing and categorising as an essentially benign, harmless compulsion, Bateman's obsession (a word that he himself uses in this passage) in *American Psycho* is anything but harmless or benign. The incongruity of this list in the context of the passage as a whole, then, is clearly ironic. More ambiguous, however, is Bateman's nomination of Talking Heads as his favourite band.

If, as James Annesley argues in *Blank Fiction*, 'Ellis orientates his text around an obviously moral position', then we would expect to see a clear divergence between Bateman's values and opinions and those of his creator.[17] Indeed, Annesley complains that 'commentators have failed to see the distinction between the views of the author and the activities of the character' (p. 12), but the implication of Ellis's choice of the Talking Heads epigraph is that he shares Bateman's estimation of them. This does not, of course, suggest in itself that he shares anything else with Bateman, but it does seem to invite a troubling identification between the two. Of Bateman's propensity for itemisation, Annesley has this to say:

> His desire to catalogue is so overpowering that it infects his whole personality and inspires not only tedious, itemised lists of his property, but also intensely detailed descriptions of his violence. The litany of atrocities constitutes . . . some kind of reflection on the power of his ownership. Bateman is a consumer with unlimited desires and as such he is unable to distinguish between purchasing a camera and purchasing a woman. The violent treatment of his predominantly female victims is thus tied to his vision of a world in which everything has been commodified. (p. 14)

There is no doubt that there is an intimate connection between Bateman's consumerism and his objectification of women, but this doesn't account for his explosive rage: to pursue Annesley's analogy, Bateman wouldn't vandalise or destroy a camera that he had bought, yet he inflicts unspeakable violence on his victims (female and male). Moreover, this violence, though metaphorically unspeakable, is, as Annesley points out, actually articulated, and while Annesley's equation of Bateman's 'lists of his property' with his 'litany of atrocities' provides a psychological explanation for these passages, it offers no moral justification for them. The problem here is that Ellis could easily have elicited the necessary outrage and indignation at Bateman's crimes without dwelling in such detail on the ordeals to which he subjects his victims. In this sense, he is implicated in Bateman's crimes: it is his decision as author to imagine, and relate, the methods, modes and minutiae of Bateman's murders. Annesley himself concedes that 'Ellis may . . . [be trying] to make a point about sex and violence in contemporary culture, but in doing so he produces a text that mimics the very processes he is criticising' (p. 21), but he doesn't explain how this can be reconciled with his earlier contention that commentators have failed to recognise the distinction between Ellis's position and Bateman's. Is Ellis satirising the values of Bateman's world or is his investment in that world too great for him to establish any ironic distance between it and him? Is he complicit in Bateman's crimes or is he condemning them? The answer is both. In the same way as Melville both parodies the dusty old scholar who assembles the 'etymologies' of the whale that preface the main narrative of *Moby-Dick* and at the same time provides evidence of his own obsession with the arcane topic, each time Bateman notes the designer labels of the clothes he or one of his acquaintances is wearing, or delivers a diatribe on the superiority of Pepsi to Coca-Cola, Ellis is simultaneously mocking his protagonist's earnest devotion to trivia and participating in it. Like Jack Gladney's shopping mall apotheosis in *White Noise* and the anecdote about Whitman's brain in Auster's *Ghosts*, at moments such as these Ellis half-offers his readers an ironic vantage point from which to judge his protagonist.

To put it another way, the conjunction of interests and knowledge between Ellis and Bateman, combined with the absence of any voice in the narrative other than Bateman's, makes it difficult to locate irony with any certainty, and yet *American Psycho* demands to be read ironically. To understand how this works, it is helpful to return to the allusions to popular music in the novel. One of the most striking features of the novel is the insertion, directly after some of its most gruesome passages, of several essays on different singers and pop groups. The first of these – an essay on Genesis, which most first-time readers might expect to refer to the first book of the Bible – immediately follows the first reported murder of the novel, in which Bateman tortures a beggar he encounters on the street, cutting out both his eyeballs and stabbing him repeatedly in the stomach before breaking the legs of his dog.[18] What is particularly shocking about this attack is the sadistic pleasure Bateman takes in it. First, he engages the man in conversation, appearing sympathetic to his plight, while waving a banknote in his view but of out of reach. Then he detaches the man's retina, 'being very careful not to kill him' and begins to stab him 'lightly' in the abdomen (p. 126). He is clearly intent on prolonging the man's agony, ensuring that he will suffer a slow death, and his reluctance to leave the scene of the crime (he 'linger[s], 'laughing' at the 'tableau') is mirrored by the length of time he devotes to narrating the episode (p. 127). It is difficult to accommodate this episode in Annesley's model of Bateman as the product of a society governed by unrestrained materialism: though Bateman taunts the beggar with a five-dollar bill, asking him why he doesn't get a job, finally calling him a 'fucking loser', his contempt for the man's low status seems to be incidental to the murder (p. 126). Indeed, Bateman doesn't discriminate when it comes to the status of his victims: they include unborn babies, children, prostitutes, ex-girlfriends, professional rivals, strangers he encounters on the street. However, an alternative framework for reading the murders is provided by the abrupt transition from this episode to the chapter entitled 'Genesis'.

Like the list of favourites that follows the references to the blood and bones of two of Bateman's later victims, this chapter relies for its initial impact on its incongruity with what has gone before. However, there are significant differences: whereas in the passage quoted above the list is brief and its contents arbitrary, here Bateman delivers a four-page disquisition on the *oeuvre* of the British rock band Genesis, which contains a number of comments that shed light on the events of the preceding chapter. In his discussion of their 1981 album *Abacab*, Bateman reveals that his favourite track is 'Man on the Corner', which he describes as 'a moving ballad' that 'profoundly equates [*sic*] a relationship with a solitary figure (a bum, perhaps a poor homeless person?), "that lonely man on the corner" who just stands around' (p. 129). There is of course a grim irony in Bateman being moved by the plight of the generic social outcast in the Genesis song, having just inflicted horrific, probably fatal wounds on a real homeless man. However, Ellis also establishes an implied ironic distance between himself and Bateman more subtly, undermining Bateman's credentials as an authority on pop music in general, and on Genesis in particular, through a number of telling details.

First, Bateman's prose is peppered with lazy clichés and hyperbole as well as the odd solecism, for example his only reservation about the 1980 album *Duke* is that he finds one of its tracks, 'Alone Tonight', 'reminiscent of "Tonight, Tonight, Tonight" from the group's later masterpiece *Invisible Touch*', whereas of course it can only be said to anticipate the later track, as it precedes it by some six years (p. 128). Second, although he gets their names right earlier in the piece, Bateman begins, about halfway through, to refer to two of the band members, Tony Banks and Mike Rutherford, as 'Mike Banks' and 'Tom Rutherland', respectively (p. 130). Third, he confesses at the start to having been a fan of the band only since 1980, after the 'complex, ambiguous studies of loss' that characterised the band's earlier work, when Peter Gabriel was the lead singer, were replaced by 'smashing first-rate pop songs' on which the band's drummer, Phil Collins, sings lead vocals (p. 128) and he concludes the piece by erasing this early period of the band's history entirely, claiming that 'Genesis is still the best, most exciting band to come out of England in the 1980s' (pp. 128, 131). The first of these statements calls Bateman's aesthetic judgement into question, since a preference for 'pop songs', even 'first-rate' ones, over 'complex, ambiguous studies of loss' suggests a superficial appreciation of the form (most critics agree that the band's creative high point came during the Gabriel era, 1969–75, though they became more commercially successful after his departure). The second reveals an ignorance confirmed by an earlier reference to 'the horns by some group called Earth, Wind and Fire' on one of the tracks from *Abacab* (p. 129). No one with any pretensions to being a pop aficionado would be unaware of the work of Earth, Wind and Fire – one of the most successful and accomplished disco/funk bands of the late 1970s and early 1980s. It may be, of course, that Bateman intends the comment to be ironically dismissive: this would be consistent with his claim that 'Land of Confusion', one of Genesis's biggest hits, 'is laid down with a groove funkier and blacker than anything Prince or Michael Jackson – or any other black artist of recent years, for that matter – has come up with' (p. 131); and with his racial insult to the beggar in the previous chapter. The final words he addresses to his victim are 'Go buy some *gum*, you crazy fucking *nigger*' (p. 127).

On the other hand, Bateman's apparent disdain for African-American music does not extend to Whitney Houston, to whom he devotes another adulatory essay later in the novel. Moreover, if it seems unlikely that Bateman would not know about Earth, Wind and Fire, it becomes more plausible when we discover later that he hasn't heard of Hank Williams (one of the most influential postwar American songwriters) (p. 342), that he thinks Phil Collins wrote 'A Groovy Kind of Love' (it was written by Carole Bayer Sager and Toni Wine) (p. 97), that 'You Can't Always Get What You Want' is by the Beatles (it is a Rolling Stones song) and that Elvis Costello's second album was called *My Aim Was You* (p. 340) (its title is *My Aim is True* and it was Costello's first album). This last error is particularly significant, given that Ellis took the name of his first novel, *Less Than Zero*, from Costello's début single and is an avowed admirer of his, whereas Bateman dismisses the album he misnames as 'thin' and 'vapid' (p. 340). This reference to Costello comes from the final pop music essay of the novel – on a band called Huey Lewis and the News – which follows Bateman's most spectacular killing spree.

The chapter that deals with this spree – entitled Chase, Manhattan (an allusion to the famous New York bank but also a pun, since it describes a chase through the streets of Manhattan) – is pivotal. At this stage of the novel Bateman is undergoing a breakdown of sorts: constantly popping pills, his murders becoming increasingly reckless, he finds himself being pursued by police after the silencer on his gun fails when he shoots a busking saxophonist. During his description of the ensuing chase, in which he kills at least seven people (including three policemen), Bateman begins to refer to himself in the third person – 'Patrick tries to put the cab in reverse but nothing happens' (p. 335). He ends the chapter by leaving an answer-phone message for one of his colleagues, making a full confession of his crimes – 'thirty, forty, a hundred murders' (p. 338). Still, Bateman remains at large: as the novel goes on, he repeatedly tries to tell people the truth, but they either think he is joking or ignore him altogether. So instead of 'Chase, Manhattan' leading to Bateman's arrest and a resolution in which some kind of moral order is restored, it precedes the most bathetic, banal chapter of the novel, in which Bateman's eulogies to mediocrity become increasingly self-contradictory and incoherent:

> [S]ide one [of Huey Lewis's most successful album, *Fore*] . . . ends with the masterpiece 'Hip to be Square' (which, ironically, is accompanied by the band's only bad video), the key song on *Fore!*, which is a rollicking ode to conformity that's so catchy most people probably don't even listen to the lines, but with Chris Hayes blasting guitar and the terrific keyboard playing – who cares? And it's not just about the pleasures of conformity and the importance of trends – it's also a personal statement about the band itself, though of what I'm not quite sure. (p. 343)

Once again, this mini-essay provides an ironic counterpoint to the extreme, cinematic violence of the previous episode but at the same time ironises that counterpoint. The irony of Bateman championing conformity having just displayed the most extreme form of anti-social behaviour imaginable seems straightforward. However, Huey Lewis and the News's hymn to conformity is itself ironic (something that renders Bateman's naive admiration for it doubly ironic). Moreover, if Bateman's private life is, as he himself puts it, 'a living hell' (p. 136), his public persona is entirely anodyne.

In the first few pages of the novel, Bateman's girlfriend, Evelyn, describes him, without irony, as 'the boy next door' (p. 11); when one of his ex-girlfriends, Bethany (whom he later tortures and kills), asks him why he carries on working when he is so wealthy, Bateman replies: 'Because . . . I . . . want . . . to . . . fit . . . in' (p. 228). So unexceptional and outwardly conformist is Bateman that he is repeatedly mistaken for one of the other twenty-something Wall Street brokers with whom he associates. Indeed, Bateman himself remarks on his resemblance to Craig McDermott, one of his colleagues, noting that 'we both look pretty much the same' (p. 240). He also concedes that 'if I were to disappear . . . the odds are good that no one would notice I was gone' (p. 217). James Annesley calls Bateman 'a yuppie everyman' (p. 19) and claims that *American Psycho* is characterised by 'the absence of any kind of existential reflection on his own behaviour or any desire to legitimate it in psychological terms' (p. 19), but in fact Bateman only *appears* to be an everyman because he makes a conscious effort to construct himself as ordinary and inconspicuous; he is in fact acutely aware of his own blankness. After he is interviewed by Donald Kimball, a detective investigating the disappearance of one of his victims, Bateman observes that Kimball is 'utterly unaware of how truly vacant I am' (p. 264), and in the latter stages of the novel Bateman repeatedly reflects explicitly on the tension between his outward normality and his internal lack of humanity. At one point he observes that 'I had all the characteristics of a human being . . . but I was simply imitating reality' (p. 271); on another occasion he claims that 'there is an idea of a Patrick Bateman, some kind of abstraction, but there is no real me' (p. 362).

Because of this self-awareness, the ironic distance established in Bateman's excursions into cultural criticism cannot be sustained. Instead, that irony itself becomes ironised, so that Bateman's enthusiasm for bland, middle-of-the-road pop, invariably expressed straight after the moments of most extreme depravity in the novel, paradoxically heightens the sense of Bateman's inhumanity precisely because it appears to relocate him safely within the bounds of conventional human values. Conversely, when Bateman confesses to his moral vacuity and claims that he has 'gain[ed] no deeper knowledge' about himself, he paradoxically demonstrates a self-knowledge (and a self-disgust) that makes him more human. As his violence becomes more extreme – encompassing rape, torture, dismemberment, cannibalism and necrophilia – Bateman's grip on reality becomes increasingly tenuous. He imagines being pursued by a park bench and being given instructions to kill cats by an ATM. This mental deterioration calls into question the reliability of Bateman's narrative as a whole, particularly after he visits Paul Owen's apartment, where he has been concealing the remains of some of his victims, only to discover a realtor showing an immaculate apartment to prospective buyers. This further complicates the question of irony in the novel: if Bateman has simply imagined committing his crimes, then the moral outrage felt by readers at these acts of depravity is misplaced, as is any indignation and incredulity at the persistent refusal of Bateman's colleagues to recognise his guilt, even when he is trying to confess it to them. By introducing these doubts into the narrative, Ellis is in a sense having his ironic cake and eating it: including material that he knows will provoke outrage while at the same time providing himself with an alibi in the form of Bateman's delusions.

Like *White Noise* and *City of Glass* then, *American Psycho* is a novel that simultaneously invites and deflects ironic readings, paradoxically making it both imperative and impossible to infer an authorial perspective that diverges from the narrator's. The moment early in the novel when Courtney tells Bateman 'You really know how to charm the ladies' and Bateman observes that 'There is no sarcasm in Courtney's voice' (p. 8) can be read as a meta-fictional reflection on Ellis's method in the novel. Like Bateman here, who knows that Courtney's compliment only makes sense if intended ironically but cannot detect any sarcasm in her voice, readers of *American Psycho* may understand that the novel is supposed to satirise Bateman's values but search in vain for evidence of authorial irony. At times that evidence is there, but it tends to rely on extra-textual knowledge and the fact remains that there are several passages in *American Psycho* that are too grotesque to be redeemed by the deferred promise of ironic distance.

CONCLUSION

I began this chapter by suggesting that irony always implies a moral position – the normative position from which whatever is ironised deviates – but I have also argued that in *White Noise*, *City of Glass* and *American Psycho* there is no stable centre of authority from which a moral position can be inferred. In fact, the clearest indicators in all three fictions of a moral agenda come in the form of what might be called millenarian references.

There is what Gladney calls a 'persistent sense of large-scale ruin' in *White Noise* that manifests itself periodically in his off-hand comments, such as 'times are bad' (p. 14), '[a]ll plots tend to move deathward' (p. 26), and '[f]orgetfulness has . . . entered the food chain' (p. 52). It is present also in Murray's analysis of the *Zeitgeist*: he explains his preference for white, non-branded supermarket goods as part of a 'new austerity', a 'kind of spiritual consensus' that is 'like World War III' (p. 18) and argues, ambivalently, that technology 'creates an appetite for immortality on the one hand . . . threatens universal extinction on the other' (p. 285). In the middle of 'The Airborne Toxic Event', Jack is waylaid by a Jehovah's Witness who hands him a pamphlet entitled 'Twenty Common Mistakes about the End of the World' (pp. 135–7). As impressed by his conviction as he is later dismayed by the nuns' lack of it, Jack 'wonder[s] about his eerie self-assurance, his freedom from doubt. Is this the point of Armageddon? No ambiguity, no more doubt' (p. 137). Babette is similarly struck by the man's wife, who tells her that 'God Jehovah's got a bigger surprise in store than this [the airborne toxic event]' (p. 132); a few moments later, Babette (consciously or unconsciously) mimics the woman's tone when she announces to Jack that '[w]e're practically at the edge' (p. 132). Later in the chapter she reads out loud stories from the tabloids to a group of 'four blind people, a nurse and three sighted people' (p. 146). One of the items she reads relates the thoughts of 'the country's leading psychics' about imminent events: these include predictions that the moon will explode, though 'UFO cleanup crews will help avert a worldwide disaster, signalling an era of peace and harmony' and that 'an air-crash cult will hijack a jumbo jet and crash it into the White House', though the President and First Lady will survive (p. 146). At first Jack is taken aback by the apparent credulity of Babette's auditors ('[t]he predictions did not seem reckless to them', he notes), but then he observes that the characteristic formula of these stories – giving a 'hopeful twist to apocalyptic events' – is 'not so very remote from our own immediate experience' (p. 146). For anyone reading *White Noise* after 9/11, the prophecy of the attack on the White House will necessarily seem less absurd than it would have done to contemporary readers of the novel. Moreover, the movement in

Jack's response from initial (ironic) distance to a recognition that the 'audience of the old and blind' (a phrase alluding to the ancient belief that these members of society possess faculties of wisdom and second sight denied to the younger and more able-bodied) may be attuned to a larger resonance of these tales, is consistent with the millenarianism that haunts the novel.

In an interview with Joseph Mallia, Paul Auster said of *The New York Trilogy*: 'these books are mostly concerned with spiritual questions, the search for spiritual grace' (p. 280). He might have added that these spiritual questions are intimately bound up with eschatological ones. From Peter Stillman Jr's portentous pronouncements, such as 'I am the last of the Stillmans . . . I am the last one . . . the end of everyone, the last man' (p. 22), to his father's invention of the aptly named Henry Dark and his apocalyptic pamphlet *The New Babel*, *City of Glass* is full of apocalyptic intimations. Towards the end of *City of Glass*, Quinn concludes that he has 'come to the end of himself', that '[t]here was nothing left', 'everything was gone' (p. 125), the tautologous nature of these phrases implying a symbolic rather than literal meaning. This is reinforced by the way in which Quinn's narrative, as recorded in the red notebook, peters out, its final entry reading: 'What will happen when there are no more pages in the red notebook?' (p. 131). When the self-cancelling mantras that punctuate Stillman Jr's speech, such as 'Yes and no', 'I am Peter Stillman. That is not my real name' (p. 15), begin to contaminate Quinn's discourse, 'My name is Paul Auster. That is not my real name' (p. 40), the nihilism of that final entry is already implicit. Aliki Varvogli argues acutely that *City of Glass* exhibits 'a certain nostalgia for the "Golden Age" of the private investigator, and nostalgia implies not only a hankering after the past but also the acceptance that a return to this past is no longer possible' (p. 25). However, it also exhibits a certain despairing longing for an end to the present, which implies an acceptance of the inescapability of the future, so that Quinn, like the narrator of *The Unnameable* (1959), the last in the trilogy of novels by one of Auster's heroes, Samuel Beckett, 'can't go on, [but] must go on'.[19]

This is also an apt description of the mixture of nihilism and resignation that characterises Patrick Bateman in *American Psycho*.

Bret Easton Ellis's novel is bookended with allusions to Dante's *Inferno*. It begins with one capitalised warning, 'ABANDON ALL HOPE YE WHO ENTER HERE' (p. 3) – implicitly addressed to readers of the novel as well as being a transcription of some graffiti that Bateman sees – which echoes the famous legend greeting those entering the underworld in Dante's poem, and it ends with another: 'THIS IS NOT AN EXIT' (p. 384). In between, we encounter horrors that drain Bateman's clichéd description of his life as 'a living hell' of any irony. If the Manhattan of Ellis's novel functions as a modern-day equivalent to Dante's mythical underworld – a notion that is reinforced by the suggestive description of Price, Bateman's symbolically named associate, running down a subway tunnel, 'disappearing into blackness' (p. 60) – then the chapter towards the close of the novel entitled 'End of the 1980s' (p. 356), whose final words are 'I feel I'm moving toward as well as away from something, and anything is possible' (p. 366), seems to herald the end not just of that decade but, in the biblical sense, the end of days.

Although all three novels have been hailed as postmodernist classics, there is an old-fashioned concern with morality and spirituality at the heart of each of them. In particular, in their very different ways, Auster, DeLillo and Ellis all seem to express a fear about the very loss of meaning and normative values which postmodernism is conventionally taken to celebrate. Perhaps the final ironic paradox shared by *White Noise*, *City of Glass* and *American Psycho* is that their rhetorical radicalism both reveals and obscures an ideological conservatism, a nihilism issuing from nostalgia.

- The use of irony in modern American fiction is fraught with paradox. It can be used to circumvent conventional morality, yet in order to use irony in this way, writers rely on a shared sense of what is morally acceptable. One ironic reading of a text can undermine another and at the same time confirm it. This chapter examines the use which the chosen authors make of these ironic paradoxes.
- Further use of paradox is evident in these novels. They exhibit the self-reflexivity, tonal ambiguity, generic hybridity and intertextuality that characterise postmodernist fiction, yet they also

invoke the conventions of the classic realist novel. They allude to various kinds of popular genre fiction, yet situate themselves in the canonical tradition of American literature. They encourage their readers to collaborate with them in the construction of meaning; on the other hand, they frustrate, alienate and antagonise them, withholding meaning.

- In the novels selected for discussion here, there is no stable centre of authority from which a moral position can be inferred. The clearest indicators of a moral agenda come in the form of what might be called millenarian references. Each author seems to express a fear about the very loss of meaning and normative values which postmodernism is conventionally taken to celebrate.

- Their radical form notwithstanding, the novels chosen might be seen as essentially conservative moral critiques of the state of the American nation in the 1980s, an aspect which has led to their current status as modern classics, widely taught and studied in the US and elsewhere.

NOTES

1. Don DeLillo, *White Noise* (London: Picador, 1986), p. 9. All subsequent references in the text are to this edition.
2. Collected in *The Whitsun Weddings* (1964).
3. Pynchon is most famous as the author of a number of experimental novels widely seen as among the foundation texts of postmodernist fiction: namely, *V* (1963), *The Crying of Lot 49* (1966) and *Gravity's Rainbow* (1973).
4. These consist of a short list (usually a trio) of products, inserted into the narrative without attribution as follows: 'The Airport Marriot, the Downtown Travelodge, the Sheraton Inn, the Conference Center' (p. 15); 'Dacron, Orlon, Lycra Spandex' (p. 52); 'Try an Audi Turbo . . . Try a Toyota Supra.' (p. 81); 'Mastercard. Visa. American Express. (p. 100); 'Krylon, Rust-Oleum, Red Devil' (p. 159); 'Leaded, unleaded, super unleaded' (p. 199); 'Clorets, Velamints, Freedent' (p. 229); CABLE HEALTH, CABLE WEATHER, CABLE NEWS,

CABLE NATURE. (p. 231); 'Tegrin, Denorex, Selsun Blue' (p. 289); 'Containing iron, niacin and riboflavin' (p. 310). DeLillo originally intended to call his novel *Panasonic* but was denied permission to use it because it is the registered trading name of a large electronics company. Instead it appears as the final, single-word paragraph of Chapter 32.

5. Cited in Daniel Septimus, 'Still Reverberating', *The Jerusalem Post*, 4 February 2005, http://www.myjewishlearning.com/blog/culture/happy-birthday-don/, p. 1.

6. Paul Auster, *The Art of Hunger: Essays, Prefaces, Interviews and The Red Notebook* (London: Faber and Faber, 1998), pp. 120, 181, 195. All subsequent references in the text are to this edition.

7. Paul Auster, *The New York Trilogy* (London: Faber and Faber, 1988), p. 3. All subsequent references in the text are to this edition.

8. The author of *Moby-Dick* (1851), a novel named after a mythical whale whose whiteness both enthrals and horrifies the novel's narrator, Ishmael. There are numerous references to Melville in the *Trilogy*, most explicitly in *The Locked Room* when the narrator is given a copy of *Moby-Dick* for his thirtieth birthday and, later, actually claims to be the famous author (pp. 233, 295–6).

9. Aliki Varvogli, *The World is the Book* (Liverpool: Liverpool University Press, 2001), p. 64. All subsequent references in the text are to this edition.

10. Because of Thoreau's belief in the value of civil disobedience (he was imprisoned on one occasion for refusing to pay his taxes) and interest in ecology he was appropriated by a number of radical movements during this period.

11. Cited in Maureen O'Brien, 'American Gothic', http://www.ew.com/ew/article/)0,,313573,00./, p. 1.

12. Reproduced in the (unnumbered) front-matter of the Picador paperback edition.

13. Larry McCafferty, 'An Interview with David Foster Wallace', *Review of Contemporary Fiction*, 13:2 (1993), p. 132 (127–50).

14. Bret Easton Ellis, *American Psycho* (London: Picador, 1991), p. 8. All subsequent references in the text are to this edition.

15. The lines are taken from '(Nothing But) Flowers', a track from the Talking Heads' final album, *Naked* (1988). There may also

be an implied allusion to the debut single from their first album, *Talking Heads: 77* (1977), 'Psychokiller', which appears to record the thoughts of a serial killer.

16. The term 'chicklit' was first coined in 1988 and became common currency in the 1990s, when it was used to describe a publishing trend exemplified by novels such as Helen Fielding's *The Diary of Bridget Jones* (1996).

17. James Annesley, *Blank Fictions: Culture, Consumption and Contemporary American Narrative* (London: Pluto Press, 2008), p. 13. All subsequent references in the text are to this edition.

18. This is not, however, the first murder Bateman has committed. As the novel proceeds, it emerges that he has killed many times before the beginning of the period covered by the narrative.

19. Samuel Beckett, *The Beckett Trilogy* (London: Picador, 1979), p. 381.

CHAPTER 2

Silence, Secrecy and Sexuality: 'Alternate Histories' in Jane Smiley's *A Thousand Acres*, Carol Shields' *The Stone Diaries* and Jeffrey Eugenides' *Middlesex*

The connection between silence and women writers of fiction has become something of a critical commonplace. Ever since Tillie Olsen's seminal *Silences* (1971), feminist critics in particular have been preoccupied with both the extra-textual silences of women writers (that is, the hiatuses in their careers) and their textual silences (that is, what is left unsaid in their work). References to these and to other kinds of silence feature prominently in Carol Shields' biography of Jane Austen. Shields begins by drawing attention to the fact that 'Austen's intractable silences throw long shadows on her apparent chattiness' and ends by noting that on her tombstone there was 'no mention of her six great novels'.[1] Writing of 'the long years of silence' in the middle of Austen's career, during which she apparently stopped writing fiction altogether, Shields suggests that this 'creative silence . . . gestures towards other silences', notably the conspicuous absence in her writing of any mention of her handicapped brother, George (pp. 103, 97). Furthermore, this period of literary inactivity 'means that everything we know of her during this period is . . . a question that leads

around to an even greater silence' (p. 102). Shields argues that
Austen's novels 'can be read . . . through the light that glances and
gathers around the many silences' (p. 111), that *Mansfield Park*
'is a novel about . . . human noise and silence' (p. 146) and that
the famous dénouement of *Persuasion* derives its power from 'the
unspoken subtext of all that has been said aloud' (p. 158).

The idea that silence can be as expressive as speech is as central
to the author of *Jane Austen* as it is to that of her subject. It is intimately connected in her fiction and in that of her contemporary
Jane Smiley, with the trope of what Hermione Lee, in her influential anthologies of women's short stories, has called (borrowing a
phrase from one of Katherine Mansfield's letters) 'the secret self'.[2]
This in turn is associated with female duality: the idea that women
lead a kind of double life. Early on in *The Stone Diaries* (1993),
Shields' most celebrated novel, Clarentine Flett, who adopts
Daisy, the novel's protagonist and narrator, after Daisy's mother
dies in childbirth, learns to cherish the long hours she spends alone
in her home, a time of 'ease and secrecy' when '[t]he silence is
perfect' and she feels 'as though she'd been given two lives instead
of one, the alternate life cloaked in secret'.[3] It is no coincidence that
Clarentine experiences at such moments 'a kind of rapturous wave
. . . bringing tightness to her female parts' (p. 12), because this
cluster of ideas – silence, secrecy and the alternate life – is invariably associated in Shields, as in Smiley, with female sexuality and
gender identity.

Jeffrey Eugenides, the third novelist discussed in this chapter,
is ostensibly the odd one out, as a male author. Yet both his novels
– *The Virgin Suicides* (1993) and *Middlesex* (2002) – are also characterised by the tension between secrecy and revelation, silence
and speech, public and private lives. Where Eugenides differs
from Shields and Smiley is in his implication of male figures in
this conventionally feminised, furtive world: the collective male
narrative voice that tells the stories of the doomed Lisbon sisters
in *The Virgin Suicides* and the female-who-turns-out-to-be-male
narrator of *Middlesex*. In this respect, and in his own incursion as
a male author into this female terrain, Eugenides complicates the
sexual politics of contemporary American fiction and undermines
essentialised notions of gendered discourse.

JANE SMILEY, *A THOUSAND ACRES*

Jane Smiley's Pulitzer Prize-winning *A Thousand Acres* (1991) was her sixth novel and the first to gain her wide recognition, becoming both a bestseller and a set text on many college courses. It is a work paradoxically both very much of its time and part of a venerable tradition. In its treatment of sexual abuse within the family and ecological issues, the novel locates itself rather precisely as the product of a particular cultural moment in the US: the chief revelations of the novel involve the protagonist's recovery of long-repressed memories of paternal incest and her discovery that her history of multiple miscarriages is likely to be the result of environmental pollution. Yet in its rewriting of Shakespeare, it forms part of a continuum that encompasses earlier postwar works, such as Edward Bond's *Lear* (1972) and Tom Stoppard's *Rosencrantz and Guildenstern Are Dead* (1966), but whose origins are to be found in the Restoration and eighteenth-century revisions of Shakespeare by writers such as William Davenant, John Dryden, Thomas Shadwell and Nahum Tate. Of course, Shakespeare's play is itself in part a reworking of an older play, *King Leir*, and many scholars now believe that Shakespeare also rewrote his own play (the Folio version of 1623 being a revision of the Quarto of 1608).

Tate's version of *King Lear*, in which, notoriously, Lear survives and Edgar marries Cordelia at the end of the play, was the only version of Shakespeare's play to be performed on the English stage for some 100 years, and has been partly defended by arguably the most influential Shakespearean critic of the twentieth century, A. C. Bradley:

> Doubtless we are right when we turn with disgust from Tate's sentimental alterations . . . But . . . I find that my feelings call for this 'happy ending' . . . What we desire for him [Lear] during the brief remainder of his days is . . . what Shakespeare himself might have given him – peace and happiness by Cordelia's fireside.[4]

Careful though he is to distance himself from Tate's sentimentality, Bradley is all too susceptible to his own, which takes the form of a beatification of Cordelia – 'to use too many words about Cordelia seems to be a kind of impiety . . . Her image comes before us calm and bright and still' (pp. 264–5) – and a demonisation of Goneril ('she is the most hideous human being (if she is one) that Shakespeare ever drew') and Regan ('less formidable and more loathsome' than her sister) (p. 249). Bradley's lectures on Lear amount to a rewriting of the play – he even goes as far as to rename it 'The Redemption of King Lear'; and Smiley's novel is clearly in part intended as a corrective to this, and other less extreme Manichean readings of Lear.

Because the transposition of the Lear story from *King Lear* into *A Thousand Acres* involves the crossing not just of historical and geographical but also of generic and gender boundaries (a twentieth-century novel written by an American woman rewriting a seventeenth-century play written by a man), it inevitably entails radical shifts in the way the story is told and in the form it takes. In choosing Ginny (the Goneril figure) as her narrator, Smiley immediately signals her intention of rehabilitating the marginalised, stigmatised sisters of Shakespeare's play; against the apparently objective mode of direct dramatisation she sets the apparently subjective mode of the first-person narrative. Many of the most dramatic episodes in Shakespeare's play (the storm scene, Gloucester's blinding, the reconciliation between Lear and Cordelia, Lear's death) are related (at second or third hand) retrospectively in Smiley's novel. Conversely, much that happens off-stage in *King Lear*, in particular the development of the relationship between the three principal villains, Edmund, Goneril and Regan, is brought to the fore in *A Thousand Acres*. As a result, it becomes clear that decisions not just about how to tell a story, but about which bits of it (or, to put it in adversarial terms, whose side of it) to tell, can never be anything but subjective and, by implication and in the broadest sense of the word, political.

The politics of storytelling is a subject on which Ginny meditates on more than one occasion. The novel begins with the return of Jess Clark (the Edmund figure) to the family home which he had left thirteen years earlier when he fled to avoid the draft for the Vietnam War. Ginny observes that during his absence 'everything about him slipped into the category of the unmentionable' and looks forward to watching him 'break through the surface of everything that hadn't been said about him over the years'.[5] In the same chapter she notes that, apart from her bond with her sister Rose (the Regan figure), 'every other relationship was marked by some sort of absence' and, after reciting some of the history of the main highway running past the family farm, she states: 'The view along the Scenic . . . taught me a lesson about what is below the level of the visible' (pp. 8, 9). From the outset, then, the novel is concerned with disappearance, absence, silence: the invisible and 'the unmentionable'. The world of *A Thousand Acres* is one of occlusion and effacement, and one of the great strengths of the novel is the skill, and timing, with which it withholds and reveals its secrets.

One of the most pivotal revelations (it occurs almost exactly at the midpoint of the novel) is that Ginny's repeated miscarriages may have been caused by the pollution of the farm's water supply as a result of the use of chemical fertilisers. The force of this disclosure is all the greater because, as Jess points out, in the wider world '[p]eople have known for ten years or more that nitrates in well water cause miscarriages and death of infants' (p. 165). When Ginny realises that her suffering might have been avoided, her bitterness focuses on the taboo imposed on the discussion of such issues by the farming community at large, and by her husband, Ty (the Albany figure) in particular: '"We never . . . told anyone we'd had miscarriages. We kept it all a secret. What if there are women all over the country who've had miscarriages, and if they just compared notes – but God forbid we should talk about it!"' (p. 259). Yet earlier in the novel Ginny herself had colluded in this conspiracy of silence by concealing her last two miscarriages from her husband and by continuing to attempt to conceive without his consent or knowledge. Indeed, she self-consciously cultivates a clandestine existence which offers her opportunities for self-fulfilment denied to her in her public roles as wife, daughter and sister.

> One of the many benefits of this private project . . . was that it showed me a whole secret world, a way to have two lives, to be two selves. I felt larger and more various than I had in years, full of unknowns, and also of untapped possibilities. (p. 26)

Susan Farrell comments that 'the only way she [Ginny] can imagine articulating her own wishes and desires is by displacing them onto a second, submerged self'.[6] Paradoxically, however, Ginny's instinctive retreat into her secret self turns out to be at least partly the consequence of the trauma of abuse: her belief as an adult, that leading a double life is liberating, is complicated by the fact that she was trained to do so as a child. When her family's dark secrets are finally brought to light, for Ginny the fragility of the familial structure itself is exposed: '[t]he last few weeks had shown well enough for anyone to understand that the one thing our family couldn't tolerate, that maybe no family could tolerate, was things coming into the open' (pp. 251–2). There is an implied ambivalence here towards the idea (enshrined in popular television shows such as Oprah Winfrey's) that baring and sharing all is of therapeutic value, an ambivalence still evident at the end of the novel when Ginny reflects on the effect these discoveries have had on her life:

One benefit, which I have lost, of a life where many things go unsaid, is that you don't have to remember things about yourself that are too bizarre to imagine. What was never given utterance becomes too nebulous to recall. (p. 305)

Just as Cordelia, in the opening scene of *King Lear*, is damned if she speaks and damned if she doesn't, so in *A Thousand Acres* the price of speech is at times as high as that of silence. In fact, throughout the novel there is an unresolved tension in Ginny between the desire to break down the barriers of silence that surround so many of the key areas of her life and the fear that to do so would cause an irreparable breach in the fabric not only of her social world, but of herself. One of these areas is occupied by her mother, whose death from cancer 'before I knew her' places her in 'the category of the unmentionable' (p. 93). At one point she contrives, then dismisses, 'a magic solution' to the enigma of her mother's life and death, imagining that her spirit has been mysteriously reincarnated in Rose: 'All I had to do was be mindful of the relationship between them [her mother and Rose] (mindful in secret, in a way no one else could be mindful), and gather up the answers, glean the apparently harvested field for overlooked bits. But no' (p. 94). It is not clear whether or not Ginny is aware of the irony of trying to discover her mother's secrets by preserving her own secretive life (being mindful *in secret* of the relationship between her older sister and her mother, from which she feels excluded). At any rate, Ginny's curiosity about her family history extends further back. Her grandmother Edith (her father's mother), Ginny tells us, 'was reputed to be a silent woman', but Ginny questions this received version of history, wondering whether 'her reputed silence wasn't due to temperament at all, but due to fear', the result of being 'surrounded by men' and the 'great plate of land they cherished', and having no means of escaping this male-enclosed world: 'She didn't drive a car. Possibly she had no money of her own. That detail went unrevealed by the stories' (pp. 132–3). As with the agricultural metaphor of 'glean[ing] the apparently harvested field for overlooked bits', so here Ginny's interest in what has been left unsaid, the details that 'went unrevealed by the stories', seems to be an analogue for Smiley's method in this novel. Digging the well-excavated site of Shakespeare's play, she disinters the fragments that critics have neglected or missed altogether, and from these she (re)constructs an 'alternate history': one that privileges the private, the domestic, the feminocentric, over the public, the national, the phallocentric.

It is has become critical orthodoxy over the past thirty years or so that *King Lear* is a political play, but the readings that begin from this premise tend to be concerned primarily with the politics of state, of kingship – what we might call macrocosmic politics. Moreover, much is made of the grand scale of *King Lear*, of its philosophical reach, its preoccupation with the condition of man, in particular 'unaccommodated man', that 'poor, bare, forked animal'.[7] What Smiley sees, and what *A Thousand Acres* highlights, is that the play's dynamics are essentially familial, microcosmic; that its central conflicts are between siblings, genders and genera-tions, rather than between rival political factions. As if to empha-sise the point, Smiley transforms Lear's kingdom into a farm and the king himself into a farmer (albeit the wealthiest and most pow-erful figure in his local community), rather than the president or the holder of another important public office. In keeping with this scaled-down version of the story, Lear's train of followers is absent from Smiley's novel (in productions of Shakespeare's play they often appear, although there are no stage-directions to justify this), the roles of the king's faithful followers, Kent (Ken LaSalle in the novel) and the Fool (Marv Carson) are reduced and the kingdom of ancient Briton becomes an estate of 1,000 acres.

Smiley is also careful, for the most part, to avoid directly rewriting particular episodes from Shakespeare's play. Two notable exceptions are Act I.4 and Act II.4 in which first Goneril, then Goneril and Regan, confront their father. Smiley conflates these scenes, so for the sake of accuracy, as well as convenience, I shall refer to this episode in the novel as the 'pre-storm scene'. In Shakespeare's play the two sisters demand that Lear live more temperately, that he be 'led / By some discretion that discerns your state/Better than you yourself' (II.4.148). Lear's response is to move from bitter recrimination and self-pity – 'She hath . . . / Look'd black upon me; strook me with her tongue, / Most serpent-like, upon the very heart' (ll. 159–61); to furious cursing – 'Strike her young bones, / You taking airs, with lameness! . . . Infect her beauty, / You fen-suck'd fogs . . . / To fall and blister!' (ll. 161–8); to wheedling ingratiation – 'Thy tender-hefted nature shall not give / Thee o'er to harshness: her eyes are fierce, but thine / Do comfort and not burn' (ll. 171–3); to hysterical invective – 'thou art . . . a disease that's in my flesh . . . a bile / A plague-sore, or embossed carbuncle,/In my corrupted blood' (ll. 221–5); to incoherent threats – 'I will have such revenges on you both / That all the world shall – I will do such things – / What they are, yet I know not' (ll. 279–81).

What is so striking, and shocking, about Lear's language in this scene, and indeed in Act I.4, in which he urges Nature to 'convey sterility' into Goneril's womb (I.4.278), is not simply its extreme violence, but its misogyny.[8] When Regan greets him with an equable 'I am glad to see your highness', Lear responds: 'Regan, I think [you] are; I know what reason / I have to think so. If thou shouldst not be glad, / I would divorce me from thy [mother's] tomb, / Sepulchring an adult'ress (II.4.129). Instead of accepting the salutation gracefully, the king immediately issues an implicit threat ('if thou shouldst not be glad') to dishonour the memory of his wife, the mother of his daughters. This is the only allusion to her in the play, and it is hardly a tender one. That Lear should think nothing of annulling his marriage might not seem particularly surprising in one who has already abdicated his throne and disowned two of his daughters, but making his wife posthumously guilty of a sexual crime is surely as perverse an act of disloyalty, an offence against 'the offices of nature', as any committed by the women whom he terms 'wicked creatures' and 'unnatural hags' later in the same scene (II.4.178, 256, 276). Yet it is of a piece with the rest of his rhetoric. That Lear views the paternal bond as provisional is reiterated in Act I.4, when he asks Goneril 'Are you our daughter?' implying that if she opposes his will, she cannot be (I.4.216). Gloucester's reaction to the revelation of Edgar's supposed treachery – 'I never got him!' (II.1.78) – suggests that he feels similarly.

Like Bradley, for whom Edmund's villainy is mitigated by the fact that he is 'at any rate not a woman' (p. 248), and Albany, who observes that 'Proper deformity [shows] not in the fiend / So horrid as in woman' (IV.2.60–1), Lear seems to find his daughters' behaviour peculiarly monstrous because they are women. At the height of his passion, he fixes on what Regan's clothing reveals of her body: 'Thou art a lady; / If only to go warm were gorgeous, / Why, nature needs not what thou gorgeous wear'st, / Which scarcely keeps thee warm' (II.4.267). The implication of this reproof is that Regan's sexually provocative attire signifies moral corruption: for Lear, his daughters' evil manifests itself in sexual incontinence. Just as the opprobrium heaped on Goneril earlier in the play focused on her 'derogate body' (I.4.280), so here Lear's rage is aimed at Regan's womanhood. In the midst of his madness, in the mock-trial scene, he returns to this theme, issuing to imaginary court officers the grotesque command to 'anatomise Regan; see what breeds about her heart' (III.4.76–7).

It is this disturbed and disturbing preoccupation with the female body that Smiley stresses in her reworking and whose implications the novel as a whole explores. In her discussion of the novel, Martha Tuck Rozett argues that 'when Smiley attempts to follow Shakespeare closely – by writing the storm scene into her book . . . she is less convincing than when she uses her own fiction-writing strategies', but in fact Smiley does not write the storm scene into her book.[9] Moreover, I would argue that her representation of the events directly preceding the storm is one of the most effective – and affecting – episodes in the novel precisely because it echoes, but also amplifies and distorts, Shakespeare. In the novel Larry Clark turns with sudden vehemence on Ginny:

> 'You barren whore! I know all about you, you slut. You've been creeping here and there all your life, making up to this one and that one. But you're not really a woman, are you? I don't know what you are, just a bitch is all, a dried-up whore bitch.' (p. 181)

There is a verbal echo of Shakespeare here: 'dried-up whore' recalls Lear's appeal to the gods to 'dry up in her [Goneril] the organs of increase' (I.4.279). But Smiley's fidelity to her source is more to the spirit than to the letter. Reflecting later that evening, Ginny 'wondered why Daddy had chosen just those terms for me, whore, slut' (p. 185), just as Smiley herself seems to have pondered the origins of Lear's prurience. In the first instance, Rose offers her sister the most prosaic of explanations: 'He is crazy . . . When they bring up sex it's a sure sign' (p. 186). The movement here from third-person singular ('*He* is crazy') to plural ('When *they* bring up sex it's a sure sign') seems to signal that, for Rose, Larry's symptoms are generic and gender-specific; that his behaviour, bizarre and unpredictable as it is, paradoxically is also typical, symptomatic of a type of male insanity. Speculating on the fate of previous generations of her family patriarchs, however, Rose admits that they may not have been 'like the others' (that is, other local farmers), and, as the conversation proceeds, the peculiarity of Larry's case becomes clear. Rose tells Ginny that their father began sexually abusing them in their early teens, soon after the death of their mother. Ginny's incredulity (at this stage of the novel her memories of this period, unlike Rose's, are completely repressed) is not shared by the alert reader, for whom the significance of several previously mysterious details suddenly becomes plain.[10]

In particular, the episode in Chapter 16 in which Ginny, arriving at her father's house to cook his breakfast, realises that she has forgotten to bring eggs and is faced with what is apparently the most mundane of dilemmas, takes on a retrospective poignancy.

It was my choice, to keep him waiting or to fail to give him his eggs. His gaze was flat, brassily reflective. Not only wasn't he going to help me decide, my decision was a test. I could push past him, give him toast and cereal and bacon, a breakfast without a center of gravity, or I could run home and get the eggs . . . I smiled foolishly, said I would be right back, and ran out the door and back down the road. The whole way I was conscious of my body – graceless and hurrying, unfit, panting, ridiculous in its very femininity. It seemed like my father could just look out of his big front window and see me naked, chest heaving, breasts, thighs, and buttocks jangling, dignity irretrievable. Later . . . what I marveled at was that I hadn't just gone across the road and gotten some eggs from Rose, that he had given me the test, and I had taken it. (p. 115)

In the light of Rose's revelation, it becomes apparent that Ginny's subservience to her father, her readiness to comply with even the most trivial of his whims rather than oppose his will, is not just analogous to, but a consequence of, being physically mastered by him. Ginny's acute self-consciousness as she runs to fetch the eggs, her feelings of vulnerability, her sense of humiliation, are prompted not just by the ignominy of her surrender, but by the associations it has with earlier surrenders. It is not just her dignity that has been sacrificed, it is her autonomy and sexuality. It is because Larry has literally penetrated her that she imagines his gaze as penetrating; it is because she has internalised his contempt for her body that its femininity has come to seem ridiculous.

The 'test' that Ginny marvels at having taken is essentially the same one that was imposed on her as a child and as an adolescent. It is a test not just of obedience, but of her ability to please him (always measured by implication against her sisters', hence her instinctive reluctance to rely on Rose for the eggs), a test Larry sets again in the scene before the storm. We can now see that the storm of Smiley's novel, like that of Shakespeare's play, has an allegorical aspect: it represents the external manifestation of the internal, psychological tempest precipitated by Rose's revelation. When Rose tells her father that he had better agree to live 'this same life, nothing more nothing less' (p. 183), Larry responds not by turning his vituperation on her, but by addressing Ginny in mollifying tones:

> Now he looked at me again. 'You hear her? She talks to me worse than you do.' Now he sounded almost conciliatory, as if he could divide us and conquer us. I stepped back. All at once I had a memory of a time when Rose and I were nine and eleven, and we had kept him waiting after a school party that he hadn't wanted us to go to in the first place. I had lost a shoe in the cloakroom, and Rose and I looked for it madly while the other children put on their coats and left. We never found it, and we were the very last, by five or ten minutes, to come out of the school . . . Daddy was seething, and we knew we would get it just for being late when we got home. There was no telling what would happen if he learned about the shoe. It was Mommy who betrayed me. When I walked in the door, she said 'Ginny! Where's your shoe?' and Daddy turned and looked at my foot, and it was like he turned to fire right there. He came for me and started spanking me with the flat of his hand, on the rear and the thighs. I backed up until I got between the range and the window, and I could hear Mommy saying, 'Larry! Larry! This is crazy!' He turned to her and said, 'You on her side?'
>   Mommy said 'No, but – '
>   'Then you tell her to come out from behind there. There's only one side here, and you'd better be on it.' (p. 183)

Again, Smiley takes her cue here from Shakespeare. In II.4, Lear begins by attempting to stir Regan's indignation at her sister's treatment of him and contrasting Goneril's ingratitude with her own sense of obligation – 'Thy half o' th' kingdom hast thou not forgot, / Wherein I thee endowed' (II.4.180–1) – but when he learns that Regan intends to allow him to retain fewer of his retinue than her sister had offered him, he decides to cut his losses and return to Goneril, on the basis that 'Thy fifty yet doth double five and twenty, / And thou art twice her love' (II.4.258–9).[11] Again, there are precedents for this earlier in the play: in the love contest of the opening scene, in which Cordelia is challenged not simply to match her sisters' extravagant declarations of love, but to surpass them, 'to draw / A third more opulent than your sisters' (I.1.85–6); and in Lear's prediction that 'When she [Regan] shall hear this of thee [Goneril], with her nails / She'll flea thy wolvish visage' (I.4.307–8).

Although there have been a number of post-*A Thousand Acres* productions of Shakespeare's play in which Lear has exerted a sexual hold over his daughters (notably Richard Eyre's National Theatre production, with Ian Holm as Lear, filmed as part of the BBC's 'Performance' series in 1997), his persistent pitting of one daughter against the other(s) is usually attributed to childish caprice and egoism. In Smiley, however, it takes on more sinister implications. Lear's exclamation when Regan holds Goneril's hand, 'O Regan! will you take her by the hand?' (II.4.194), is of wounded self-pity; Larry's remark, prompted by the same gesture in Smiley ('That's right. Hold hands'), is a sardonic sneer at the female solidarity that he has always sought to prevent, either through the use of physical violence (as in the lost shoe incident, which Ginny recalls at this moment through association), or by threatening to withhold or promising to grant his approval, his love, as punishment/reward for disloyalty/loyalty (as in the incident of the eggs).

For Larry loyalty is an absolute: others are either on his side or against him (it is in this that he most closely resembles Lear, whose treatment of Kent is a fine illustration of his inability to distinguish between criticism and opposition). To be wholly on his side they must not be on anyone else's, he must have exclusive rights to their fealty. When Rose tells Ginny that Larry began to abuse her after having started with Ginny, she confesses: '"I was flattered . . . I thought that he'd picked me, me to be his favorite, not you, not her" [Caroline, the Cordelia figure]' (p. 190). By deliberately fostering this sibling rivalry, by encouraging his daughters to compete for his love, Larry preserves his authority and ensures that his side remains the only one: Ginny observes 'when my father asserted his point of view, mine vanished' (p. 176). Although his strategy founders in the face of the sisters' joint resolve to stand firm, its legacy continues to divide them in their love for Jess, who, as Ginny notes, 'in some sense, usurp[s] Daddy's place' (p. 225), just as Edmund supplants Lear in the affections of Goneril and Regan. Always overshadowing this sibling rivalry (which is echoed in the sub-plot by the struggle over their patrimony between Edgar and Edmund in the play and Loren and Jess in the novel), however, is the conflict between the genders.

What is clear throughout the play is that Lear's battle with his daughters is not just an internecine power struggle, but an ideological battle between the genders and generations. When Lear implores the gods to 'let not women's weapons, water-drops, / Stain my man's cheeks!' (II.4.276–7), echoing his earlier shame that Goneril should have the 'power to shake my manhood thus, / That these hot tears . . . [should] break from me' (I.4.297–8), or when he praises Cordelia's unassuming manner of self-expression ('Her voice was ever soft, / Gentle, and low, an excellent thing in woman' (V.3.273–4)), he is employing a patriarchal discourse that is rigidly conservative in its assumptions about gender roles (emphasised by the way in which Goneril and Regan are repeatedly labelled 'unnatural', referred to as 'monsters' and 'hags' and likened to a veritable menagerie of animals). In Smiley's novel, however, patriarchy is not merely conservative and misogynistic, a way of keeping women in their place: it is a system of mental and physical abuse.

This system manifests itself in the first instance as a discourse of distrust among the men in the novel, in which the female is figured as Other and everything associated with her is tainted by fear, suspicion and intolerance. After the storm, Harold (the Gloucester figure) goes to see Ginny on Larry's behalf to demand that she and Rose apologise to him. He begins by announcing '"You got a problem, girlie"' (p. 202) and ends by lecturing her on the community work ethic, the importance of subordinating one's personal interests to the larger interests of the farm: 'One person don't break a farm that lots of people have sweated and starved to put together . . . Women don't understand that"' (p. 204). As it turns out, then, the ethic is not a communal one at all, but a specifically masculine one, one that demands a selflessness Harold considers inherently alien to women. That Harold should hold such views is hardly surprising: Gloucester's irreverent reference to Edmund's mother – 'there was good sport at his making' (I.1.23) – and his largely unsubstantiated claim that Lear's 'daughters seek his death' (III.4.164), suggest that he may share Lear's misogynist tendencies (in Smiley the kinship between the two men is suggested by the resemblance of their surnames, Cook and Clark). More insidious, however, because he seems at first to be a decent man, is the way in which Ty (the Albany figure) repeatedly addresses Ginny and Rose in terms that reveal a deep-seated sexism.

Discussing Larry's eccentric behaviour in the second section of the novel, Ty tells his wife, '"you women don't understand your father at all"' (p. 103) and '"you women could handle it better"' (p. 104), and later reproaches her bitterly for what he perceives as her and Rose's failure to reach a compromise in their dispute with Larry over the management and ownership of the farm: '"I was so excited about the hog operation . . . and then you women just wrecked it"' (p. 261). In his final conversation with Ginny, towards the end of the novel, he continues to draw gendered battle-lines between the daughters and their father, claiming '"he [Larry] always threw you women into a panic"' (p. 343) and attributing to Ginny and Rose the same intractability and irrationality he had seen in his own mother: 'The thing I don't understand about women is how cut and dried they are' (p. 341). The echo here of Larry's insult to Ginny ('dried-up whore') seems to confirm that Ty's apparent bewilderment at the ways of women masks a suspicion of, and hostility towards, them. This is true even of Jess, who initially seems to be a liberal, progressive, even heroic figure, but ends the novel, having used and deceived Ginny and ruined the farm, by abandoning a terminally ill Rose and her children to their fate. What these attitudes reveal is that all the men in the novel are complicit in the maintenance and preservation of a brutal and brutalising system in which women are disenfranchised and dispossessed.

If Ty, Jess, Harold and the other men help to perpetuate this system, it is of course Larry who is its chief agent and embodiment. Early on Ginny observes: 'My mother died before she could present him to us as just a man, with habits and quirks and preferences' (p. 20). However, as the novel proceeds, it becomes increasingly clear that Larry's 'quirks and preferences' are legitimised by, if not the product of, a particular community, a history, an ideology. Commenting on the way that her husband, Pete (the Cornwall figure), viewed Larry's abuse of her as a threat to his own masculine authority rather than in terms of her suffering, Rose tells Ginny:

> 'At the core they're all like that . . . He [Larry] fits right in. However many of them have fucked their daughters or their stepdaughters or their nieces or not, the fact is that they all accept beating as a way of life. We have two choices when we think about that. Either they don't know the real him and we do, or they do know the real him and the fact that he beat us and fucked us doesn't matter.' (p. 302)

Towards the end of the novel, when Ty visits her to ask for a divorce, Ginny decides which of these versions she believes is the correct one:

> 'I can remember when I saw it all your way! The proud progress from Grandpa Davis to Grandpa Cook to Daddy. When "we" bought the first tractor in the county, when "we" built the big house, when "we" had the crops sprayed from the air . . . But then I saw what my part really was . . . You see this grand history, but I see the blows . . . Do I think Daddy came up with beating us and fucking us on his own? . . . No. I think he had lessons, and those lessons were part of the package, along with the land and the lust to run things exactly the way he wanted to no matter what, poisoning the water and destroying the topsoil and buying bigger and bigger machinery, and then feeling certain that all of it was "right", as you say. (pp. 342–3)

In this passage Ginny addresses explicitly the way in which her family history (and, by implication, history in general, the authorised or official version of events) is gendered; the way it is used as a tool of patriarchy, a way of explaining and justifying a fundamentally oppressive system, a way of representing tendentious and self-interested views as though they were absolute, inviolable truths. In fact, as Ginny notes early in the novel, any given story, or version of history, can provide only part of the truth: the same events, the same period of time, will disclose different meanings to different people.

This does not amount to historical relativism in which the very notion of verifiable truth is rejected; on the contrary, it is Ginny's insistence that her father, and the other men in the novel, confront and acknowledge their true family history (and their insistence on avoiding and denying it) that lies at the heart of the book. It is precisely the denial of family history that enables Larry to continue to exercise tyrannical control over his children: "'Daddy thinks history starts fresh every day . . . That's how he keeps betraying us'" (p. 216). Moreover, again the point is made that he is aided and abetted in this denial by the farming community at large: "'People pat him on the head and say what bitches we are, and he believes them, and that's that, the end of history'" (p. 303). Yet, in the end, this denial is self-destructive. Faced for the first time with the reality of what he has done to his daughters, Larry descends rapidly into dementia, while Pete commits suicide and Ty has to give up his cherished dreams of hog farming. If patriarchy in this novel is predicated on secrecy and silence (of Larry's sexual abuse Ty remarks, "'I think people should keep private things private'" (p. 340), presumably unaware that it is precisely this keeping of privacy that has allowed it to happen in the first place), Smiley proposes a feminocentric alternative, based on the sharing of stories, the construction of 'alternate histories'. For Ginny, it is this ability to articulate and analyse their experiences that distinguishes women from men:

> There seemed to be a dumb, unknowing quality to the way the men had suffered, as if, like animals, it was not possible for them to gain perspective on their sufferings. They had us, Rose and me, in their suffering, but they didn't seem to have what we had with each other, a kind of ongoing narrative and commentary about what was happening that grew out of our conversations. (p. 113)

This is not to suggest, however, that the novel presents a picture of sororal solidarity. Tim Keppel is right, up to a point, when he suggests that Smiley 'provides a psychological complexity for the female characters . . . by focusing on the positive relationships of women among women', but not when he claims that 'the only friction between the sisters is Ginny's envy of Rose's two daughters'.[12] In fact, the sisters' rivalry over Jess Clark, which culminates in Ginny's attempt to poison Rose, is simply the most obvious breach in a friendship that is always fragile. Moreover, the fact that Caroline never accepts her sisters' stories, preferring instead to explain them (as Lear and critics such as Bradley do the behaviour of Goneril and Regan) with the belief that 'some people are just evil' (p. 363), seriously undermines any notions of sisterly unity. When Caroline makes this remark, Ginny, in one of the most chilling moments of the novel, confesses that 'for a second I thought she was referring to Daddy. Then I realised she was referring to me' (p. 363).

In allowing Ginny to 'speak again', not at the bidding of the father figure (as Cordelia is invited to in *Lear*), but as a means of explaining herself and her story without recourse to reductive moralising, Smiley's project is clearly feminist. Yet, as Caroline's remark illustrates, Ginny is figuratively as well as literally her father's daughter: that is to say, by the end of the novel her voice, like Rose's, is uncompromising, abrasive and absolute in its conviction of rectitude. Her side has become the only side. Indeed, if the men are destroyed by their attempts to evade and erase history, Ginny and Rose are damaged by their inability to escape it (the ambivalence to the discovery and sharing of painful history which I identified at the start of the chapter remains unresolved). Whether one sees Ginny as an unreliable narrator or not, her narrative is undoubtedly coloured by her experiences: although she survives, she remains to an extent a victim, embittered and alone. This is what Keppel's feminist reading of the novel misses in its enthusiasm for Kathleen McCluskie's vision of 'new forms of social organisation and affective relationships' (p. 114). Smiley's novel is indeed a version of the Lear story (though I think it is misleading to call it Goneril's version, for reasons I have made clear), with all that the word implies of subjectivity. Where Keppel argues that the novel 'reverses the emotional structures of *King Lear*' (p. 112), I would say that it complicates them, exposing and exploiting their ambiguities; where Keppel and Martha Tuck Rozett see the end of the novel as 'life-affirming' (p. 113) and 'affirmative' (p. 172), respectively, I see it as being, in its own way, as bleak as Shakespeare's play. Unlike Tate's and Bradley's versions of *King Lear*, then, Smiley offers no consolation, no happy ending; what she does offer, however, is an alternative, feminocentric reframing of the Lear story which is also a compelling work in its own right.

CAROL SHIELDS, *THE STONE DIARIES*

The Stone Diaries was Carol Shields' seventh novel and represented something of a breakthrough for her. Until this point in her career, Shields had received polite but often somewhat patronising reviews, some of which she satirised in her final novel, *Unless* (2002), and was not particularly widely known outside her adoptive Canada. With *The Stone Diaries*, however, she received not only the premier Canadian award for fiction, the Governor General's Award, but also the Pulitzer Prize, arguably the most prestigious prize for fiction in America, the country of her birth and formative years. Since then, Shields has been acknowledged as an important postwar novelist, sometimes bracketed with Margaret Atwood and Alice Munro in a mighty triumvirate of Canadians, sometimes (re) claimed, as I am doing here, as a contemporary American author with affinities to contemporaries such as Alison Lurie and Anne Tyler.

Like Tyler and Lurie, Shields is known primarily as a realist, the author of conventional, if not conservative, novels. However, there has always been an experimental aspect to Shields' work. *Mary Swann* (1987) was in part an exercise in point-of-view, telling the story of a fictional poet's life and death from the perspective of four narrators; *Happenstance* (1980) was divided into two narratives, 'The Wife's Story' and 'The Husband's Story', which meet in the middle of the book, so that the reader has to choose which to read first. *The Stone Diaries* goes further, however, in terms of formal innovation. It begins with a family tree, has a number of black-and-white photographs, ostensibly of members of that family, inserted into the middle of the book and is told partly by a third-person narrator, partly by a first-person narrator, partly in the voices of a number of minor characters, partly in epistolary form and partly through a series of lists that summarise the life of the protagonist, Daisy Goodwin, in comically elliptical terms. The first of these, which takes the form of a mock-obituary, consists of experiences that Daisy has never had, ranging from oral sex to jalapeno peppers (p. 344).

Defining her life negatively – in terms of what has not happened to her, the things she has missed out on – might seem appropriate for a heroine of whom her children say: 'She just let her life happen to her' (p. 356) and who professes to have 'a talent for self-obliteration' (p. 124). Certainly, Daisy's life is punctuated by absence and loss, from the death of her own mother in childbirth, to the demise of her first husband on their honeymoon, to the loss of the gardening column, 'Mrs Green Thumb', which sustains her after the death of her second husband. Her image is conspicuous by its absence from the gallery of photographic portraits in the book and Chapter 6 consists entirely of a series of letters addressed to her, the responses to which can only be inferred since they are not included in the text. Many of the crucial encounters of her life – from her first meeting, at the age of eleven, with her father (who had left her to the care of Mercy's friend and neighbour, Clarentine, after his wife's death), at which they sit like 'two strangers in a glare of silence' (p. 77), to her premarital interview with the mother of her first husband, Mrs Arthur Hoad, during which she doesn't utter a word, to her long-awaited reunion with her adoptive uncle and soon-to-be second husband, Barker, at which she 'can think of nothing to say' (p. 152), to her visit to Barker's elderly father, a senile centurion in an old people's home, at which she 'would have liked to have said the word "father"' (p. 307) – are notable for her inability, or unwillingness, to speak out. Her dreams 'release potent fumes of absence' (p. 281) and even on her deathbed, Daisy remains preoccupied by 'the deep, shared common distress of men and women, and how little they are allowed, finally, to say' (p. 359). Her last words – '"I am not at peace"' – are 'unspoken' (p. 361) and after her death, her children are startled to discover that she had been briefly married to another man before her marriage to their father but had never mentioned it: 'All those years – saying nothing' (p. 351).

Yet Daisy's silence is fundamentally paradoxical because, as the implied narrator of the novel, it is she who reports the words that she does not say, just as, earlier in the novel, she discloses the details of 'a very private moment, she will not discuss it with anyone, though she records it here' (p. 230). Although she repeatedly draws attention to the inherent inaccuracy of biography ('The recounting of a life is a cheat', she observes) and autobiography (which she claims is 'full of systemic errors'), as well as to her unreliability as the author of her own and other's life-stories ('much of what she has to say is speculative, exaggerated, wildly unlikely'), it is precisely these departures from fidelity that enable Daisy to 'rescue' her life 'by a primary act of imagination' (pp. 28, 196, 148, 76).

At one point Daisy is moved by a newspaper report of the mysterious death of a young woman, who fell, or possibly jumped, to her death from a bridge, to reflect on all that is left unsaid about her life:

> Her beauty, her intelligence, her years of inspired teaching . . . all are lost to history. She will always be 'that woman who jumped or fell' . . . The rest is a heap of silence. (p. 123)

Although the allusion to Hamlet's famous final words ('The rest is silence') is mischievous, this revelation enables Daisy to try to rewrite her own history (that is, effectively, to write the novel itself) so that it takes account not simply of the bare facts of her life, but also all its potentialities, the other possible lives that it contained. *The Stone Diaries* is, among other things, the story of Daisy's struggle to find an appropriate form for her story, a way of overcoming her early conviction that '[h]er autobiography, if such a thing were imaginable, would be, if such a thing were ever to be written, an assemblage of dark voids and unbridgeable gaps' (pp. 75–6). The tautologous use of the double subjunctive here ('if such a thing were imaginable . . . if such a thing were ever to be written') is an indication of just how insuperable the obstacles to such a project seem at first. Like George Gissing, whose contention that 'the only good biographies are to be found in novels' Shields quotes approvingly in her biography of Austen (p. 10), Daisy soon decides to reject 'the straight-faced recital of a throttled and unlit history' and to rely instead on 'the efforts of her imagination' (p. 190). Where autobiography had seemed a dead end, fiction liberates Daisy:

> The narrative maze opens and permits her to pass through. She may be crowded out of her own life . . . but she possesses, as a compensatory gift, the ability to draft alternate versions. She feels, for instance, the force of her children's unruly secrecies . . . the notion that Mrs Flett has given birth to her mother, and not the other way around. (p. 190)

A maze may not seem a very promising metaphor for the possibilities of fiction (most mazes, after all, have many dead ends but only one route through to the centre), but for Daisy (as for Larry Weller, the protagonist of Shields' novel *Larry's Party* (1997), who becomes a designer of mazes) it is a symbol of the imaginative power of the artist. That she implicitly connects her capacity to 'draft alternate versions' of her own life with a mysterious access to the most private thoughts of her children and a counterintuitive sense that her mother is her own creation is apt, since the novel of which she is the author reaches back before her birth to recreate her mother's life and beyond her death to imagine her children's mourning of her.

Appropriating for herself the knowledge of an omniscient narrator, Daisy begins the novel by reconstructing the day of her birth and her mother's death, and the events leading up to it. Her mother, Mercy Stone, an orphan, is created in Daisy's image, if not physically – she is obese and lethargic, whereas Daisy is slim and 'sprightly' (p. 146) – then in terms of her painful reticence. When Cuyler, Daisy's father, begins his courtship, Mercy is able to provide no more than 'a kind of mute encouragement' (p. 84). When she finds herself continually afflicted by what she believes to be indigestion (but are actually symptoms of pregnancy), she has no one to confide in, since 'she would never speak to Dr. Spears of such a thing, she would speak to no one, not even her husband'

(p. 5). Later, Cuyler is unable to decide whether she deliberately withheld the truth from him or simply couldn't find the right moment or means of expression to convey the momentous news: 'He supposes he must look upon her silence as an act of betrayal . . . but he is reminded, always, of her old helplessness with words' (p. 60). At any rate, Daisy tells us, 'his love for his dead wife has been altered by the fact of her silence' (p. 61), just as Barker Flett, Daisy's second husband, dies 'mourning the waste of words between us and the thought of what we might have addressed had we been more forthright' (p. 198).

If the taciturnity of Mercy and Daisy dismays their husbands, silence in *The Stone Diaries* also sometimes empowers the women who employ it as a shield of sorts, behind which their secret selves can flourish. There is a strong sense of this at the start of the novel, not in the case of Mercy (whose trouble with words, like her trouble with food, seems to be a manifestation of what modern psychologists would call low self-esteem), but that of her neighbour, Clarentine Flett. Clarentine, who secretly harbours a strong homoerotic attraction for Mercy, enjoys 'the oval of silence' (p. 13) in which she spends her days, marvelling at 'how not one pair of eyes can . . . regard her as she moves through her dreamlike days' (p. 11). She uses her private, sacrosanct space to reflect on her 'unlived life' (p. 37) and ultimately resolves to 'rema[k]e her own history, abandoning a husband and her wifely duties' (p. 113), and forging a new, alternative life for herself. Leaving her unhappy marriage to the flinty Magnus Flett, Clarentine goes to live with her eldest son, Barker, a professor of botany at Wesley College, and devotes herself to bringing up Daisy and tending her garden.

Clarentine is not just a surrogate mother to Daisy but a precursor, providing her with a feminist model of self-determination. Just as Clarentine defies convention by leaving her husband and home for a new life, setting up her own 'wholesale flower enterprise' (p. 127), so Daisy, after being widowed on her honeymoon (her drunken husband falls to his death from the window of their bedroom, perhaps partly propelled by Daisy's explosive sneeze), decides to leave her father's home and make a new life for herself as the wife of Clarentine's son, Barker, and later as the author of the weekly newspaper column dispensing gardening advice under the by-line 'Mrs Green Thumb'. Like Clarentine, who 'likes to study' the 'grey-green leaves' of her 'prized star of Bethlehem' 'for secrets' (p. 16), Daisy has a quasi-mystical relationship with the plants she tends, 'yearn[ing] to know the true state of the garden, but . . . understand[ing] perhaps, a quarter of its green secrets, no more' (p. 196). Like Clarentine, too, she fiercely preserves a secret self, an identity independent of her roles as daughter, wife, mother and grandmother, symbolised by the bracelet that she receives when admitted to hospital during her final days, mistakenly bearing her maiden name, Daisy Goodwill. Instead of correcting the error, Daisy 'cherishes' this 'secret known only to her' (p. 320). This specifically female sensibility also appears to have been passed on to a third generation, as Daisy's daughter, Joan, is 'so full of secrets that sometimes she thinks she's going to burst . . . [she] understands that she is destined to lead two lives, one existence that is visible to those around her and another that blooms secretly inside her head' (p. 172).

Reta Winters, the protagonist of Shields' last novel, *Unless*, observes that 'we carry a double history in our heads, what is and what could be',[13] and much of her fiction can be read as an exploration of what Shields elsewhere calls a 'world of dreams and possibilities and parallel realities', a world that is divided along gendered lines.[14] One of the pivotal moments in *Unless* occurs when Reta finds an unopened invitation to a baby shower behind a bathroom radiator, addressed to the previous occupant of her house, a Mrs McGinn. Initially, Reta dismisses the significance of the invitation:

> It mattered so little, this 1961 women-only social evening. John Fitzgerald Kennedy was president of the United States. The country was exploding with consciousness and guilt . . . Around the world the political forces eclipsed an event as neutral and trivial and miniscule as a baby shower in a small Canadian town; a lost invitation weighed nothing at all on the scale of human concerns. (p. 38)

Yet the invitation haunts her, not simply because, as she observes later (in what might be read as an apologia for the novelist who concentrates on domestic, rather than national politics),[15] 'we know how inconsequential the unfolding of political events really is. People enter and exit the world; that's the real news' (p. 130), but because it represents for her the poignancy of one of the many roads not taken or, as Daisy puts it in *The Stone Diaries*, 'alternate histories'. In this sense, the context of the social event that Mrs McGinn presumably failed to attend is significant. The fact that it was a 'women-only' event that took place during Kennedy's presidency, an era of momentous political change, not least for women (it was at this time that 'second-wave' feminism in the United States began in earnest), is of symbolic importance, as becomes clear if it is juxtaposed with the fleeting references to Kennedy in *The Stone Diaries*.

In *The Stone Diaries* Kennedy is mentioned just twice: once when Daisy's old friend, Fraidy, writes that she disapproves of the fiancé of the third member of their clique, 'Beans', because of 'the way he sneers at the Kennedys' (p. 224), and again when news of Kennedy's assassination is filtered through a letter from Jay Dudley, the editor of the local newspaper for which Daisy writes her weekly gardening column (and with whom she has a brief affair), informing her that her by-line will not appear that week, since 'Most of the Sports and Home section will be cancelled because of the Kennedy coverage'. The pointed obliqueness of this allusion to arguably the most traumatic event in postwar American history prior to 9/11 (the assassination itself is not mentioned, only implied in the euphemistic term 'Kennedy coverage') might seem implicitly to anticipate Reta's claim that political events are actually 'inconsequential' compared to the daily dramas of human existence and extinction that generally go unreported. While the opening and closing chapter titles of *The Stone Diaries* ('Birth, 1905' and 'Death') fulfil Reta's criteria for 'real news', the section in which the references to Kennedy occur ('Work, 1955–1964') is the most apparently inconsequential of the novel. Although the chapter begins with a number of letters commiserating with Daisy on the loss of her second husband, many more of the letters that make up this section are concerned not with matters of life or death but with the gardening tips she gives in her guise as 'Mrs Green Thumb'. On the face of it, there could not be a greater gulf between the subject-matter of the fan letters that Daisy receives from readers of her column and the Kennedy assassination. Yet, when Daisy is replaced by a colleague who exercises his right as a 'full-time staffer' to have 'first choice of columns' (p. 226), it is as catastrophic for her as Kennedy's death was for many Americans. Her displacement from her regular newspaper slot hits Daisy harder than any of the bereavements she has suffered, precipitating a lengthy depression exacerbated by her recognition 'that her immense unhappiness is doomed to irrelevance' (p. 263).

If, as I am suggesting, the 'Work' section of *The Stone Diaries* provides an 'alternate history' of the period from the mid-1950s to the mid-1960s to the one that we encounter in history books – one characterised not by the struggle for civil rights, Cold War brinkmanship and the emergence of the counterculture, but by Daisy's emergence as a working woman and as a writer who has, as two of her correspondents put it, 'a way with a phrase' (p. 208) and 'a real gift for making a story out of things' (p. 222) – then it is a counter-history that offers an implied feminist critique of the male authority and authorship with which, and in which, history is traditionally invested.[16] This is made clear first by the terms in which Daisy's column and that of her rival, Pinky Fulham, are described. The author of one of the first fan letters Daisy receives reports how happy she was 'to see the Tulip Festival through female eyes for a change' (p. 205), while Fulham, in a letter to Daisy defending his decision to take over her column, cites the positive response he has received when standing in occasionally for her, the 'appreciative letters from readers who especially like the fact that my columns . . . take the male point of view' (p. 226).

At one point, Daisy remarks on the way in which '[m]en . . . were uniquely honoured by the stories that erupted in their lives, whereas women were more likely to be smothered by theirs' (p. 121). Although this observation is prompted by Daisy recalling how her 'honeymoon tragedy' had defined her in the eyes of others, even though she actually 'live[d] outside her story as well as inside' (p. 123), it resonates well beyond the immediate context. Indeed, the novel as a whole can be seen as Daisy's refusal to be smothered by her story: wresting control of it, remaking her own history as her Aunt Clarentine did, and also redefining the parameters of history itself. For while she describes her mother, Mercy's, hapless sense of existing 'apart from any coherent history' (p. 7), she also describes Mercy's death in childbirth as 'a moment in history' (p. 39). Even though she immediately appears to retract this, dismissing the incident as a 'paltry slice of time' that hardly 'deserves such a name' (p. 39), *The Stone Diaries* itself, by chronicling the lives of three generations of unremarkable women, is a testament to the importance of that alternative, female history that has conventionally remained shrouded in secrecy and occluded by silence.

Towards the end of the novel, when Daisy appears to be constructing her own posthumous history, someone (it is not clear who) asks, would Daisy's 'life would have been different if she'd been a man?' (p. 353), a question that brings to mind the famous prelude to George Eliot's *Middlemarch* (1871–2), Shields' great heroine, along with Jane Austen. The Victorian novelist, whose decision to write under a male pseudonym was itself an implicit recognition of the way in which the reception of stories is influenced by the perceived gender of their author, writes of the many women throughout history 'who found for themselves no epic life wherein there was a constant unfolding of far-resonant action; perhaps only a life of mistakes . . . a tragic failure which found no sacred poet and sank unwept into oblivion'.[17] Daisy's life has its share of mistakes and of tragedy but no great claim to epic grandeur, but it is, paradoxically, its very ordinariness that lends it a far-reaching resonance. At one point the very ordinary hero of the novel that followed *The Stone Diaries*, Larry Weller, observes that 'history was [rarely] what it claimed to be . . . history was exactly the reverse – what *wasn't* written down . . . most of life fell through the mesh of what was considered to be worthy of recording'.[18] What *The Stone Diaries* does is to rescue the (fictional) lives of a number of ordinary women from oblivion; to write an 'alternate history' that records precisely the kinds of life-stories that usually fall through the mesh of what is considered to be worthy of recording.

This is not to say that the novel lacks incident or drama: it contains numerous births, deaths, marriages, separations, divorces, affairs and betrayals. It also boasts many memorable characters, from the tragic Mercy Goodwill to the grotesquely comic Mrs Arthur Hoad and her feckless, self-defenestrating son Harold, to the tragic-comic

Magnus Flett, who is abandoned by his wife partly because of his incapacity for romance but in later life commits the whole of *Jane Eyre* to memory like a character from a Luis Borges story. For all that, it is neither the characters themselves nor the circumstances they find themselves in that make *The Stone Diaries* such a compelling book. It is not the case, as Daisy claims, that she (and, by extension, Shields herself) 'lacks a tragic register' (p. 263), but rather that she refuses to elevate the tragic above other aspects of life. Perhaps Shields' most remarkable feat is to write about men and, primarily, women who, though they suffer, are generally, in the words of Bibbi, the sister of Fay McLeod, the heroine of *The Republic of Love* (1992), '[h]appy enough';[19] who, though they are flawed, are basically good;[20] who, though they make their fair share of mistakes, love and are loved in return, without any hint of sentimentality or threat of tedium. In this sense, her whole *oeuvre* can be seen as a triumphant refutation of the famous opening line of *Anna Karenina* that 'All happy families are alike but an unhappy family is unhappy after its own fashion'.[21] In writing about happy (enough) families who are happy (enough) after their own fashion, Shields paradoxically highlights secret lives – those that have often been neglected by writers of fiction – giving a voice to silent women and, in the process, constructing her own 'alternate history' of the novel form.

JEFFREY EUGENIDES, *MIDDLESEX*

Middlesex is Jeffrey Eugenides' second novel, following the critical and commercial success of *The Virgin Suicides* (augmented by the film adaptation with which the director, Sofia Coppola, made her name). It won the Pulitzer Prize for Fiction in 2003, firmly establishing Eugenides as one of the most ambitious and accomplished American novelists of his generation. Like *A Thousand Acres*, *Middlesex* explores a taboo area of gender identity and sexual politics – in this case hermaphroditism. Like *The Stone Diaries*, *Middlesex* employs a first-person narrator who is at times also the protagonist of his own story, but at other times takes on the attributes of an omniscient third-person narrator, relating events that lie outside his own experience. Whereas *A Thousand Acres* and

The Stone Diaries are preoccupied with the silences that aggregate around female experience, *Middlesex* is narrated by a protagonist whose very gender identity is shrouded in silence for most of his life. While Smiley's and Shields' novels give up their secrets gradually, Eugenides boldly announces the central revelation of his novel at the outset; if Smiley and Shields posit a feminocentric form of fiction predicated on the notion that ordinary events and people are paradoxically remarkable, Eugenides' novel proposes that extraordinary events and people are paradoxically unexceptional.

Middlesex tells the story of three generations of the Stephanides family: Lefty and Desdemona, siblings who fall in love, fleeing from a small Greek village after the Turkish invasion of 1922 and settling in America, where they live as husband and wife; their son, Milton, and his cousin, Tessie, who marry and give birth to a boy, Chapter Eleven, and the narrator of the novel, Calliope (Callie for short). At birth, Callie appears to be a girl and is brought up as a female until she is diagnosed, at the age of fourteen, with a rare genetic mutation (5-alpha-reductase deficiency) that has concealed her male genitals beneath what appears to be a clitoris. When she discovers the truth, Callie renames himself Cal and decides to live out the rest of his life as a man.(For the sake of clarity, during the remainder of this discussion, I use the male name and male pronouns when referring to the narrator.)

The doubling of names and genders that attends Cal is just one aspect of a leitmotif that runs through *Middlesex*. Midway through the novel, Cal describes the conclusion of a Super-8 film that his father made of his seventh birthday party. In keeping with convention, the grand finale of the party is blowing out the candles on the birthday cake:

> In the film I lean forward and, Aeolian, blow the candles out. In a moment, they re-ignite. I blow them out again. Same thing happens. And then Chapter Eleven is laughing, entertained. That was how our home movies ended, with a prank on my birthday. With candles that had multiple lives.[22]

As far as the plot is concerned, this incident is inconsequential, except insofar as it marks the end of an era of prosperity for the

Stephanides family: Cal speculates that his father stopped record-ing such events because his business began to falter, drawing him away from the domestic realm (a scenario anticipated by the naming of Cal's brother Chapter Eleven, after the protection from bankruptcy proceedings legislation in America). In other respects, however, it is central: the allusion to the Greek god of wind, Aeolus, is one of many such references that punctuate the novel, from Cal's full name (Calliope, the Muse of Poetry) to the com-parison of the teenage Cal to the Delphic Oracle (p. 373). The fact that Cal is describing this episode from his childhood as it replays on film is also significant, since cinematic techniques are a recur-ring trope of the novel's narrative rhetoric.[23] Finally, the practical joke that Chapter Eleven plays on Cal functions as a metaphor for his life. The 'multiple lives' of the reigniting candles anticipate the different chapters in Cal's existence. In this sense, it forms part of one of the key discourses of the novel; the candles are simply one of many instances when Cal's dual gender identity is figured in terms of doubling or dividing metaphors.

This trope is evident from Cal's description of the moment of his conception, at which 'a pair of miscreants [genes] . . . siphon off an enzyme, which stops the production of a certain hormone, which complicates my life' (p. 16), through to the narrative present from which the novel is retrospectively related, in which Cal is employed by a 'Foreign Service [that] is split into two parts' (p. 40), in Berlin, a 'once-divided city . . . still cut in half by racial hatred' (p. 106). Indeed, the novel begins by drawing attention to this doubling:

> I was born twice: first, as a baby girl . . . and then again, as a teenage boy . . . Specialised readers may have come across me in Dr Peter Luce's study, 'Gender Identity in 5-Alpha-Reductase Pseudohermaphrodites,' published in the *Journal of Pediactric Endocrinology* in 1975. (p. 3)

The terms in which Eugenides couches Cal's dual identity here implicitly invoke mythological figures – notably Tiresias, the blind prophet in Greek mythology, who was transformed into woman for seven years, whom Cal later plays in a high school production of *Antigone* and to whom he compares himself explicitly, 'Like

Tiresias, I was first one thing and then the other' (p. 3) – and literary precursors (notably the eponymous protagonist of Virginia Woolf's *Orlando* (1928), who lives one life as a man and then another as a woman, and Rose Tremain's *Sacred Country* (1992), whose protagonist, Mary Ward, lives an outward life as a female and an inner life as a male). It also borrows a trick from Philip Roth's *Portnoy's Complaint* (1969), which begins, in the form of an epigraph, with a (fictional) citation from a medical paper in which the protagonist's condition is diagnosed and classified. Here, too, Eugenides invents a fictional article with a fictional author to emphasise that Cal's gender identity has entered public discourse – it has been officially recorded, analysed and categorised – in order to contrast this reductive scientific case study with the more complex literary account that follows. However, there is a crucial difference between Roth's and Eugenides' strategies: Portnoy's complaint exists as a condition only within the larger fictional world of the novel, whereas the genetic mutation that afflicts Cal exists in the real world. Although Luce's article is fabricated, the condition he analyses, and the journal in which his article is supposed to have been published, are not.

Realistic though the framework of *Middlesex* is, it is nonetheless a highly stylised novel – one that constantly draws attention to its own literary strategies. On the face of it, Eugenides' decision to open the novel with the revelation of his narrator's hermaphroditism might seem perverse: had he withheld this information until the moment (late in the novel) when Cal himself realises that he is biologically male, it would have been a formidable coup – comparable perhaps to the moment in *A Thousand Acres* when Ginny finally recovers the memories of being abused by Larry. However, whatever the novel loses in terms of dramatic suspense, it gains in terms of dramatic irony.

When, as a young girl, Cal practises kissing with Clementine, the girl next door, Clementine reproves him for imitating her movements, telling Cal, 'You're the man' (p. 265). Without knowing Cal's ambiguous sexuality, this would seem like the simple role-play of a childish game: Clementine casts Cal in the role of 'the man' in the kissing game because she wants to play the role of 'the woman'. But with foreknowledge of Callie's metamorphosis into Cal, Clementine's words take on a different, literal meaning. This is also true of the name of the house, 'Middlesex', which gives the novel its title – the house that the Stephanides family move into with the proceeds of the insurance money that they receive after the family restaurant is burned down during the Detroit riots of 1967. When Cal wonders at 'the effort of delivering a sermon each week twice, first in Greek and then again in English' (p. 12) undertaken by the priests in the Greek Orthodox Church her family attends, the reader will infer a connection between the bilingual religious services and the bisexual nature of Cal's own life, first as a female and then as a male. Similarly, the funeral obsequies at her uncle's funeral, at which '[f]lags were held over the coffin, the Greek flag on one side, the American flag on the other' (p. 128), becomes a buried allusion to the duality of Cal's sexual identity. The description of the attitude adopted by one of the women whom his grandfather courts ('Victoria Pappas stood half in and half out of the light', p. 35) and the 'halfway house' where Cal takes refuge after his flight from the family home (p. 491) also hint at the narrator's hybridity, as do the references to his 'amphibian' heart (pp. 265, 383). In an excellent article on *Middlesex*, Deb Shostak argues that Eugenides' 'attachment' to metaphors of 'hybridity, doubleness, the middle, between-ness' is part of a struggle to 'devise figures of the newly thinkable with which to rescue the hermaphrodite from the position of the strange'.[24] Yet it seems to me that Cal's rhetorical strategy is not so much to redeem his hermaphroditism from what Shostak (after Judith Butler) calls 'the position of the strange', but rather to appropriate it as a figure for other kinds of strangeness whose very familiarity paradoxically renders them invisible.

Knowledge of his hermaphroditism colours every aspect of Cal's narrative: in the manner of Christian scholars who reconstitute episodes from the Old Testament as prefigurations of the New, Cal invariably interprets incidents from his pre-male existence typologically. With hindsight, as Cal himself puts it, 'all the mute objects of my life seem to tell my story . . . if I look closely enough'; his second birth seems to be foretold from the moment of his first (p. 397). Hence Cal claims that even '[a]s a baby . . . [there was a] changeableness . . . as if beneath my visible face there was another, having second thoughts' (p. 218). These 'second thoughts' are accompanied by a sort of second sight, a 'latent . . . ability to communicate between the genders, to see not with the monovision of one sex but in the stereoscope of both' (p. 269). When the dormant second (male) self emerges, it does not entirely eclipse the original (female) one. Instead, the female becomes the submerged other, occasionally 'surfac[ing] . . . ris[ing] up inside me, wearing my skin like a loose robe' (pp. 41–2), so that Cal's amphibian nature survives the transition from female to male self-identification.

In narrative terms, Cal's second sight extends back in time, so that he is able to function as a near-omniscient narrator, locating the origins of his condition in the roots of his family tree. Once again, this involves retrospectively encoding his gender duality in incidents from the past. Describing the symbiotic relationship of his grandparents during their childhood as brother and sister, for example, Cal conflates their bodies, likening them to 'a four-legged, two-headed creature' and to conjoined twins who, when alone, 'seemed cut in half' (p. 25). This imagery anticipates the physical union of the two when they become lovers (the phrase that Iago uses to describe the lovemaking of that other literary Desdemona with Othello – 'the beast with two backs' – springs to mind in this context), but it also initiates a chain of associations that continues with his father's conception, which is inspired by Lefty and Desdemona's attendance at a performance of *The Minotaur*, 'a play about a hybrid monster' (p. 109), and concludes with Cal's dismayed discovery of the cross-reference in the second Webster's Dictionary definition of hermaphrodite: 'See synonyms at MONSTER' (p. 430). The implied link between the (supposed) moral monstrosity of Lefty and Desdemona's incestuous intimacy and their grandchild's (supposed) physical freakishness is spelled out in Cal's exposition of the perverse proliferation of relationships between the various members of his immediate family:

So, to recap: Sourmelina . . . wasn't only my first cousin twice removed. She was also my grandmother. My father was his own mother's (and father's) nephew. In addition to being my grandparents, Desdemona and Lefty were my great-aunt and -uncle. My parents would be my second cousins once removed and Chapter Eleven would be my third cousin as well as my brother. (p. 198)

Like that most infamous of dysfunctional Greek families, in which Oedipus is both son and husband to his mother, both father and brother of his siblings, the original act of incest produces a progeny of double-headed monsters, rendering ironic Milton's salutation, addressed to the foetus in his wife's body: 'Lucky two!' (p. 16). Just as Oedipus' sin pollutes his family and the entire state of Thebes, so in *Middlesex* the unnatural shift from a brother–sister to a husband–wife relation between Lefty and Desdemona anticipates, and is responsible for, the unnatural shift in sexual identity from female to male that Cal experiences.

If *Oedipus Rex* is one of the ur-texts that inform *Middlesex*, then another is Ovid's *Metamorphoses*; but whereas Sophocles provides Eugenides with a discourse of tragic duplication, Ovid offers a more redemptive framework for figuring Cal's predicament. If the Oedipus analogy tends to stigmatise and at the same time elevate Cal (Oedipus' sin makes him both a pariah and a seer of legendary wisdom), then the Ovidian model tends to normalise him, presenting his peculiar circumstances not as perverse deviancy but rather as a permutation of the evolutionary changes seen everywhere in nature. At high school, Cal observes the progress of puberty among his classmates with particular intensity, fearing that 'as most of the other girls in my grade began to undergo their own transformations, I [was being] left behind, left out' (p. 285). Referring to himself in the third person (as he does with increasing frequency as the novel proceeds, reflecting the demarcation between his present, male, narrating self and his past, female, narrated self), Cal notes that '[o]nly Calliope . . . takes in the true extent of the metamorphoses around her' (p. 286).

As with the instances of doubling and dividing, moments such as these signify at two levels: they pertain both to the adolescent anxieties that Cal shares with his peers (and indeed all teenagers) and to the peculiar circumstances that separate him from his classmates (and all but a tiny number of human beings). However, by using words such as 'transformation' and 'metamorphosis' to describe the ordinary transition from childhood to sexual maturity, Eugenides and his narrator implicitly situate Cal's extraordinary evolution within the parameters of familiar change. As Cal himself puts it: the 'change from girl to boy was far less dramatic than the distance anybody travels from infancy to adulthood' (p. 520). In this sense, Cal's hybridity might even be said to function as a paradigm of the universal fluidity of human identity, as is implied by his claim that '[w]e're all made up of many parts, other halves. Not just me' (p. 440). Certainly, the novel offers numerous examples of transformations that contextualise Cal's: from the silkworms that Desdemona carefully cultivates, and to whom she is compared when she tries on her mother's bridal gown, 'awaiting metamorphosis' (p. 36); to the Greeks who take to 'wearing a fez in order to pass as . . . Turk[s]' during the invasion of Greece by the Turks in 1922 (p. 53); to the passengers on the *Giulia* (including Lefty and Desdemona), bound for America, for whom '[t]he driving spirit . . . was self-transformation' (p. 68); to Cal's 'Obscure Object of Desire' (the nickname he gives to the classmate with whom he falls in love at high school), 'discovering the self it could be' when she performs the title role in a production of *Antigone* (p. 338); to his uncle, Father Mike Antoniou, who 'amaz[es]' him with 'the transformation . . . [he goes] through every Sunday' when he dons his priestly robes (p. 351); to his uncle-in-law, Jimmy Zismo, who 'change[s] past understanding' (p. 125), faking his own death and re-emerging as Minister Fard, the founder of the Nation of Islam, propounding the bizarre theory that the 'white race' was created by an evil genius who, 'OVER MANY, MANY YEARS . . . GENETICALLY CHANGED THE BLACK MAN . . . MAKING HIM PALER AND WEAKER' (p. 155).[25]

Taken together, these various metamorphoses might seem to suggest that Cal's journey from girl to man is more a matter of volition than one of genetic destiny. Indeed, Cal reinforces this idea when he recognises that his early attempts to appear and behave like a man were akin to 'a convert to a new religion', who 'over[does] it at first' (p. 449), or to 'an immigrant, putting on airs' (p. 471). At one point Cal explicitly compares his decision to flee his old life with that of his grandparents: 'I was becoming a new person too, just like Lefty and Desdemona, and I didn't know what would happen to me in this new world to which I'd come' (p. 443). There are echoes here of the utopian rhetoric of the early colonial settlers of the United States, as there are also in Cal's description of himself as a 'new creation' (p. 445) when he emerges from Ed's barbershop with his first haircut as a male and in his conviction (expressed on the final page of the novel) that Middlesex itself was 'designed for a new type of human being, who would inhabit a new world' (p. 529). There is, too, a happy ending for Cal, who finally finds a sympathetic companion in Julie Kikuchi, a fellow expatriate in Berlin. Nonetheless, *Middlesex* is not a sentimental novel – ultimately, it undermines rather than endorses the fashionable theory that sexual and gender identities are social constructions rather than biological facts.

The chief advocate of the precedence of nurture over nature in the novel is Dr Peter Luce, a 'famous sexologist' and 'regular contributor to *Playboy*', for whom Cal is 'a living experiment', an ideal case study, 'arriving out of the woods of Detroit like the Wild Boy of Aveyron', 'a sexual or genetic Kaspar Hauser' (p. 408). Cal's contempt for Luce is clear in the tone of this passage, and although the comparisons with the infamous feral children are Cal's rather than Luce's, they reflect the way in which Cal is objectified by Luce (which in turn ironically echoes his own objectification of the 'Obscure Object of Desire'). Personable and charming, Luce nonetheless repeatedly displays Cal, without seeking his permission, to eminent colleagues as evidence of his theory that 'a patient's gonadal sex often didn't determine his or her gender identity' (p. 411). Ironically, Cal convinces Luce that in his case 'chromosomal status has been completely overridden by rearing' (p. 421) by tailoring his responses to match what he thinks Luce wants to hear, in the hope that he will then be able to go home without being subjected to more tests and examinations. Because Luce does not tell Cal that he is chromosomally male, Cal decides to feign conventional femininity in the hope that 'if I seemed normal enough he might send me back home' (p. 418). In fact, by duping Luce, Cal only confirms him in his conviction that surgical intervention is required to ensure that Cal can continue to live his life as a female. Reflecting on these events, Cal comes to the paradoxical conclusion that '[n]ormality wasn't normal', since 'people – and especially doctors – had doubts about normality' and 'felt inclined to give it a boost' (p. 446). On the face of it, this might seem like a critique of the very idea that there might be a norm when it comes to matters as complicated as sexuality and gender identity. In fact, it is precisely this position – Luce's *distrust* of the medical evidence that Cal is emotionally and sexually a normal male – that puts Cal in danger of undergoing an invasive surgical procedure that would have made him conform to Luce's thesis that a child brought up as a member of a gender group not his or her own will identify with that group in contradiction to the normal feelings of his or her biological gender. This is not to say that there are no deviations from the norm – there are of course many variations of sexual identity (heterosexuality, homosexuality, bisexuality, trans-sexuality) and some of gender identity, of which hermaphroditism is one. Luce's assumption that because Cal has been brought up as a girl he will be sexually attracted to males (as he pretends to be when cross-examined) might have proved correct, but only if Cal had been a gay man. In fact, Cal is neither a female, a gay male, 'a new type of human being', nor, as Zora (with whom he performs as 'the God Hermaphroditus' in a sexual freak show in San Francisco) informs him in yet another reference to classical Greek literature, one of the 'original human being[s]' who, according to Plato's theory, were composed of male and female halves that were later split (p. 489), but a heterosexual male. He is not a hermaphrodite in the strict medical sense as he does not possess both male and female genitalia, but rather a pseudo-hermaphrodite – that is to say, a normal human male except insofar as his male genitalia are obscured by tissue that resembles female genitalia.

At one point, Cal complains about the limitations of the discourse available to him, on the grounds that:

> Emotions, in my experience, aren't covered by single words . . . Maybe the best proof that the language is patriarchal is that it oversimplifies feeling. I'd like to have at my disposal complicated hybrid emotions, Germanic train-car constructions like, say, 'the happiness that attends disaster'. (p. 217)

Cal's desire to articulate 'complicated hybrid emotions' is implicitly connected to the complex hybridity of his gender identity, but as the reference to patriarchy makes clear, he is also making a feminist point about the phallocentric nature of language. Growing up as a girl, Cal recalls that his (ostensibly female) genitalia were 'shrouded in a zone of privacy and fragility'; whereas 'Chapter Eleven's apparatus was called a "pitzi" . . . for what I had there was no word at all' (p. 226). Again, there is a double meaning here: Cal is alluding both to the taboo that surrounds the female sex organs of young girls and to the literal lack of a term to describe his own unusual genitals. As if to compensate for this lack, Cal's narrative bristles with details; for in contrast to his parents' reticence, Cal's narrative voice is prolix. Although he is characteristically scathing about Luce's attempts to gender his discourse ('Luce even analyzed my prose style to see if I wrote in a linear, masculine way, or in a circular, feminine one'), elsewhere Cal seems to subscribe to the view that feminine discourse differs essentially from male; that it has softer, rounder contours. Early in the novel, for example, he observes that 'despite my androgynised brain, there's an innate feminine circularity in the story I have to tell' (pp. 19–20); and much later he attributes his adolescent enthusiasm for *The Iliad* to his emerging male sexuality:

> (Maybe this was another sign of the hormones manifesting themselves silently inside me. For while my [exclusively female] classmates found *The Iliad* too bloody for their taste, I thrilled to the stabbings and beheadings, the gouging out of eyes, the juicy eviscerations.) (p. 322)[26]

In fact, *Middlesex*, as might be expected, occupies the middle ground. Or it might be more accurate to say that there is a tension throughout the novel between an explicit, expansive, at times excessive, public, masculinist discourse (the novel contains many Whitmanian lists, many detailed descriptions of teeming, urban life, many invocations of different historical contexts) and a covert, submerged, secretive, private feminist discourse. Perhaps the best example of this occurs in the opening line of the chapter entitled 'Flesh and Blood'.

> I'm quickly approaching the moment of discovery: of myself by myself, which was something I knew all along and yet didn't know; and the discovery by poor, half-blind Dr Philobosian of what he'd failed to notice at my birth and

continued to miss during every annual physical thereafter; and the discovery by my parents of what kind of child they'd given birth to (answer: the same child, only different); and finally, the discovery of the mutated gene that had lain buried in our bloodline for two hundred and fifty years, biding its time, waiting for Atatürk to attack, for Hajienestis to turn into glass, for a clarinet to play seductively out a back window, until, coming together with its recessive twin, it started the chain of events that led up to me, here, writing in Berlin. (p. 361)

On the one hand, this long sentence (so long it is also a paragraph), with its iteration of different discoveries, its references to grand historical events and its apparent faith in a linear, cause-and-effect narrative, seems to conform to the classic tradition of masculine rhetoric. On the other, it implicitly accords domestic detail (the clarinet playing seductively, a reference to the courtship of Milton and Tessie) the same status as public history and is hedged about with qualifications (the 'moment of discovery' is at the same time not the moment of discovery, since the reader has been made aware of Cal's secret from the beginning, and because he himself has been aware of it all along, the revelation makes him into a different child who is, paradoxically, still the same child). In this respect, it has close affinities with the feminocentric narratives of writers such as Shields and Smiley. And the sentence concludes by drawing attention to the writing subject, which, in his present incarnation as Cal in Berlin, is masculine, but at the moment of discovery alluded to, still self-identified as feminine.

This paradoxical quality invariably attends those moments in the narrative when Cal refers self-consciously to the act of writing. Earlier in the novel he confesses that he has no desire to write 'a great book anymore, but just one which, whatever its flaws, will leave a record of my impossible life' (p. 302). On the one hand, Cal uses the language of authenticity, of history: if he narrates his life history, it will become a matter of record. Then again, the life that he wishes to document is 'impossible', so that any attempt to record it will inevitably appear inauthentic, fictional. Like Shields and Smiley, Eugenides here represents the act of writing one's life-story as at once an act of imagination – the construction of an 'alternate history' – and an act of historical recuperation and revisionism: if Cal's autobiography is published, it will discredit Luce's publication of his distorted case history, setting the record straight. Like Smiley and Shields too, Eugenides locates this project in a specifically female-gendered space. As a schoolgirl, Callie habitually retreats to the basement bathroom, for, as Cal puts it: 'Where else would a girl like me, hiding from the world a knowledge she didn't quite understand herself . . . feel more comfortable than in this subterranean realm where people wrote down what they couldn't say, where they gave voice to their most shameful longings and knowledge?' (p. 329). The familiar association of female-authored writing with secrets, subterfuge and silence is given a peculiar poignancy here because Cal's shameful secret is precisely that he does not belong in this space in which young girls' desires are made public (by being scrawled on lavatory walls), but paradoxically remain private (since their authors are anonymous). The metaphorical power of these school toilets resides not just in the fact that they provide a forum for these girls to 'give voice' to matters too taboo to be spoken, however, but also in its location. Literally in the basement, they also offer Cal a symbolic 'subterranean realm' that corresponds perfectly to his secret teenage life and to his later vocation as a writer. As he puts it: 'Writing is solitary, furtive, and I know all about those things. I'm an expert in the underground life' (p. 319). If *The Virgin Suicides* established Eugenides' credentials as a chronicler of the solitary and furtive pursuits of teenage Americans, *Middlesex* confirms that he is indeed an 'expert in the underground life' – the private, secret inner world that is the counterpart to every public existence.

CONCLUSION

Early in *Middlesex* Cal draws attention to the logical impossibility of his account of the circumstances his own conception: 'Of course, a narrator in my position (prenatal at the time) can't be entirely sure of any of this' (p. 9). There's a similar moment in *The Stone Diaries* when Daisy describes the moment of her birth:

It is a temptation to rush to the bloodied bundle pushing out between my mother's legs, and to place my hand on my own beating heart, my flattened head and infant arms amid the mess of glistening pulp. There lies my mother, Mercy Stone Goodwill, panting on the kitchen couch . . . Her blood-smeared drawers lie where she's thrown them, on the floor probably, just out of sight. (p. 23)

The detailed description of Mercy's labour, with its implicit claim to narrative omniscience, is so vivid that the narrator feels as though it might be possible to intervene and become a midwife to her own birth. At the same time, however, the word 'probably' implicitly discloses that everything that precedes it is speculative. Just as Daisy must imaginatively reconstruct her mother's experience, having never known her, so Ginny in *A Thousand Acres* can only speculate about her mother's true nature, as she was only a young girl when her mother died. She considers embarking on 'a quest' to discover her mother's history, becoming 'her biographer', before rejecting the idea: 'I was, after all, my father's daughter, and I automatically did believe in the unbroken surface of the unsaid' (p. 94). There is, of course, dramatic irony in Ginny declaring herself to be her father's daughter (at this stage she remains unaware that he abused her), and in the fact that her qualms about writing the history of her mother's life derive from her father's indoctrination of the importance of keeping family matters private. Although she decides not to become her mother's biographer, the very fact that Ginny contemplates doing so, while 'form[ing] my mother's maiden name with my lips', constitutes an attempt to retrieve a maternal history that has always seemed inaccessible (p. 94). Later, she speculates about her grandmother's life: 'Possibly she had no money of her own. That detail went unrevealed by the stories' (pp. 132–3). Again, the word 'possibly' indicates that Ginny's reconstruction of her female progenitor's history, like Cal's and Daisy's, is necessarily conjectural, but it is precisely this imaginative licence – this paradoxical impulse to reveal, through stories, the 'details . . . unrevealed by the stories' – that makes the 'alternate histories' of *A Thousand Acres*, *The Stone Diaries* and *Middlesex* so compelling.

There was a significant trend in American fiction of the 1980s and 1990s towards what Linda Hutcheon has called 'historiographic metafiction': that is to say, a

> kind of postmodern novel which rejects projecting present beliefs and standards onto the past and asserts the specificity and particularity of the individual past event . . . [insisting] that . . . historical knowledge . . . is semiotically transmitted . . . [and] using the paratextual conventions of historiography to both inscribe and undermine the authority and objectivity of historical sources and explanations.[27]

The three novels discussed in this chapter have affinities with this sub-genre and with the notion of 'counter-history' advanced by Don DeLillo in his essay 'The Power of History', where he argues that the language of fiction 'can be . . . the thing that delivers us, paradoxically, from history's flat, thin, tight relentless designs . . . and that allows us to find an unconstraining otherness, a free veer from time and place and fate'.[28] Certainly, these novels all express scepticism about 'the authority and objectivity of historical sources and explanations' and reject 'history's flat, thin, tight relentless designs' in favour of an 'unconstraining otherness'. On the other hand, their preoccupation with the relationship between history and fiction is, crucially, inflected by questions of gender and sexuality that complicate the models described by Hutcheon and DeLillo. In breaching 'the unbroken surface of the unsaid', Smiley, Shields and Eugenides all establish a complex set of relations between silence, secrecy and sexuality, which continue to have important implications for contemporary debates about gender identity and narrative form long after the moment of historiographical metafiction has passed.

- Silence, secrecy and the notion of the alternate life lived by women is associated in the work of Carol Shields and Jane Smiley with female sexuality and gender identity.
- Jeffrey Eugenides' novels *The Virgin Suicides* and *Middlesex* are also characterised by the tension between secrecy and revelation, silence and speech, public and private lives, though he differs

from Smiley and Shields in the way he introduces a male narrative voice into the conventionally feminised, furtive worlds he evokes. *Middlesex* shows that Eugenides is an 'expert in the underground life' – the private, secret inner world that is the counterpart to every public existence.

- Whilst in giving the reviled Goneril a chance to 'speak again' as Ginny in *A Thousand Acres*, Smiley's project is clearly feminist, she exposes and complicates the emotional structures of *King Lear* rather than reversing them, to offer an alternate, feminocentric version of the Lear story.

- In writing about happy families and women who are basically good, Shields highlights secret lives, giving a voice to silent women and, in the process, constructing her own 'alternate history' of the novel form.

- Smiley, Shields and Eugenides breach 'the unbroken surface of the unsaid' to establish a complex set of relations between silence, secrecy and sexuality, which has implications for contemporary debates about gender identity and narrative form.

NOTES

1. Carol Shields, *Jane Austen* (London: Phoenix, 2001), pp. 5, 163. All subsequent references in the text are to this edition.
2. The first of these was published in 1985 and featured fiction by several American contemporaries of Shields and Smiley, such as Joyce Carol Oates, Jayne Anne Phillips and Bobbie Ann Mason.
3. Carol Shields, *The Stone Diaries* (London: Fourth Estate, 1993), p. 12. All subsequent references in the text are to this edition.
4. A. C. Bradley, *Shakespearean Tragedy* (Basingstoke: Macmillan, 1994), pp. 205–7. All subsequent references in the text are to this edition.
5. Jane Smiley, *A Thousand Acres* (London: Flamingo, 1992), pp. 6, 7. All subsequent references in the text are to this edition.
6. Susan Farrell, *Jane Smiley's A Thousand Acres: A Reader's Guide* (London: Continuum, 2001), p. 31.

7. William Shakespeare, *King Lear* in *The Riverside Shakespeare* (Boston, MA: Houghton Mifflin, 1974), (III.4.105). All subsequent references in the text are to this edition.

8. Lear's misogyny has, of course, been the subject of much comment in feminist criticism. For example, Joyce Carol Oates – like Smiley a contemporary American novelist and short-story writer – sees it as expressive of the 'anti-feminine brutality' of the play, which in turn is part of 'a general fear and loathing of Nature itself' ('Is this the Promised End?: The Tragedy of King Lear', in *Contraries: Essays* (New York: Oxford University Press, 1981), p. 66 (51–81)). Oates points out that in the story in Sidney's *Arcadia*, which is one of Shakespeare's sources, it is the king's sons-in-law, rather than his daughters, who rebel against him.

9. Martha Tuck Rozett, *Talking Back to Shakespeare* (Newark, DE: University of Delaware, 1994), pp. 170–1.

10. For example, Rose's decision to send her children to boarding school, and her warning to them not to open the door to Larry when on their own (p. 83); Ginny's conversation with an old friend of her mother's, Mary Livingstone, who tells her that her mother 'was afraid for you girls . . . For the life you would live after she died' (p. 91); Ginny's habitual 'feeling of forgiveness [when looking at her father working in the fields] when I hadn't consciously been harbouring any annoyance' (p. 136) and of unease whenever Caroline kisses Larry: 'it always made me feel odd, as if a heavy stone were floating and turning within me, that stone of stubbornness and reluctance that kept any more from being asked' (p. 64). Many of Rose's earlier remarks, for example, when she says of Caroline, 'she's the one who got away' (p. 99), or of Larry that 'he thinks he has a right to everything. He thinks it's all basically his' (p. 119), are also invested with dramatic irony.

11. Lear's tendency to value his daughters in such crude commercial terms is apparent as early as the opening scene of the play, when he tells Burgundy: 'When she [Cordelia] was dear to us we did hold her so, / But now her price is fallen' (I.1.195–6).

12. Tim Keppel, '"Goneril's Version": *A Thousand Acres* and *King Lear*', *South Dakota Review*, 33.2 (Summer 1995), p. 111 (105–17).

13. Carol Shields, *Unless* (London: Fourth Estate, 2002), p. 149.

14. Carol Shields, 'Arriving Late: Starting Over', in *How Stories Mean*, ed. John Metcalf and J. R. Struthers (Erin, Ontario: Porcupine's Quill, 1993), 244–51, quoted by Coral Ann Howells in 'In the Subjunctive Mood: Carol Shields' *Dressing Up for the Carnival*', in *The Yearbook of English Studies* 31 (2001), p. 144 (144–54). I am indebted to Professor Howells' excellent article for opening up the critical territory of Shields' use of 'parallel realities', territory that I have tried to explore further in my discussion of *The Stone Diaries*.

15. A charge which has, of course, often been levelled at Jane Austen, and against which Shields defends her: 'By indirection, by assumption, by reading what is implicit, we can find behind Austen's novels a steady, intelligent witness to a world that was rapidly reinventing itself' (Shields, *Jane Austen*, p. 4).

16. Alex Ramon observes that 'It is the hierarchical division between the celebrated "public" life . . . and the uncelebrated "non-public" life that her [Shields'] fiction seeks to critique' (Alex Ramon, *Liminal Spaces: the Double Art of Carol Shields* (Cambridge: Cambridge Scholars, 2008), p. 129). For a discussion of 'Shields' scepticism about the tenability of phallocentric historical narratives' in the larger context of Canadian fiction, see Ramon, pp. 128–30.

17. George Eliot, *Middlemarch* (Harmondsworth: Penguin, 1965), n.p.

18. Carol Shields, *Larry's Party* (Harmondsworth: Penguin, 1997), p. 107.

19. Carol Shields, *The Republic of Love* (London: Fourth Estate, 1992), p. 116. This phrase also appears in *Larry's Party*, where it is used as the title of the book on women saints published by Beth Prior, Larry's second wife.

20. Their names often subtly suggest this: for example, the Goodwills in *The Stone Diaries*, Larry Weller in *Larry's Party* and Hap Lewis, Brenda Bowman's best friend, in *Happenstance*.

21. Leo Tolstoy, *Anna Karenina* (Harmondsworth: Penguin, 1986), p. 13.

22. Jeffrey Eugenides, *Middlesex* (London: Bloomsbury, 2003), p. 227. All subsequent references in the text are to this edition.

23. The second paragraph of the novel offers a series of snapshots of the whole narrative in a literary equivalent to the opening sequence of Nic Roeg's film *Don't Look Now* (1973), and the rest of the novel is punctuated by episodes in which the narrator 'unspools', 'replays' or provides a 'stock . . . montage' (p. 203) of images as a way of compressing a long period of time into a short narrative frame.

24. Debra Shostak, 'Theory Uncompromised by Practicality: Hybridity in Jeffrey Eugenides' *Middlesex*', *Contemporary Literature* 49:3 (Fall 2008), p. 401 (383–412).

25. Like the narrator himself, who is variously called Calliope, Callie and Cal, Zismo in his incarnation as the minister 'had many names', including 'Mr Farrad Mohammad, or Mr. F. Mohammad Ali . . . Fred Dodd, Professor Ford, Wallace Ford, W. D. Ford, Wali Farad, Wardell Fard or W. D. Fard' (p. 146).

26. Certainly, the Homeric influence on Cal's narrative is conspicuous. On the second page of the novel, Cal invokes the Muses ('Sing now, O Muse, of the recessive gene on my fifth chromosome!') in a direct echo of the opening of *The Iliad*. Afterwards he apologises for his rhetorical excesses ('Sorry if I get a little Homeric at times'), explaining that his predilection for such flights of poetry is 'genetic', a reference not just to his Greek ancestry but to the fact that he has been named after the Muse of epic poetry, Calliope (p. 4). He reprises this apostrophe on two other occasions and *Middlesex* as a whole is clearly epic in its scale and ambition, covering three generations of the Stephanides family and taking in many key historical events along the way.

27. Linda Hutcheon, *A Poetics of Postmodernism: History, Theory, Fiction* (New York: Routledge, 1988), pp. 122–3.

28. Don DeLillo, 'The Power of History', *New York Times Magazine*, 7 September 1997, www.nytimes.com/library/books/090797article3.html.

CHAPTER 3

'Nes and Yo': Race, Ethnicity and Hybridity in Gish Jen's *Mona in the Promised Land*, Philip Roth's *The Human Stain* and Richard Powers' *The Time of Our Singing*

No Western society has been so riven by race as the United States. Although the intention to abolish slavery in the South was enshrined in the Emancipation Proclamation of 1862, confirmed by the subsequent victory of the Union in the Civil War and partly implemented during the Reconstruction period (1864–77), by the end of the nineteenth century white Democrats had effectively established political hegemony in the South, founded on the so-called 'Jim Crow' laws which enforced racial segregation throughout most of the southern states until the 1960s. These laws, together with extra-legal action, such as the intimidation and violence practised by white militias like the Ku Klux Klan, as well as continuing widespread racial discrimination throughout the US, ensured that for a century after the end of the Civil War which had supposedly freed them, black Americans were anything but equal citizens.

The legacy of slavery can still be felt in every dimension of life in the US. The outcomes of two of the three most recent presidential elections have arguably hinged on what is often called 'the race question': many analysts claimed that George W. Bush's first victory was secured only as the result of the illegal disenfranchisement of thousands of black voters in Florida, while Barack Obama's victory was achieved partly as the result of mobilising large numbers of African-Americans (95 per cent of whom voted for him) and in spite of the fact that the majority of whites voted Republican. As the notorious (first) trial of O. J. Simpson proved, public opinion still often divides along racial lines: according to several polls taken at the end of his acquittal in 1995, almost all white respondents believed that Simpson was guilty of the murder of his former wife, Nicole Brown Simpson, and her friend, Ronald Goldman, while the vast majority of blacks were convinced of his innocence. If the fault-lines between black and white still dominate the American cultural and political landscape, however, it must be remembered that there are many Americans who cannot be comfortably accommodated in either of these categories. Of all the other ethno-racial groups who inhabit the United States – for example, Native Americans, Latinos, Asians – one in particular has muddied the waters of racial relations because of their ambivalent attitudes towards, and the ambivalence with which they in turn are viewed by, both sides of the racial divide.

Although Jews make up only between 1.4 and 2.5% of the total population of the US (the figures vary according to the criteria used to define Jewishness), they occupy a central position in the symbolic imagination of both blacks and whites because, paradoxically, they fit into neither and both camps. It is this equivocal position – compounded by the ambiguity of the term 'Jewish' itself, which conflates racial, religious, ethnic and cultural characteristics – together with the complex history of black–Jewish relations in the postwar period, that makes Jewishness such a useful prism through which to refract contemporary racial politics in the US.[1] As Jonathan Freedman puts it in *Klezmer America: Jewishness, Ethnicity, Modernity* (2008), 'the example of Jewishness powerfully and uniquely . . . disrupt[s] the certitudes and rigidities that mark not only American race thinking, but race thinking across the board'.[2]

In this chapter, I look at three novels – Gish Jen's *Mona in the Promised Land* (1996), Philip Roth's *The Human Stain* (2001) and Richard Powers' *The Time of Our Singing* (2003) – in which Jewishness and other liminal, 'yellow' identities, such as Chinese-American and mixed-race, are used to dramatise the paradox at the heart of all discourses about race, as articulated by Erika Lin. In her article on *Mona in the Promised Land*, she asks:

> [H]ow do we talk about race in a way that does not naturalize race as a category but is still culturally intelligible? . . . when we talk about race at all, we *must* cite because there is no discursive practice that does not include citation . . . we do reinforce normative notions . . . but we also circulate [alternative] notions of identity.[3]

Lin identifies here the catch-22 in which these novels find themselves: even as they radically challenge the very notion of race, they partly reinstate it, since they must repeatedly cite the term, implicitly reinforcing the 'normative notions' that the nomenclature of race assumes. In a sense this is the dilemma faced not only by the authors of these novels but also by their protagonists: Mona Chang, Jonah Strom and Coleman Silk all try to invent for themselves alternative notions of identity – to situate themselves outside the ordinary parameters of racial categories – but in the very act of doing so they confirm the idea that race defines their identity, whether positively or negatively. In Lin's words, they 'naturalize race as a category'. In this sense, all three novels engage ambivalently with what Andrew Furman calls 'the paradigm shift regarding the immigrant ethos, precipitated in large part by the multicultural enthusiasms of the 1960s that continue apace today'.[4] To put it another way, they can be read both as products and critiques of multiculturalism: on the one hand, their heightened awareness of the problematic nature of all discourses of race is consistent with, and arguably has been enabled by, the project of multiculturalism; on the other, their recognition of the invidiousness of the kind of identity politics that has come to dominate contemporary race relations in the US puts them at odds with that project.

GISH JEN, *MONA IN THE PROMISED LAND*

Mona in the Promised Land is Jen's second novel, a sequel of sorts to her first, *Typical American* (1991), which follows the fluctuating fortunes of Ralph Chang, Mona's father, after he emigrates from Shanghai province in China. Mona is first mentioned early in that novel, cross-examining her father about his account of his train journey from San Francisco to New York, during which 'famous mountains lumbered by, famous rivers, plains, canyons, the whole holy American spectacle, without his looking up once'.[5] '"So how'd you know what you were *passing*, then," his younger daughter would ask. (This was Mona, who was just like that, a mosquito)', the narrator comments drily (p. 7). In an interview with Yuko Matsukawa in 1993, Jen claimed not to have any plans to write a novel about Mona (though she had by then published a story that featured her as its protagonist, later incorporated into her second novel), but the germs of *Mona in the Promised Land* are nonetheless present in this brief aside early in the first novel.[6] The juxtaposition of the narrator's lyrical description of the Arcadian American scene – the 'Promised Land', as the title of *Mona* has it – and Ralph's indifference to it establishes one of the tensions that animates both *Typical American* and *Mona*. Moreover, the inquisitive, sceptical nature that draws Mona towards Judaism in *Mona* ('[t]he whole key to Judaism is to ask, ask', she explains) is clearly visible in this, her first appearance as a character in Jen's *oeuvre*.[7] Finally, the italicisation of the word 'passing', even though in this context it refers to the sights that Ralph misses, also implicitly points towards the other meaning of the word: the phenomenon of members of one racial group representing themselves, and being accepted as, members of another, which is one of the central preoccupations of *Mona*.

Mona in the Promised Land begins with the Changs – Ralph, his wife, Helen, Mona, and her elder sister, Callie – moving into a predominantly Jewish neighbourhood, Scarshill, 'a liberal place, not like their old town, where [local kids] used to throw crab-apple mash at Callie and Mona, and tell them it would make their eyes stick shut' (p. 6). Although Scarshill is characterised more by the absence of intolerance than by the presence of tolerance, Mona soon finds that she is 'popular for a new girl' (p. 5) and feels at home with her (mainly Jewish) classmates. In time, this leads to a growing curiosity about Judaism, and Mona begins to attend classes with the local Jewish minister, Rabbi Horowitz, with a view to converting. During this process, Mona is invited by Horowitz to help initiate another newcomer to the fold: 'Eloise Ingle with the Rapunzel hair, who everyone thought was WASP, seeing as how she thought so herself until just recently' (p. 55). It turns out that Eloise's late mother was Jewish – a fact her stepmother had deliberately concealed from her stepdaughter 'in the name of sensitivity' (p. 55) – but when Eloise belatedly 'discover[s] her identity' (p. 56) she decides to explore her unexpected inheritance by joining the weekly synagogue discussion groups attended by Mona and her Jewish peers. As the other outsider in the group, Eloise feels a natural bond with Mona but at the same time, although a newcomer, she clearly feels more authentically Jewish than Mona, in spite of the latter's superior knowledge of Judaism. This is made clear by the patronising tone with which (in the narrator's free indirect discourse), she 'says how splendid [it is] to see a Chinese girl turn Jewish' and 'hopes that Mona feels welcome' (p. 56). Condescending though her attitude might be, she at least makes a genuine effort to befriend Mona, whereas she 'feels less pressed to extend her welcome to anyone else in the class; and after a few weeks, she has no need at all – having decided to go back to being a WASP' (p. 56).

This, even though she is actually still a Jew, according to some people (staunch adherents of the what-the-mother-is-the-child-is rule). Others, though, think how she was brought up determines at least as much who she is, if not more. 'Think about what she grew up eating,' they say. 'That's who she is, you can't deny it.' 'Like an Eskimo who prefers hamburgers to walrus meat is American,' says somebody. 'That's assuming walrus meat is what Eskimos eat,' says someone else. 'And why can't a person be both?' People nod. Yet another person thinks Eloise can be what she wants. Who are they to say what she is actually, because of her blood or her diet, either? Like the Changowitz, says this person, meaning Mona. People nod again. Should Mona take offense, though, that with this the conversation ends? (p. 56)

Jen's treatment of Eloise's brief flirtation with Judaism, and the responses that her caprice engenders, exemplify her strengths as a novelist. Economically, unpretentiously and comically she draws attention to the tensions at the heart of multiculturalism. Eloise's stepmother's 'sensitivity' to the question of Jewishness is of the self-serving, anti-Semitic kind, rather than the result of any real concern about her stepdaughter's feelings. Rather than having Eloise reclaim her Jewish heritage, however, and thus delivering a neat moral lesson, Jen has her quickly revert to her more convenient WASP lifestyle. The ensuing discussion about whether biology or culture determines ethnicity, whether it is possible to choose your ethnic identity and whether you can belong to more than one ethnic group, despite the absurdity of the example of the Eskimo and the walrus meat/hamburger, touches on many of the contemporary academic debates about race and ethnicity in the US. The reference to Mona's hybridity – expressed through the addition of the suffix 'owitz', commonly found at the end of Jewish names, to Mona's surname, Chang, and the use of the definite article preceding this compound title – is ambiguous: is it facetious proof that the other Jewish girls have not accepted her conversion or an affectionate indication that they have adopted her as one of their own? It is of course both: the girls want to include Mona but cannot help but draw attention to her difference even as they extend that welcome. Mona's 'conversion' demonstrates both the possibilities and the limitations of ethnic self-determination, both the potential for transcending conventional racial boundaries and the impossibility of ever fully doing so.

This idea is explored elsewhere in the novel: when Mona blithely informs her first love, a Japanese boy named Sherman Matsumoto, that he can 'become American anyway' (p. 14) only to be told years later (by a boy impersonating Sherman) that, conversely, she 'will never be Japanese' (p. 82); when the family of Mona's best friend, Barbara Gugelstein, try to dissociate themselves from their Jewish origins by refusing 'to talk Yiddish, or to vacation on the east coast of Florida, where . . . there are too many Jews' (p. 125); and, most importantly, in a conversation between Mona, Barbara, Seth Mandel (who later becomes Mona's lover), Alfred, an African-American cook who works at the Changs' restaurant, and three of Alfred's black co-workers, about Mona's conversion to Judaism.

> 'Mona is Jewish now, and it's made a big difference in her life.'
> 'You trying to convert us, sister?'
> 'She's trying to educate you,' says Mona. 'So you can have a big house and a four-bay garage and a gardener too.'
> 'We're never going to have no big house or no big garage, either,' explains Alfred. 'We're never going to be Jewish, see, even if we grow our nose like Miss Mona here is planning to do. *We be black motherfuckers.*'
> 'You can be Jewish too,' says Barbara.
> 'Even Stokely Carmichael originally wanted to go to Brandeis,' Seth says. 'He learned a lot from the Jews.' (p. 137)

Again, Jen uses comic dialogue to highlight a problem that is central to postwar race relations in the US: namely, the tensions between blacks and Jews. While Barbara earnestly tries to persuade Alfred of the virtues of Jewish values, Mona provides an ironic commentary, emphasising the material rewards rather than the moral benefits that can be attained as an American Jew, parodying both Barbara's naive enthusiasm and the allegations made by some African-Americans that Jews 'bought their way into whiteness'.[8] Seth's invocation of the militant black activist Stokely Carmichael is also (unwittingly) ironic, since Carmichael became notorious during the 1980s for his anti-Semitism – an anti-Semitism that is also implicitly present in Alfred's aside about Mona growing her nose (an allusion to the stereotype of the long-nosed Jew). Alfred himself appears to conform to stereotypical images of black-ness here, with his (feigned?) ignorance of the concept ('Typing? Stereo? I've never heard of no stereo that could type') and his idiomatic, ungrammatical speech, peppered with profanities ('*We be black motherfuckers*'). These black–Jewish tensions reach their height later in the novel when a silver flask goes missing from the Gugelstein house, which Alfred and a number of his (fellow black) friends are using while Barbara's parents are on holiday. This incident breaks the fragile trust between the two camps who constitute (the self-consciously named) Camp Gugelstein: Barbara assumes that one of Alfred's gang has stolen the flask, and one of them, Luther, retaliates by referring to Barbara's father as a 'Jew-daddy' (p. 204).

However, the ostensibly clear-cut opposition between the blacks and Jews in *Mona* is complicated by a number of factors. First, Barbara's parents are self-hating Jews whose decision to have Barbara's nose remodelled by cosmetic surgery suggests that they share Alfred's prejudices about Jewish physiognomy. Second, Alfred's apparent anti–Semitism does not prevent him from having a secret affair with, and eventually marrying, Barbara's cousin. Third, Seth is an atheist who explains his own indeterminate identity in terms that parody the subtle distinctions between different types of Jew made by Jean-Paul Sartre in *Anti-Semite and Jew* (1946), telling Mona that he is 'an authentic inauthentic Jew . . . in the process of becoming an inauthentic inauthentic Jew' (p. 112). He also spends much of his adolescence in a tepee in his backyard, reinventing himself as a Native American Jew, a version of ethnic hybridity that mirrors and perhaps mocks Mona's. Finally, Mona herself both is and is not Jewish. Rabbi Horowitz tells her, paradoxically, that '*The more Jewish you become, the more Chinese you'll be*' (p. 190) and the narrator likewise poses the question of whether, since Jewishness seems to depend on 'remembering that you are', 'the fact that Mona remembers all too well who she is make[s] her more Jewish than, say, Barbara Gugelstein' (p. 32). In fact, her dual identity as Chinese and Jewish makes Mona an ideal lightning rod with which to register all the complex racial currents flowing through contemporary multicultural America.

As the daughter of Chinese immigrants, Mona is exposed to all the ambivalence towards their adopted nation her parents, Helen and Ralph, feel. In Jen's first novel, the phrase 'typical American' (p. 67), which gives the novel its title, is a mantra uttered by the Changs to express their incredulity and derision at the customs of their new countrymen. However, Mona's aunt, Theresa, notes astutely that the reason her generation '*used to say* typical American good-for-nothing . . . *was because we believed we were* good for nothing' (p. 126). This is lent credence by the fact that the phrase crops up only once in *Mona in the Promised Land*, when the Changs use it ironically of themselves, vowing to stop being 'typical American parents' who have 'let the kids run wild', and to revert to being more responsible 'Chinese parents' (p. 246). Their resolution is made more ironic by Mona's response, which is to tell her parents that they 'sound like the Puritans' (p. 246) – the first American settlers and hence quintessentially typical Americans.

If, as Theresa suggests, self-hatred haunts the Changs' uneasy negotiations with American culture, then that internalised preju-dice is intimately linked with their perceptions of the status of other minority groups in America. Of these, the most important are the Jews and blacks. The former represent a model for their own aspirations; on the opening page of the novel we are told that the Chinese-Americans are 'the new Jews, after all, a model minor-ity and Great American Success', who 'belong in the promised land' (p. 3). In stark contrast, the Changs 'don't want to have too much to do with blacks' because they fear that they will be associ-ated with them. In *Typical American* the narrator had recorded the Changs' reaction to moving into a predominantly black neigh-bourhood in equivocal terms: 'So many Negroes! Years later, they would shake their heads and call themselves prejudiced, but at the time they were profoundly disconcerted' (p. 65). The narra-tor of *Mona* puts it more baldly: Ralph and Helen are prepared to employ black workers but 'they don't want to turn into blacks' (p. 118), which is to say they don't want to be bracketed with them as 'people of color' by the WASP majority.

Chinese-Americans may well be America's 'new Jews', but if so they have in a sense displaced the blacks, who were often called 'America's Jews' by postwar Jewish immigrants who identified with their historical suffering as the result of racial discrimination. Like American Jews, Chinese-Americans occupy a liminal posi-tion on the colour line that divides black from white, being neither one nor the other. When Alfred tells Mona that 'White is white . . . Everything else is black. Half and half is black' (p. 155), Mona flippantly asks whether this makes her black, but the logic of her belief that being 'American means being whatever you want' (p. 49) dictates that she might just as easily become black as Jewish, a fact recognised by her mother when she expresses the fear that, since Mona has decided to become Jewish, 'Tomorrow you'll come home and tell me you want to be black' (p. 49). Helen's comment is partly facetious but it has a real undercurrent of anxiety, just as there is in the jibes directed at Ralph in *Typical American* after he gets sunburnt on one side of his body while on holiday: 'They called him half-cooked, half-black, half-and-half' (p. 180).

Although Mona points out to Helen that she can't 'turn black' since it is 'a race, not a religion', her assurances are disingenuous, both because Jewishness has, historically, been regarded as a race as much as a religion and because, as the narrator notes in parenthesis, 'Mona . . . knows some kids [who] . . . call each other brother . . . eat soul food . . . and wear their hair in the baddest Afros they can manage' (p. 49). Indeed, Mona herself, though she never indulges in this *ersatz* blackness, does come under the influence of Naomi, her older sister Callie's African-American college roommate. When Callie asks Mona whether she is aware of the mixed feelings their parents had about their Chinese identity even before they emigrated to the United States, Mona confesses that she 'never thought about it before', at which point Naomi chips in:

'But here you are now,' says Naomi. 'Thinking.'
'And here I am too,' says Eloise.
'Half Jewish,' Mona says.
'Maybe starting to turn part black too,' says Naomi.
'Why not?' Eloise raises her fist proudly, the way Miss Montana did in the Miss America pageant one year.
Mona and Callie raise their fists as well. 'Black is beautiful!'
(p. 184)

The sisters' Black Power gesture is at once parodic and sincere, reflecting both the sense of solidarity that they feel with African-Americans and their awareness of the gulf that separates them. Whereas the first generation of Chinese-Americans feared that to identify too strongly with blacks might result in their being identified *as* black, Mona and Callie, American-born, are more secure about their position in relation to other ethnic groups and more likely to assert and celebrate the difference from WASPs that their parents underplayed or denied. In this respect, too, they are following a trajectory established by American Jews.

Early on in the novel, Barbara 'announces that she's Jewish' to a bemused Mona, who wonders, 'what were you before?' (p. 30). Of course, Barbara has always been Jewish in the ethno-racial sense, but is referring to her newfound interest in Judaism. Similarly, late on in the novel, Callie begins 'using her Chinese name', Kailan, as a sign that 'she's proud to be Asian American' (p. 301). Whereas Barbara is renewing her links with a tradition that has been rejected by her parents, who 'spent their whole lives getting out of the ghetto' (p. 125), Callie is embracing a new ethnic identity which her parents do not recognise:

> But what in the world is an Asian-American? That's what Ralph and Helen want to know. And how can she lump herself together with the Japanese? . . . And what, friends with the Koreans too? And the Indians? The parents shake their heads. Better to turn Jewish than Asian American, that's their opinion these days. (pp. 301–2)

What Callie sees as a way of connecting herself to an older, more authentic culture (she refers to Kailan as her 'original name'), her parents regard with a mixture of incomprehension and disdain: by aligning herself with Americans from Japan, China's bitter enemy, Callie is, in their eyes, betraying rather than honouring her history. What both episodes reveal, however, is that ethnicity in America is not fixed, but fluid, contingent on historical circumstances.

Whereas many of the Jews who settled in America during the two 'great waves' of immigration at the end of the nineteenth and beginning of the twentieth centuries accepted that they would have to assimilate thoroughly, sacrificing their old-world customs and beliefs in order to thrive in their newly adopted nation, the Holocaust and the establishment of the State of Israel brought about a fundamental change in the way that many American Jews felt about their Jewishness. As Jen's narrator puts it, with a characteristically epigrammatic brevity, by the time the Changs move to Scarshill in 1968, far from having dissolved in the melting pot, 'the Jews have become The Jews, on account of the Six Day

War' (p. 3). A Chinese-American identity has also evolved. If the first generation of immigrants, like Ralph and Helen, felt at once superior to, and envious of, the 'typical Americans' whom they encountered, Mona's generation feels both more at home in the US and, paradoxically, more keenly aware of their status as 'ethnics', having more in common with other 'Asian-Americans', or even with Jewish and African-Americans, than with the WASPS whom their parents had identified as the 'typical Americans'.

For Mona's parents in *Typical American*, the only effective defence against racism seemed to be economic success, so that Ralph exclaims that in America, if '"You have no money, you are nobody. You are Chinaman!"' (p. 199). In *Mona*, however, 'Chinaman' is no longer a synonym for 'nobody', not only because many Chinese-Americans, like the Changs, have moved up the economic ladder, but because the notion of the 'Chinaman' itself has become anachronistic in the era of multiculturalism, a fact that the narrator constantly emphasises. At the start of the novel the narrator observes that, in 1968, 'the blushing dawn of ethnic awareness has yet to pink up [the Changs'] inky suburban night', but of course the narrative itself is suffused with this 'awareness' as this phrase itself demonstrates, with its arch poetic idiom and sly allusions to colour, reinforced by the pink/ink rhyme (pink, like yellow, being a traditional marker of mixed race, of someone who is 'neither one thing nor the other'). So, for example, when Mona and Callie first enrol at their new Scarshill school, we are told that they seemed 'like permanent exchange students', but that '[i]n another ten years, there'll be so many Orientals they'll turn into Asians' (p. 6). Later, as the adolescent Mona worries about her lack of body hair and other ways in which she seems to differ from her Jewish peers, the narrator breaks off from the free, indirect discourse with which Mona's thoughts are characteristically conveyed, to comment:

> Of course, this whole train of thought will one day prove not her own train at all, but a train set on track by racist sexist imperialists. She will one day discover that it is great to be nonhairy, and what's more that not all Asians are areolaless, just her and some others. Plus that she is yellow and beautiful

– baby boobs, hammy calves and all. She will ask for an extra print when people take her picture. She will come to recognize, with a little squinting, her goddess within. (p. 76)

In her essay 'The (Re)Birth of Mona Changowitz: Rituals and Ceremonies of Cultural Conversion and Self-making in *Mona in the Promised Land*', Begoña Simal González observes that the phrase 'of course' is 'the author's ironic mark' in *Mona*.[9] However, the tone of this passage is not straightforwardly ironic. Certainly, Jen's narrator implies scepticism of the new postmodernist pieties through what Erika Lin (borrowing the term from Judith Butler's *Bodies That Matter*) calls 'hyberbolic citation', the restating of 'a normative notion in an exaggerated way in order to simultaneously work against it' (p. 49). Mona's anxieties are clearly not simply the product of colonialist brainwashing, but also of the kinds of insecurities suffered by all pubescent girls, whatever their ethnicity. However, this is not to say that Mona is not beautiful. Conversely, although her lack of body hair does not signify abnormality, it is not necessarily 'great to be nonhairy'. Finally, the narrator neither scornfully rejects nor wholeheartedly approves of the enlightenment offered by multiculturalism. Like Mona assessing herself, she can see its virtues if she squints, while remaining aware of its absurdities and excesses.

Mona in the Promised Land ends with an epilogue which finds Mona 'sort of married' to her Jewish boyfriend, Seth, and about 'to be more married soon', with a 'pink-prune child' named Io, but estranged from her mother (p. 296). On the final page, Mona's dearest wish – 'that her parents [would] burst through the door, if only so that her mother could judge for herself whether Io could pass for pure Chinese with that nose' (p. 298) – is fulfilled, giving rise to a tearful reunion. However, the belated marriage and family reconciliation cannot resolve the tensions that have been troubling Mona and her family. The indeterminacy of Mona's matrimonial status, though described with characteristic dry irony, echoes that of her ethnicity, and the joke about Io's ability to 'pass for pure Chinese with that nose' similarly serves as a reminder of the Jewish self-hatred that prompts Barbara's parents to arrange cosmetic surgery for her and of the anti-Semitic jibes of the Changs'

African-American employees, who tell Mona that she must 'grow [her] nose' if she wants to pass as Jewish. In *Klezmer America*, Jonathan Freedman points out that what he calls 'the race plot' of *Mona* (by which he means the sub-plot involving Alfred and his African-American friends) 'strikes a discordant note that remains to complicate the novel's comic celebration of a new, multicultural America' (p. 299), but I would argue that the ending of *Mona* is in any case too equivocal to be celebratory. If Mona's inter-racial marriage with Seth seems to be blessed by both the previous generation (when her mother sees Mona again, she cries so that 'anyone would think that Helen is the person Mona's taking in sickness or in health') and the next (the final image of the novel is of Io clapping), there are a number of details that qualify the apparently happy ending and hint at persistent problems with the ethno-racial status of Mona and her new family (p. 304).

When Mona tells Theresa that she intends to change her name, not to Mandel (her husband's name), but to 'Changowitz' – the Jewish version of her family name which her Jewish high school friends had coined – Theresa, clearly incredulous, asks if she is serious. Mona's answer – 'Nes and Yo' – again expresses, facetiously, an anxiety about the hybridity of her identity, as does the name of her daughter, Io (who, in Greek mythology, undergoes her own metamorphosis, when Zeus changes her from a nymph into a heifer in an unsuccessful attempt to shield her from the vengeance of Hera). Michelle Byers, in her essay 'Material Bodies and Performative Identities: Mona, Neil and the Promised Land', argues that Jen 'looks for a resolution for all her characters within a single version of American multicultural hybridity, a watered down vision of hybridity in which identities simply "mix" as though outside the historical and material realities of power'.[10] However, it seems to me that the novel's vision of hybridity is hedged about everywhere with qualifications and reservations. In spite – or because – of her attempts to carve out a particular ethno-racial niche for herself, Mona ends the novel by defining herself only in negative terms – 'not wasp, and not black, and not as Jewish as Jewish can be; and not from Chinatown, either' (p. 231). If *Mona* suggests, as one reviewer put it (in a comment that is included on the back page of the Granta paperback edition), that 'perhaps there is more melting in the pot than [one might have] imagined' (n.p.), it also suggests that the 'Promised Land' invoked in its title is as mythical and unattainable – as perpetually deferred – for a new generation of multicultural American families as it was for their immigrant parents and grandparents.

PHILIP ROTH, *THE HUMAN STAIN*

The third in Philip Roth's 'American Trilogy' – following *American Pastoral* (1997) and *I Married A Communist* (1998) – and the twenty-fourth book of his prolific career, *The Human Stain* tells the story of Coleman Silk, an African-American professor of Classics at the fictional Athena College, who spends his adult life passing as a Jew. When Silk flippantly asks a class whether two persistent absentees are 'spooks', his life rapidly unravels. Although he uses the word as a synonym for 'ghosts', the two students turn out to be African-Americans and they lodge a formal complaint on the grounds that 'spooks' is a pejorative word for blacks. Rather than fight the allegations, Silk leaves in disgust – and in disgrace. After the death of his Jewish wife (from whom he had kept his identity secret), the octogenarian Silk begins an affair with a much younger woman, Faunia Farley, who also pretends to be someone she isn't: for reasons that remain obscure, she claims to be illiterate. She is also being stalked by her ex-husband, Les Farley, a psychopathic Vietnam veteran who blames her for the death of their two children. Apart from Faunia, Silk's only confidant is his near-neighbour, Nathan Zuckerman, a reclusive Jewish-American author whom Roth uses as the narrator of this, and many other, novels.

Like Mona, Coleman grows up under the influence of those other ethnic 'others', the Jews. Although he lives in a neighbourhood where 'mostly everyone was white' and 'there were fewer Jews even than there were Negroes', 'it was the Jews . . . who . . . loomed larger than anyone in Coleman's extracurricular life'.[11] When Coleman takes up boxing, his Jewish coach encourages Coleman not to challenge the assumption that others might make that he is one too. As far as Coleman's father is concerned, the

Jews provide a model for assimilation that blacks might emulate: 'the Jews . . . were like Indian scouts, shrewd people showing the outsider his way in . . . showing an intelligent colored family how it might be done' (p. 97). Mr Silk's argument here deconstructs itself, since the terms in which he suggests that American Jews have blazed a trail of assimilation into mainstream America that blacks might follow implicitly invokes the tragic consequences of America's historical intolerance of outsiders. First, the analogy with Indian scouts hints at the costs of assimilation – the scouts were initially employed by the US military to fight in the so-called 'Indian Wars' and therefore arguably betrayed their own people, as well as being representatives of them.

Second, while ostensibly establishing the common ground shared by Jews and blacks as fellow outsiders, Silk actually draws attention to the fundamental differences between them: paying tribute to the ingenuity of American Jews by comparing them to Indian scouts ironically serves as a reminder that it is African-Americans, rather than Jewish-Americans, who have most in common with the Native Americans as the two great historical victims of the territorial and economic expansionism of the United States.

Although the Jews endured a unique genocidal catastrophe in Europe, in America they have never suffered from the kind of systematic racial discrimination that has disenfranchised native and black Americans for so long. This distinction is demonstrated dramatically by the episode in which the Jewish father of one of Coleman's classmates, Dr Fensterman, offers Silk a bribe of $3,000 for Coleman to deliberately underachieve in two of his exams in order to allow Fensterman's son to graduate as class valedictorian. In a bid to establish his liberal credentials, Fensterman tells Silk that he has observed anti-black racism at first hand:

> Because of the tiny Jewish quotas in most medical schools, Dr Fensterman had had himself to go down to Alabama for his schooling, and there he'd seen at first hand all that colored people have to strive against. Dr Fensterman knew that prejudice in academic institutions against colored students was far worse than it was against Jews. (p. 86)

Even while he is acknowledging that racism against blacks is 'far worse' than that Jews experience, Fensterman implicitly invokes the connection between the two, first by explaining that he was forced to study at Alabama because of the anti-Semitic 'quotas' in 'most medical schools' – that is, the practice of restricting the number of Jews admitted to any given college according to a specific formula; and second, by suggesting that the prejudice against African Americans differs from that against Jewish-Americans only in degree.

In fact, Fensterman's professional and economic status illustrates the gulf between the Jewish-American and African-American experience: though his medical degree may have been awarded by a provincial college rather than one of the Ivy League elite, Fensterman has nonetheless had a successful career as a hospital consultant, while Silk, though also a college graduate, only finds employment as a waiter on a train. In addition to paying the $3,000 bribe, Fensterman also offers to help Mrs Silk, who works as a nurse on the same wards as him, get the promotion that has been denied her because of the colour of her skin. But this unwittingly undermines Fensterman's earlier attempts to establish that there is common ground between Jews and blacks due to their shared status as marginal groups suffering from discrimination. Fensterman's offer of patronage is not simply patronising but also shameful, since it contains an implicit threat – if the Silks do not agree, he will not help (and may even hinder) her progress – and an implicit admission: he has done nothing until now to help her, even though he can see that she 'should long ago have been appointed the head nurse on the medical-surgical floor' (p. 86). Furthermore, his argument that if Coleman comes second in his class this will have 'negligible' consequences since he will still 'be the highest-ranked colored student ever to graduate' from his school and 'his having finished high school as salutatorian rather than as valedictorian would make no difference whatsoever when he enrolled at Howard University', whereas for his son the place he covets at Harvard or Yale will remain a realistic goal only if he graduates first in his class, reveals the doctor's double standards (p. 87). Coleman is to be judged only by comparison to other 'colored' students and his destiny is to attend a black-only college (Howard);

whereas Fensterman's son (if Coleman gives him a helping hand) can compete with the WASPs for a place at one of the country's elite medical schools.

Naturally, the Silks reject Fensterman's proposal, but the lesson is not lost on Coleman; when he does enrol at Howard and is called a 'nigger' at a local store during his first week on campus (p. 102), Coleman decides to leave college and join the Navy. On his return to civilian life, he finds himself once again inhabiting a world in which Jews loom large. Remembering how he had 'passed' as Jewish as a teenager under the tutelage of his boxing coach, Coleman decides to reinvent himself permanently. Unlike Mona's conversion, Coleman's is purely opportunistic: he decides to 'become' Jewish not out of religious conviction or even because he admires the industry and ingenuity that his father attributes to the Jews, but rather because he *can* – and because in doing so he can exploit the historical moment at which 'Jewish self-infatuation was at a postwar pinnacle' and the Jewish intellectuals of Greenwich Village have 'an aura of cultural significance' (p. 131).

If Coleman's assumption of Jewishness smoothes his path to prosperity, however, he also paves the way for other 'ethnics' to follow in his footsteps. In the opening pages of the novel, before Silk's secret has been disclosed, Nathan Zuckerman observes that 'Coleman was one of a handful of Jews on the Athena faculty when he was hired and perhaps among the first Jews permitted to teach in a classics department anywhere in America' (p. 5). When he is promoted to the post of Dean, he wastes no time excising the 'deadest of the deadwood' from the Faculty, hiring new faces from diverse backgrounds and creating a meritocracy (p. 8). In this sense, Silk is both the beneficiary of cultural change and its agent. Ironically, he also becomes its victim, as the new era of multiculturalism that he helps to usher in ultimately destroys him.

Although the novel weaves a complex tapestry of allusions that connects the scapegoating of Silk by his colleagues at Athena with contemporary attempts to impeach President Clinton for the scandal that became known as 'Monicagate',[12] the ancient 'purifying rituals' practised in Greek society and dramatised in the tragedies of Aeschylus and Sophocles, and the stigmatising of Hester Prynne in Nathaniel Hawthorne's *The Scarlet Letter* (one of the foundational texts of American literature), it also provides the occasion for a scathing critique of contemporary identity politics. Whereas Oedipus' patricide and incest make him first a pariah (in *Oedipus Rex*) and later a holy man (in *Oedipus at Colonnus*), Hester Prynne is similarly transfigured from a reviled adulteress to a revered wise woman, and the stain on Clinton's reputation has been largely erased by the nostalgic affection with which many Americans now look back to the economic prosperity that coincided with his two terms as president, no such redemption is forthcoming for Silk. Instead, he is punished twice over for his decision to disown his origins and his family. When he decides to marry the woman whom Zuckerman describes, in characteristically paradoxical terms, as 'non-Jewish [i.e. secular] Jewish Iris' (p. 132), Silk tells his mother that in order to preserve his own version of non-Jewish Jewishness he intends to sever all links with his family. The comparison with Oedipus is made implicitly at this moment:

> He was murdering her. You don't have to murder your father. The world will do that for you . . . Who there is to murder is the mother, and that's what he saw he was doing to her, the boy who'd been loved by this woman. (p. 138)

Yet it is made on the basis not of similarity but of disjunction. Whereas Oedipus unwittingly loves his mother too much – uxoriously and incestuously – Silk sins against his mother not by being too intimate but by renouncing all intimacy with her. Furthermore, however ruthless and unfilial his actions may be, his description of himself as a murderer is self-dramatising hyperbole. The awkwardness of the syntax in the phrase 'Who there is to murder is the mother' manifests an anxiety about the sentiment that it expresses. As Jonathan Freedman points out,[13] this aspect of the plot conforms to – perhaps parodies – the conventions of other passing narratives, one of which Coleman's sister, Ernestine, refers to explicitly in a long conversation she has with Zuckerman towards the end of the novel:

> '[T]he decision that he made, despite his Negro ancestry, to live as a member of another racial group – that was by no

means an uncommon decision before the civil rights movement. There were movies about it . . . One was called *Pinky*.'
(p. 323)

In spite of superficial affinities, Coleman's story differs radically from these traditional passing narratives. First, because the other 'racial group' that Coleman elects to join is not that of the white majority but of another minority (a distinction that is evaded by the vagueness of Ernestine's formulation); and second, whereas the protagonists of these older passing narratives fall victim to the racism endemic in postwar American society once their true identities are exposed, Coleman, precisely because of his success in passing as a Jew, is ironically undone by the determination of college authorities in 1990s America to eradicate racism.

If multiculturalism is very much a product of late twentieth-century politics, Zuckerman nonetheless locates its origins much farther back in history. When he describes Silk as having been '[e]xcommunicated by the saved, the elect, the ever-present evangelists of the mores of the moment' (p. 315) and subjected to 'public stoning' (p. 289), Zuckerman implicitly equates the zeal of the Athena academics with what Hawthorne called the 'moral rigidity' of the Puritan settlers, as well as with the punitive Old Testament attitude to moral transgression on which they modelled their own. Finally, he finds in the treatment of Silk an echo of the Communist witch-hunts of the 1950s (with which the previous novel in Roth's 'American Trilogy', *I Married a Communist*, was concerned). Reflecting on the credulity of the Athena college community, who readily believe the accusation of Silk's embittered colleague, Delphine Roux (made to cover her own tracks) that he broke into her office and sent an email to all her colleagues containing a lonely hearts advertisement in which she professes to be looking for a man whose profile matches Silk's, Zuckerman observes that:

No motive for the perpetrator is necessary, no logic or rationale is required. Only a label is required. The label is the motive. The label is the evidence. The label is the logic. Why did Coleman Silk do this? Because he is an *x*, because he is *y*, because he is both. First a racist and now a misogynist. It is too late in the century to call him a Communist, though that is the way it used to be done. (p. 290)

Once again, the details of Zuckerman's diction are revealing: in this highly rhetorical passage (featuring a negative catalogue, two tricolons and a form of *occupatio*) it is easy to miss the larger resonance of the formulation: 'Because he is an *x*, because he is *y*, because he is both'. Although Zuckerman glosses this phrase in the following line, supplying the terms 'racist' and 'misogynist' to fill the categories of 'x' and 'y', they also seem to allude to Silk's dual identity, providing a distorted echo of his own description of Silk as 'neither this nor that but something in between' (p. 130) and of the words of Silk's coach: 'You're neither one thing nor the other . . . . you're Jewish' (pp. 98–9). Just as having an equal number of x and y chromosomes (like Cal/Callie in *Middlesex*) produces an individual who defies normative gender definitions, so being both x and y (where x is white-skinned and y is black) produces someone who doesn't fit neatly into any racial pigeon-hole. In other words, this passage implicitly deconstructs itself, suggesting that multiculturalism, in its anxiety to indict those guilty of intolerance, paradoxically itself becomes a tool of intolerance.

This point is reinforced during the conversation between Ernestine and Zuckerman at Coleman's funeral. Although Ernestine playfully rebukes Zuckerman for his ignorance of the black explorer Matthew Henson, she is ambivalent about Black History Month, a product of multiculturalism, seeing it as symptomatic of a decline in educational standards. At the school where she taught, she tells Zuckerman, 'they stopped long ago reading the old classics' (p. 329).

They haven't even heard of *Moby-Dick*, much less read it. Youngsters were coming to me . . . telling me that for Black History Month they would only read a biography of a black by a black. What difference, I would ask them, if it's a black author or a white author? (p. 329)

That Ernestine chooses *Moby-Dick* as her exemplary classic is surely no coincidence: Melville's novel tells the story of how the multicultural crew of the *Pequod* is undone by the 'appalling whiteness' of the whale and the monomania of the white man who hunts it. The pun on 'appalling', which means both 'horrific' and 'become pale', demonstrates that for Melville, as for Roth, the 'myth of purity' is pernicious. Yet Meville is also one of the Dead White Males targeted in the 1990s by some of the more radical advocates of multiculturalism, and this is what, for Ernestine, connects the neglect of *Moby-Dick* with the insistence of her students on reading black-authored versions of black history and with the resignation of her brother from Athena College:

> What happened to Coleman with that word 'spooks' is all a part of the same enormous failure . . . it used to be the person who fell short. Now it's the discipline . . . Today the student asserts his incapacity as a privilege . . . There are no more criteria . . . only opinions. (pp. 330–1)

According to Ernestine, the reaction of the college authorities to her brother's unfortunate choice of words is emblematic of a wider malaise in higher education that has, in the name of empowering students, undermined the foundations of their learning. For Ernestine's students, however, whether or not a book is authored by a black or white writer matters because of the privileging of white authors over many centuries. One of the lasting legacies of multiculturalism has been to redefine the literary canon so that it includes more authors from ethnic minorities, mostly not at the expense of established white authors (Ernestine's comments about *Moby Dick* notwithstanding), but in addition to them. In spite of Zuckerman's professed affection for her, then, Ernestine is not necessarily the mouthpiece for Roth that Freedman takes her for: her contention that Coleman is the victim of an intellectual relativism in which there are 'no more criteria . . . only opinions' is at best misguided, at worst disingenuous.[14]

Context is everything. In itself, the authorship of the biography of a black person should be irrelevant, but in the context of Black History Month, the aim of which is to redress the historical neglect of the achievements of African-Americans, the identity of the author is as important as the subject of the study. Similarly, if

Coleman had been identified as a black man when he used the word spooks, the response would have been entirely different to the one he encounters as a putative Jew. Early in the novel, Zuckerman observes that when Coleman introduces competition to Athena, 'an early enemy' attributed his reforming zeal to his race, remarking that this '"is what Jews do"' (p. 9). Although the source of this anti-Semitic comment is not identified, the implication is that it issues from the WASP college old guard, who are affronted by their new Dean's readiness to unseat them from their sinecures. When Coleman falls foul of the new regime that he has helped to install, his Jewishness again exacerbates the situation, if indeed it does not precipitate it. That many of Coleman's colleagues at Athena are 'not at all displeased' (p. 10) by the scandal that engulfs him can be partly explained by Coleman's confrontational style during his term as Dean, but it is also, ironically, a product of the very racism that it professes to oppose, at least as far as he is concerned. In Coleman's view, the alacrity with which many of his colleagues pursued the case against him is connected with the propaganda circulated by many prominent African-American activists, from Malcolm X to Louis Farrakhan, from Jesse Jackson to Al Sharpton, that Jews are, in Coleman's satirical formulation, 'the major source of black suffering on this planet' (p. 16).

Referring to an incident when, as a sailor stationed at a naval base in Virginia, he was 'identified, in a brothel, as a nigger trying to pass', Coleman complains to Zuckerman that he has been 'Thrown out of a Norfolk whorehouse for being black, thrown out of Athena College for being white' (p. 16). Of course, Zuckerman is ignorant at this stage of Coleman's true identity, so the irony of his situation seems only to derive from the familiar scenario of the Jew who is identified as black by white racists and as white by black anti-Semites. Furthermore, Zuckerman reports Coleman's 'ravings about black anti-Semitism' with more scepticism than sympathy. In particular, Coleman's conviction that the vindictive actions of the college authorities caused the death of his wife strikes Zuckerman as wildly implausible expressions of rage and grief. In fact, this aspect of Coleman's story seems likely to derive from a previously unacknowledged source that makes its connection with the issue of anti-Semitism clearer than it appears to be in the novel.

Many critics have pointed out that Coleman seems partly to be based on Anatole Broyard, an eminent postwar cultural critic and, in Ross Posnock's words, 'a light-skinned black man who passed as white (but not as a Jew) his entire adult life, only, like Coleman, to be outed posthumously'.[15] However, the fate of Coleman's wife, Iris, and his response to it suggest an alternative model for Coleman: R. B. Kitaj. Kitaj was an American-Jewish artist who spent most of his life in England, originally making his name in the late 1950s as a pop artist and then as one of the loose association of artists (which included Francis Bacon, Lucien Freud, Frank Auerbach and Leon Kossoff) sometimes known, in a phrase coined by Kitaj himself, as the 'School of London'. A long-standing friend of Roth's, whose portrait he drew brilliantly in charcoal, Kitaj's career has a number of affinities with Roth's, notably an increasing preoccupation in the 1970s and 1980s with Jewish identity. As I have argued elsewhere, Roth makes use of an essay by the artist entitled 'First Diasporist Manifesto' (1989) in his earlier novel, *Operation Shylock* (1993).[16] Some of the episodes in *Sabbath's Theater* (1995) may also have been based on Kitaj's experiences as a young man in the Merchant Navy. These may also feed into Silk's biography (like Kitaj, as a young man he runs away to join the Navy), but I want to focus on the use Roth makes in *The Human Stain* of a crisis late in Kitaj's life that led to the artist returning to the United States and, indirectly, to his suicide.

In 2004, the Tate Gallery, London hosted a major retrospective of Kitaj's work. Although the exhibition was acknowledged by some critics as cementing his reputation as one of the key postwar figures in British and American art history, the response, in Janet Wolff's words, was 'overwhelmingly hostile' and characterised by a number of *ad hominem* attacks of 'extraordinary viciousness'.[17] Soon after the exhibition closed, Kitaj's wife, Sandra Fisher, a fellow artist, died of a brain aneurysm. Kitaj blamed the critics who had savaged his work for her death, saying, 'They tried to kill me and they got her instead' and exhibiting paintings at successive Royal Academy Summer Exhibitions in 1996 and 1997 – 'The Critic Kills' and 'The Killer Critic Assassinated by His Widower, Even' – in which his bitter sense of injury was articulated literally and symbolically.[18] Feeling betrayed by the art culture in London that had long sustained him, Kitaj left his adopted homeland, living out his final years in Los Angeles, where he continued to paint, among other things, a number of fantastic portraits of Sandra, sometimes reincarnated, together with himself, in the form of angels. In 2007, he took his own life.

The parallels with Coleman's story are striking. Iris is 'an abstract painter', an 'energetic . . . woman of commanding presence and in perfect health', who, in the midst of the legal wrangling that ensues after the students' complaint is taken up by a 'pro bono black lawyer' and a 'black activist group from Pittsfield', wakes up one morning 'with a ferocious headache and no feeling in one of her arms', is rushed to hospital, but dies 'the next day' (pp. 12, 13). Coleman's paranoid conviction that his 'enemies . . . in striking out at him, had instead felled her' and the way in which this becomes an *idée fixe*, so that he 'made sure to tell everyone at the funeral the following afternoon' that '[t]hey meant to kill me and they got her instead' (pp. 11, 13), closely echoes Kitaj's response to his wife's death (this last phrase is an almost verbatim quotation from Kitaj). Just as Kitaj expressed his grievances obsessively in his art and in a number of interviews in which he accused his critics of anti-Semitism,[19] comparing his case to the infamous nineteenth-century trial in France of Alfred Dreyfus, so Coleman compulsively scribbles notes for a book, *Spooks*, in which he presents himself as a martyr sacrificed on the altar of racial politics. As he explains to Zuckerman, the 'spooks' incident provided a focal point for black activism at Athena – a *cause célèbre* which was 'exploited' in order to press for '[m]ore black students, more black professors' (p. 17). Ironically, one of the leaders of this campaign is Herb Keble, an African-American social scientist appointed by Coleman as 'the first black [at Athena] in anything other a custodial position' (p. 16). Once again, Coleman attributes Keble's refusal to support him to the wider state of black–Jewish relations, commenting bitterly that he has been 'radicalized by the [alleged] racism of Jews like me' (p. 16). Just as Kitaj fell foul of the conjunction of what Wolff calls 'a certain anti-literary prejudice in art criticism . . . and a persistent . . . anti-semitism' in 1990s London, so Coleman finds himself flying in the face of the winds of political correctness and black–Jewish relations in 1990s Massachussetts (p. 32). As Debra

Shostak puts it, the 'sliding of black into Jew [in Coleman] evokes by implicit contrast the vexed and at times over-wrought history of conflict between blacks and Jews over competition for a position in American life'.[20] Finally, whereas Coleman is a black man who identifies with Jews, Kitaj was a Jew who often identified with blacks. In an interview with Timothy Hyman in 1980, for example, he talked of 'the Negro Tragedy, a Black unhappiness I have felt deeply all my life',[21] and in a discussion with Richard Morphet he equated the black experience with that of the Jews: 'Jews will always be in trouble, so will blacks.'[22]

The presence of Kitaj as a source may also partly account for the dramatic shift in the way that Coleman is represented in the course of *The Human Stain*. In the opening pages, Coleman is utterly consumed by a sense of injustice, a paranoid obsessive whose insistence that Zuckerman must tell his story so that the truth about his case can be brought to the attention of the wider world makes him resemble comic figures from earlier Roth novels such as Alvin Pepler in *Zuckerman Unbound* (1981) and Moishe Pipik in *Operation Shylock* (1993). At this stage Coleman appears 'completely unhinged' and Zuckerman unkindly compares him to a headless chicken: 'His head had been lopped off . . . and what I was witnessing was the amputated rest of him spinning out of control' (p. 11). By the end of the novel, however, Zuckerman's view of Coleman has changed completely: he is now a tragic figure, his dignity restored, his grievances legitimised, his story given the grandeur denied to the absurd Peplers and Pipiks. The grotesque image of the decapitated Coleman has been displaced by the grand vision of a man 'the fullness of [whose] . . . life as a created self' Zuckerman sees as part of 'the great frontier tradition' (pp. 335, 334). Viewed psychoanalytically, Coleman's apotheosis may be Roth (over)compensating for his unflattering depiction of the grieving Kitaj/Coleman at the start of the book.

At any rate, the manner of Coleman's death according to Zuckerman (who believes that he is run off the road by Les Farley, crazed with jealousy at the idea that Faunia is 'giving blow jobs to old Jews', p. 259) suggests that Coleman is undone by his decision to pass as Jewish and therefore implicitly vindicates Coleman's (and, by extension, Kitaj's) conviction that he was being targeted by anti-Semites. If Coleman is right about Iris and Zuckerman is right about Coleman, then both husband and wife are effectively, albeit indirectly, killed by anti-Semitism. Zuckerman's portentous comment at Coleman's funeral – that the message of the Kaddish (the Hebrew prayer for the dead) recited at Coleman's funeral by his son, Mark, is that each Jew dies not simply as the natural 'consequence of life but [as] a consequence of having been a Jew' – only serves to reinforce this idea (p. 314). Some very perceptive critics, such as Debra Shostak, Ross Posnock and Amy Hungerford, have argued that, in Hungerford's words, Coleman's 'true identity has nothing to do with race – understood either biologically or as a social construction' – but the circumstances of Silk's death suggest otherwise, as does the title of the novel.[23] Moreover, most of the pivotal moments in the book turn on the use of words with racial connotations: not just 'spooks', but 'lilywhite', which is the term Coleman uses to indicate his disgust at the patronising tone adopted by his lawyer, Nelson Primus (p. 81), unconsciously echoing his brother, Walter, who told him never 'to show [his] lilywhite face' (p. 145) at the Silk home again after hearing of Coleman's decision to live out his life as a Jew. The word 'nigger' also appears twice in the novel: once when Coleman is refused a hot dog at a Woolworth's on a visit to Washington and insulted on his way out of the store (p. 102) and again when Coleman himself uses the term when explaining his actions to a boxing promoter dismayed at how quickly Silk had despatched his opponent: 'I don't carry no nigger' (p. 117). Finally, there is Coleman's misreading of the word 'neck' as 'negro', in a poem written by his first serious girlfriend, Steena Palsson (p. 113). Although Coleman is abused by others, both for his blackness (at Woolworth's) and for the paleness of his complexion (by his brother), it is his sense of himself as stained by his blackness that is most striking. Like Freud's return of the repressed, this expresses itself in disguised form (as in his choice of the words 'spooks' and 'lilywhite' and his mistaken reading of Steena's verse), revealing both the intensity and ultimate futility of the psychic effort his conscious mind expends in avoiding the taboo subject of his racial origins.

When Zuckerman finally discovers Coleman's secret, he responds, in characteristically paradoxical fashion, by reflecting that 'I couldn't imagine anything that could have made Coleman more of a mystery to me than this unmasking' (p. 333),[24] but in fact the novel he has written discloses the secret almost from the outset precisely in order to make it clear that Coleman's mask was never truly opaque. When he first encounters Coleman, Zuckerman notes that he possessed the 'ambiguous aura of the pale blacks who are sometimes taken for white' (pp. 15–16); reflecting on the incident when Coleman was thrown out of a brothel, Zuckerman rationalises that such a mistake was possible 'because his name didn't give him away as a Jew – because it could as easily have been a Negro's name' (p. 16); and after Coleman decides to abandon his 'Spooks' project, Zuckerman compares him to 'Nelson Mandela . . . forgiving his jailers' (p. 20). In other words, Coleman's blackness is constantly manifesting itself in the narrative long before (the narrated) Zuckerman is aware of it, so that his belated recognition of the truth reveals as much about the limitations of his perception as it does about the existential 'mystery' of Coleman Silk. The stain of the novel's title has many connotations, from the historically specific reference to the DNA evidence on Monica Lewinsky's notorious dress which exposed Bill Clinton's secret, to the universal idea of original sin, but primarily it denotes the skin pigmentation that, for all his slippery silkiness, fixes Coleman to his fate as surely as the mythological Ixion to his fiery wheel.

RICHARD POWERS, *THE TIME OF OUR SINGING*

Although he won the National Book Award in 2006 for his novel *The Echo Maker*, Richard Powers is still something of a well-kept secret. The author of nine novels, Powers' fiction has generally been well reviewed, but he has yet to receive any serious scholarly attention. *The Time of Our Singing*, his eighth novel, tackles a number of weighty themes – the theory of relativity, the mysterious power of music, the nature of time – but its treatment of race is what distinguishes it. The novel, which is narrated partly by an anonymous third-person narrator and partly by a first-person narrator, tells the story of a mixed-race family in postwar America. David Strom, a German-Jewish physicist, escapes Nazi persecution by emigrating to the US in 1942 where he marries Delia Daley, a light-skinned African-American who dreams of emulating her heroine, the famous black singer Marian Anderson. They have three children, Jonah, Joseph and Ruth. All three children are extraordinary musicians, but whereas Jonah becomes a virtuoso vocalist of minor celebrity, Joseph earns a meagre living as a club pianist and Ruth becomes a militant black activist.

The novel begins with the first-person narrator, Joseph Strom, eulogising Jonah:

> In some empty hall, my brother is still singing . . . The rooms where he sang still hold an impression, their walls dimpled with his sound, awaiting some future phonograph capable of replaying them.[25]

He then goes on to describe the recital at which Jonah first made his name as a singer. It is the final of a national vocal competition and Jonah is singing 'Time Stands Still', a ballad by the English Renaissance composer John Dowland, to a rapt audience at Duke University, North Carolina, Joseph accompanying him on the piano. According to Joseph, this moment of triumph also marks the beginning of a trajectory that will end in Jonah's premature death: as Jonah sings, he 'holds his audience stilled for a few stopped seconds', before their 'noisy gratitude . . . starts time up again, sending the dart to its target and my brother on to the things that will finish him' (p. 4). Jonah wins the contest and receives many tributes as he makes his way through the crowd afterwards. In the midst of the well-wishers, however, is a 'ramrod retired colonel' whose face 'is a hostile muddle', 'twitch[ing]' with 'righteousness' and 'rage' (p. 6). When he reaches the head of the queue, he 'studies' Jonah's face 'like a thwarted anthropologist', before demanding to know: 'What exactly *are* you boys?' (p. 6).

This opening subtly sets out all the main preoccupations of the novel and illustrates perfectly the way in which Powers' prose accumulates resonance through the use of a nexus of interrelated, multivalent terms. The ambiguity of the word 'still' in the phrase 'my brother is still singing', the word means both that Jonah's singing continues to ring out and that when he sings his body is immobile, which reverberates throughout these first pages, forms part of a discourse exploring the theories of time that haunt David Strom, one of the leading physicists in the field of relativity. It also initiates the novel's thorough interrogation of the ways in which identity is, paradoxically, both fixed and fluid. When Joseph writes of the audience's applause propelling his brother towards 'the things that will finish him', he is positing a chain of cause and effect, initiated by Jonah's anointment as 'America's Next Voice'; but the phrase also refers to the series of experiences that will refine and polish his raw talent and 'finish' his voice in the sense of perfecting it. Jonah's performance is, according to Joseph, '[t]he moment when the world first finds him out' (p. 4) – after winning the contest, 'the word is out' (p. 5). Again, Powers chooses his words carefully: the world has found Jonah out both in the sense of discovering his prodigious talent and in the sense of exposing his racial identity: the word is out because Jonah's fame as a singer will now spread, but so will his notoriety as a black interloper in the white domain of classical music.

The belligerent, bigoted colonel's indignation and incomprehension at the fact that the Strom brothers have stormed the white citadel of high culture is only exacerbated by the fact that their ethnicity is indeterminate: Joseph is dark-skinned but Jonah is light-skinned. When Joseph sings he 'stands fixed' (p. 3) and he transfixes his auditors; at the same time, he has 'a hatred of being fixed' (p. 8). The key to this paradox lies in Joseph's description of the favourite family game, 'Crazed Quotations', in which the Stroms collaborate and compete to overlay melodies with contrapuntal musical 'quotations'. Joseph recalls that the game 'produced the wildest mixed marriages, love matches that even the heaven of half-breeds looked sidelong at' (p. 13), but he also comments that 'the Stroms sang with a skill built into the body, a fixed trait, the soul's eye color' (p. 14). In other words, the racial hybridity of the family manifests itself in the unorthodox juxtapositions of different musical genres and traditions thrown up by the game. At the same time, their shared musical dexterity unites them and provides a permanent point of reference, 'a fixed trait' that blends their different physical hues into a common metaphysical colour, 'the soul's eye color'.

This is the first of numerous instances in the novel when race and music are linked through the metaphor of colour. On their début at Orchestra Hall, Chicago, the brothers' '[n]erves and over-learning get [them] through in a splash of color' (p. 109); when he begins to learn to sing opera, '[e]verything Jonah lost in pitch, he stood to gain many times over in color and sweep' (p. 111); and in their rehearsals, Joseph struggles 'to match my shaky color to his exact shade' (p. 531). Most importantly, when Marian Anderson (one of the first African-American singers to gain national recognition) sings at an historic free concert at the Lincoln Memorial in 1939, the event where Delia and David meet, she does so in 'a voice that is steeped in color, the only thing worth singing' (p. 45). It is their shared love of music that brings David, the German-Jewish atheist, and Delia, the African-American, church-going Christian, together, but their first encounter is overshadowed by the history of racism that haunts the country. Delia and David meet when they both notice a little lost black boy at the concert. When they take him up the steps of the Lincoln Memorial to help him try to spot his parents, the boy tells them that '*Lincoln was a Nigger-hater*' (p. 225). Even if unfounded, the boy's conviction that the man credited with emancipating African-Americans was himself a racist demonstrates the enduring bitterness of the division between blacks and whites. Though Anderson's concert is attended by a 'mixed crowd' whose 'tone changes with every turn of light and tilt of head' (p. 40), Joseph reminds us that 'color will forever be the theme' of the concert, 'the reason she'll be remembered when her sound is gone' (p. 45). If music in this novel paradoxically seems both to transcend and be defined by race, skin colour remains an indelible marker of racial identity which ultimately frustrates the Stroms' dream of creating a 'post-race place' (p. 345).

The tension between the potential of music to promote racial unity and that of racism to undermine such harmony manifests itself again in an episode in which Delia takes the children to a park, where 'her boys climb on a set of concrete stairs as if it's the greatest playground ever built' (p. 479).

Each step is a pitch they cry out as they pounce on. They turn the staircase into a pedal organ, chasing up the scale, hopping in thirds, stepping out simple tunes. Two other children, white, see their ecstasy and join, hurtling up and down the flights, screaming their own wild pitches until their parents come shepherd them away, their averted glances apologizing to Delia for the universal mistake of childhood. (p. 479)

Here, as elsewhere in the novel, music seems to offer the possibility of transcending racial difference whilst reinforcing the impossibility of doing so. The white children, infected by Jonah and Joseph's enthusiasm, innocently attempt to copy them, but their 'screaming . . . wild pitches' strike a discordant note and in any case their parents quickly intervene to ensure that no harmony – musical or racial – can be achieved. The Christian resonance of the word 'shepherd' is perhaps an allusion to the professed religious devotion of many apologists for racial segregation and this incongruity is amplified by the perversity of the white parents' 'averted glances': instead of expressing contrition for their racism, they appear ashamed at the alacrity with which their children 'join' their black playmates. In crossing the colour line, the white children commit the 'universal mistake of childhood' (an ironic phrase in this context), by exposing the irrationality and artificiality of their parents' prejudices. The parents' refusal to allow their children to join in the game that Jonah and Joseph are playing and their reluctance to meet Delia's eye demonstrate both the tenacity of racism and the refusal to acknowledge that it exists. This incident has something of the force of a parable: the harsh lesson that Delia and her children learn is that they will always be defined not by their actions, their interests or their talents, but by the colour of their skin. Although Jonah and Joseph's game attracts their peers, in the same way that their musicianship later wins them the admiration of their fellow musicians, the precipitate withdrawal of their companions demonstrates that, for white society, they will always pose a threat.

The overt hostility of the colonel and the more surreptitious discrimination of the white parents in the park demonstrate the tenacity and ubiquity of racial intolerance in postwar America. Jonah may have been awarded the title of 'America's Next Voice' but it is his face that determines his destiny. When Jonah receives an adulatory review from an eminent critic which concludes by predicting that he will become 'one of the finest Negro recitalists this country has ever produced', he is indignant at being labelled in this way: 'I don't mind being a Negro. I refuse to be a Negro tenor' (p. 393). Joseph observes that although Jonah 'had never tried to pass . . . it staggered him to discover that he couldn't' (p. 313). Jonah should not be staggered, for he has encountered racial prejudice throughout his life, from the boys who 'covered [his] offending face in caked mud' (p. 10) and called him '[y]ellow boy' and '[h]alf breed' (p. 24) on his way to and from school, to the student at the music college of Boylston who tells him that he is 'not supposed to eat with anyone with black blood' (p. 51), to the innocent inquiry of his first girlfriend – 'Are the two of you Moors?' (p. 59) – with its unfortunate echo of the colonel's question. Indeed, when Jonah's 'inexplicable coloring' (p. 120) doesn't provoke outrage, it invites curiosity, even from its owner. As a young boy, Jonah seeks guidance from his mother on the issue of his and his siblings' identity: 'You are a Negro, right? And Da's . . . some kind of Jewish guy. What exactly does that make me, Joey and Root?' (p. 29). The word 'exactly' again implicitly connects Jonah's query with the colonel's, but of course there can be no satisfactory answer to these questions, because the concept of race itself has no real scientific basis and because there is no convenient alternative nomenclature to describe the Stroms' situation.

Delia and David invariably answer their children's questions by encouraging them to look beyond racial categories and determine their own identities. David deflects the issue with a pun, repeating the mantra 'You must run your own race', while Delia appeals to the idealistic belief that identity is determined internally, insisting that 'You're whatever you are, inside' (p. 29). When her mother asks Delia what she and David will tell their children 'to call themselves', she replies, 'We're trying to raise them . . . beyond race' (p. 487), while for David, '[t]here is no such thing as race', since it is refuted by the laws of physics which are his speciality:

> Race is only real if you freeze time, if you invent a zero point for your tribe. If you make the past an origin, then you fix the future. Race is a dependent variable. A path, a moving process. We all move along a curve that will break down and rebuild us all. (p. 94)

Characteristically, David frames the problem of race in the abstract terms of science, but he and the other Stroms constantly find that the reality of the society they live in confounds logic. David's conviction that the very notion of race is nonsensical doesn't alter the fact that '[h]is marriage makes him a criminal in two-thirds of the United States' (p. 89). Delia may aspire to raise children 'beyond race', but each time she gives birth, 'the state puts 'Colored' on the birth certificate' (p. 334). Growing up, Delia 'never steps out in a public place without carefully averaging the color around her, the measure of her relative safety' (p. 40); after she marries, she must pretend to be David's maid or servant whenever she ventures out with him.

The Stroms are given a brutal reminder of the dangers faced by blacks in postwar America when Emmett Till, a fifteen-year-old black boy, is beaten, mutilated and murdered for allegedly flirting with a white woman in a Mississippi village. Brought together by the neediness of a young black boy at the Anderson concert, the couple are divided for the first time by the infamous case of this other young black boy. Delia is 'fixed by the image' of the dead boy's body (p. 103) and believes that Jonah and Joseph should see the photograph of Emmett's disfigured face which his mother insisted should be published, while David thinks that children of their age should be protected from something that distressing. Ultimately, Delia herself becomes a victim of race hatred: although it is never proved, there is a strong suspicion that the fire in which she dies is the result of an arson attack.

Jonah and Joseph also come close to being killed on more than one occasion, as they find themselves caught up in the race riots that erupt across the states they visit when on tour, but Jonah ironically dies not by violence but as the result of respiratory problems. If race does not kill him, however, it certainly circumscribes his achievements. '[R]aised to believe in self-invention' (p. 564), Jonah may think of himself as *sui generis*, 'the first of all the coming world's would-be nations of one' (p. 62) – one of the 'great *pioneers* of the I', as Zuckerman describes Coleman Silk (p. 108) – but he finds that the nation he lives in prevents him from becoming 'the nation of one he knows himself to be' (p. 257). Whereas Coleman's project of self-invention unravels as a consequence of the heightened consciousness of race fostered on the campuses of US colleges in the 1990s, so Jonah's ambitions founder on the intractability of race relations in the US of the 1950s and 1960s.

Powers explicitly invokes America's foundational myths to emphasise the disjunction between utopian ideas of the US as a haven of equality and the reality of the '[c]aste-crazed country' (p. 481) in which the Stroms live. When Jonah and Joseph are admitted to Boylston, a prestigious musical academy in Boston, their presence disrupts the usual dormitory arrangements:

> In August . . . the headmaster decreed that I should bunk with Jonah and two other older midwestern boys. By rule, the younger grades slept in long wards on the building's top floor, while the smaller dorms below were reserved for the senior students. But we two had brought havoc into this orderly musical Eden. The parents of one classmate had already removed their boy from school, and two others threatened the same action if their children were forced to sleep in the same room with us. This was the year Brown allegedly beat the Topeka Board of Education. (p. 67)

The metaphor of Boylston as Eden implicitly places the Strom brothers in the position of the serpent that corrupts Adam and Eve's idyll, but of course it is the racism of their fellow pupils' parents that poisons this paradise. Moreover, the reference at the end of the passage to the *Brown v. Board of Education of Topeka* Supreme Court judgement of 1956 that racial segregation in state schools was unconstitutional – a landmark in the nascent civil rights struggle – functions as a reminder that the larger new Eden of America had lost whatever innocence it might have had long ago. At Boylston, Jonah becomes the protégé of the school's director, a Hungarian operatic tenor, János Reményi. For Reményi, Jonah is 'his American Adam, his . . . tabula rasa' (p. 113). Just as Delia and David hope that their children will, paradoxically, help 'make an America more American than the one the country has for centuries lied to itself about being' (p. 233), so Reményi envisages Jonah becoming, under his guidance, not merely a marvellous singer but a symbol of renewal, an embodiment of the idea of America as a land of limitless possibility, a vindication of his meritocratic vision. However, Reményi's idealism, like his adopted nation's, is compromised by the politics of race: when he discovers that Jonah is having an affair with Kimberley Monera, the daughter of a world-renowned conductor, he breaks the pair up and she is hurriedly withdrawn from the college. Jonah may be light in appearance, but, as Joseph points out, 'America says "light" to mean "dark, with a twist"' (p. 72): it is Kimberley who leaves Boylston, but Jonah who is exiled from paradise. While touring with Jonah, Joseph observes wryly that 'Like America, we had to be discovered again and again' (p. 308), but the allegorical force of the analogy between the fate of the brothers and the country that both owns and disowns them lies not so much in this process of perpetual (re)discovery, but in the tension between idealism and pragmatism which characterises their struggle for self-determination.

Although Jonah 'resembles . . . a blood-drained, luminous Arab' (p. 17) and makes a living by performing predominantly white-authored music for predominantly white audiences, it is only when he moves to Europe that he finds he can escape the racial categorisation that even the most sympathetic of American reviewers feels obliged to attach to him. At his first public performance, at the age of nine, before a Lutheran congregation on the Columbia campus where his father works in the Physics Department, Jonah is congratulated by a dewy-eyed matron, who tells him 'how much it means to me . . . to have a little Negro boy singing like that . . . for us' (p. 28). Jonah politely corrects her, announcing that 'we're not real Negroes. But our mother is' (p. 28). What Jonah comes to realise is that such fine distinctions are lost even on liberal white Americans; that he is doomed 'to be a fixed category, no matter how he sung' (p. 314). Historically, there has been a tendency in the US to maintain a convenient antithesis between white and black, so that children with mixed parentage have been classified as black on the basis of hypo-descent, the principle which stipulates, as Jonah's maternal grandfather puts it, that 'a half-caste child must belong to the caste with the lower status' (p. 563).[26] Given that, as Joseph points out, '[t]hree-quarters of all American Negroes have white blood – very few of them as a matter of choice' (p. 72), this was a way of ensuring that the offspring of (usually coercive) relations between white slave-owners or overseers and black slaves could be excluded from the line of descent.

The Time of Our Singing presents a disillusioning view of the rigidity of racial definitions in the US throughout the twentieth century. Delia and David Strom's hallowed principle that 'family should trump race' (p. 385) is undermined by the possible racist murder of Delia and by the radicalisation of their daughter, Ruth, for whom David becomes, as he himself puts it bitterly, 'the evil one . . . the enemy . . . [who] killed [her] mother' (p. 358). All their hope and optimism, their utopian vision of a world 'beyond race', is 'reduced to one [lesson]: No one marries outside their race and lives' (p. 503). This grim conviction prevents Joseph from marrying his white lover, Teresa. Although – or perhaps because – she thinks of him as 'half white', for Joseph the racial divide between them is so absolute that they are not 'even close enough to be different species' (p. 504). Jonah finds that, in spite of all his efforts to be judged as an artist in his own right, he is repeatedly 'driven out of the self-made self, forced to be an emblem, a giver of pride, a betrayer of the cause' (p. 314). Patronised by white critics and accused of being 'a flunky of the white culture game' (p. 381) by black writers, Jonah's story is in this sense perhaps a metaphor for the fate of that generation of African-American writers who came to prominence in the postwar years: Richard Wright, James Baldwin and, most notably, Ralph Ellison.[27]

Like these novelists, Jonah finds that the struggle to find one's own voice – to be recognised for one's talent and not as a representative of black people – inevitably attracts accusations of self-hatred; of being, as Joseph puts it, 'the white man's nigger' (p. 377). Indeed, both brothers reproach themselves in these terms. Jonah wonders whether he has indeed been 'passing', 'granted the safe passage of lightness' while his black contemporaries were being 'ground down, locked out, threatened, beaten, killed' (p. 381). Similarly, Joseph at one point concludes that '[f]rom the beginning, Jonah's and my performance had been whiteness' (p. 586). What the novel makes clear again and again, however, is that, while their musical talent and ambiguous appearance may have given them certain privileges, the Strom brothers are never fully accepted in the white world and never pass as white. In fact, whiteness in the novel is represented as paradoxically both a ubiquitous signifier of cultural dominance and a mythical ideal no American can attain. Because it defines itself negatively – as that which has no taint of blackness in it – whiteness is always embattled, always vulnerable, always a precarious condition. Although conceived of as a safeguard against the contamination of the *soi-disant* white race, the 'one drop' law, which stipulated that only those with no trace of black ancestry could enjoy the status of full citizens, actually endangered rather than protected ideas of racial purity. As Ruth sardonically points out, the appeal to an idea of pure whiteness is absurd: 'Pure invention. One drop? One drop, as far back as you can go? Every white man is passing' (p. 563). Joseph agrees, pointing out to his sceptical nephew that 'White's got to prove white, all the way back', before asking rhetorically: 'Who can do that?' (p. 602).

In common with *The Human Stain* again, *The Time of Our Singing* represents the idea of purity – whether in moral or racial terms – as a pernicious fiction that paradoxically pollutes everything and everyone it touches. Opposition to this idea unites Delia and David: David's parents are the victims of what Powers refers to as 'the final nightmare of purity' (p. 478) – the Nazis' extermination of the Jews in the name of the ideal of Aryan racial hegemony – while Delia, the grandchild of slaves, fears that 'the world's relentless purifiers would come after their [the Stroms'] happiness' (p. 9). However, it also divides them, as they become embroiled in the souring of black–Jewish relations which accompanies the increasing economic success of Jewish Americans and the rise of black militancy after the first phase of the Civil Rights Movement.[28] When the light-skinned Nettie (Delia's mother) teases William Daley (Delia's father) for his infatuation with the (white-authored) classics of Western literature, he claims, 'I am *not* black . . . It's the other side that makes us *black*' (p. 79). In doing so, he is expressing his indignation at the literal inaccuracy of the label, since no human beings are black, and drawing attention to the injustice of its metaphorical connotations: African-Americans are implicitly 'blackened' in a moral sense by the use of the term. However, he is also implicitly reinforcing the idea that there exists an absolute demarcation between 'black' and 'white' people by referring to 'the other side' – and attributing to this 'other' the power of defining his identity: it is the other who 'makes us black'. Moreover, it soon becomes clear that it is not just 'the other side' for whom race and colour are inviolable. When he first hears of Delia's engagement to David, William's response echoes the charge that Nettie had made against him: '"You are a colored woman. Colored. I don't care how high-toned you are. I don't know what the world of that white music has been leading you to – "' (p. 217)

Once again, race and music are linked by the word 'tone'. Here 'high-toned' refers to Delia's light skin, to her voice and to her refinement, expressed through her interest in the rarefied culture of 'white music'. William's insistent definition of his daughter in terms of race, evident in his repetition of the word 'colored', directly contradicts his earlier conviction that she can 'Be anything. Do anything' (p. 36). Moreover, his implicit assumption that her interest in 'white music' has led to her interest in a white man is both patronising and misleading.

David is variously described as a 'colorless man' (p. 352), 'the single whitest man in the world' (p. 460) and as a 'Jew [with] . . . two light black sons' (p. 159). At one point in the novel, Ruth, armed with a new political consciousness of her black heritage acquired through her affiliation with the Black Panthers, cross-examines him on his motives in marrying 'a black woman' (p. 304). When he claims that Delia's colour was irrelevant, she informs him, in words that echo her grandmother's admonition of her mother, that '[o]nly white men have the luxury of ignoring race' (p. 304). Just as David rejected the label 'black' as a valid description of Delia, so he takes issue with his daughter's classification of his own race: 'I'm not a white man; I'm a *Jew*' (p. 304). An atheist who 'never checked "Jewish" on any form in his life' (p. 20), David nonetheless embraces this category insofar as it defines him negatively as *not white*. For David, '[a] Jew was geography, not nation, not language, not even culture' (p. 345) – and, one might add, not colour. Ruth also defines her father negatively, but for her the fact that he is *not black* means that he is white. This exchange between the refugee from Nazi-occupied Europe, whose own parents were the victims of genocidal racism, and the embittered black radical, who is convinced that her mother was killed by

American racists because she married a white man, encapsulates the contradictions and tensions that plague and ultimately destroy the Strom family.

As in *Mona in the Promised Land* and *The Human Stain*, *The Time of Our Singing* uses Jewishness as a way of complicating the black/white dichotomy which conventionally defines race relations in America. After experiencing the legalised anti-Semitism of the Nuremberg Laws, David initially views America as a refuge from racism, a place where '[n]o one stops him or asks for identification' (p. 43) because race is not important. When she first meets him, Delia wonders if there might 'be whites who might not, after all, hate her on sight for the ungivable forgiveness they needed from her?'(p. 222), but she soon realises that his uncritical acceptance of her stems from the fact that 'he knew nothing of her country' (p. 222). Once married to Delia, however, he soon learns that blacks are 'America's Jews'.[29] The union of a European Jew and one of 'America's Jews' produces children who are, as Delia realises, '*a different race from either of* [them]' (p. 523). Towards the end of the novel, William reflects ruefully on the idealism of his daughter and son-in-law, telling Joseph that '[t]hey wanted a place where everyone was his own tone . . . But that's blackness. There is no shade it doesn't already contain' (p. 562). But again he is wrong, for the shade that blackness does not contain is Jewishness. Because of David's Jewishness, the Strom children are not 'mixed-race' in the usual sense of that term – the product of one white and one black parent – but rather a new hybrid, something closer to what Zuckerman in *The Human Stain* calls 'a heretofore unknown amalgam of the most unlike of America's historic undesirables' (p. 132). When Ruth asks Jonah and Joseph to tell her '[h]ow black' (p. 296) their mother was (she has only hazy memories of her as she was young when her mother died), Jonah's sardonic response – 'Ruthie wants to know if she's a *Schwarze*, a half *Schwarze*, an anti-*Schwarze*, or what' (p. 304) – is instructive on several levels. First, he pointedly reminds Ruth by using the Yiddish term for black, 'Schwarze', of the fact that she has a dual inheritance. Second, his reference to 'a half *Schwarze*' highlights the absurdity of her assumption that blackness can be quantified. Finally, his invention of the term 'anti-*Schwarze*' is a sly reference to the enmity between

Jews and blacks fomented by groups such as the Black Panthers, the implication being that, for black militants, Jews are inherently anti-black.

When David falls out with his father-in-law, their relationship fractures not along the old American fault-line dividing black from white, but rather along the more recent bifurcation between Jews and blacks over their respective historical claims to victimhood. As David puts it, explaining the rift regretfully to Joseph from his death-bed:

> We played 'Who owns pain?' 'Who has suffered the greater wrong?' I told him the Negro had never been killed in the numbers of the Jews. He said they *had*. This I didn't understand. He said that no killing could be worse than slavery . . . The Jews had never been enslaved, he said . . . They were, I said; they were enslaved. (p. 466)

This exchange reproduces, albeit crudely, one of the most contentious issues in postwar American race relations: one that, along with the Israeli/Palestinian conflict, the rise of black militancy and the growing chasm between the economic status of most blacks and most Jews, led to a worsening split between two minority groups who had once seemed to have much in common. The inability of David Strom and William Daley to understand each other's grievances and their unwillingness to acknowledge their mutual suffering replicate the polarised positions taken up by many African-American and Jewish American political leaders from the mid-1960s onwards. As these former allies become antagonists, the entrenched nature of race as the key determinant of identity in America once again undermines David and Delia's vision of a 'post-race' nation in which their children can live free of all labels.

Towards the end of the novel, Jonah returns from his long exile in Europe and marvels at a cereal packet he discovers in Joseph's kitchen 'with a picture of two little mixed-race kids, their smiling faces labelled TWIN PACK' (p. 598). Joseph tells his brother, by way of explanation, that 'Multiracialism's hot' (p. 598). Joseph means, of course, that the language of multiculturalism is now fashionable (though 'hot' also may have the secondary meaning of 'controversial'), but again this ostensible sign of progress is also, paradoxically, a proof that nothing much has changed. By making the implicit connection between the double quantity of the product and the biracial identity of the children whose faces adorn it, the manufacturers of the cereal are actually drawing attention to their racial difference. Similarly, Joseph (and by extension Powers), in describing the children as 'mixed-race kids', reinscribes essentialist ideas of race, even while citing them as symbols of a new era of tolerance.

CONCLUSION

In her essay '"Delusionary Thinking, Whether White or Black or in Between": Fictions of Race in Philip Roth's *The Human Stain*', Julia Faisst perceptively argues that '[b]y definition a performance of passing cannot escape the confines of racial demarcation; it can only subvert racial markers of identity to a certain degree by finding an identity that, indeed, can be called neither simply black nor quite white' (p. 123). *Mona in the Promised Land*, *The Human Stain* and *The Time of Our Singing* are all unconventional passing novels in that their protagonists perform identities that are themselves no less racially ambiguous than their original identities. For some commentators, Jews in postwar America have essentially become 'whitefolks',[30] but as Alan Dershowitz has pointed out, anti-Semitism in America is far from a thing of the past.[31] Jonathan Freedman points out that, in 'the black/white dichotomy, Jewishness often functions . . . not only as a signifier of whiteness but also as a sign of multiple affiliation and fluid identity construction' (p. 195) and this is certainly the spirit in which it is appropriated by Mona Chang and Coleman Silk.[32]

Similarly, the election of Barack Obama as the 44th President of the United States was widely interpreted as definitive evidence of what the political commentator Simon Jenkins, writing in the *Guardian*, called 'the advance of a once-oppressed group of Americans'.[33] Obama was almost universally hailed as America's first black president. Yet he is not black, but mixed-race, for like the Strom brothers, he has one white and one black parent. During an election campaign in which a significant minority of Americans were apparently convinced that Obama was a practising Muslim, if not an Arab who consorted with terrorists, it should come as no surprise that this distinction was too subtle for many to grasp. For the veteran civil rights campaigner and former candidate for the Democratic presidential nomination, Jesse Jackson, to claim, as he did during an interview with the BBC on the night of the election, that Obama's victory proved that 'there is nothing blacks can't do, not just in this country, but in the rest of the world' (Jackson 2008), however, displays an astonishing naivety.[34] Groundbreaking though Obama's win undoubtedly was, it can hardly be said to have consigned racism in America to history. African-Americans are, *pace* Jenkins and Jackson, still an oppressed people whose opportunities are often circumscribed by entrenched notions of race. Moreover, the alacrity with which Obama was identified as a black man by all sections of the media suggests that the 'one drop' rule still applies when it comes to defining blackness in America, that American society is still uncomfortable with the idea of people of mixed race.

When Alfred asks Mona whether her family's gardener is black or white and Mona confesses that she is unsure, Alfred tells her that '[i]n that case, she's black' (p. 155) and this is indeed the principle on which racial classification relies. The naturalisation of race as a category depends on certainty and absolutism. It cannot abide uncertainty or ambiguity, but rests on a binary opposition between black and white. As the third-person narrator of *The Time of Our Singing* puts it: 'We do not fear difference. We fear most being lost in likeness. The thing no race can abide' (p. 630). Hence the particular threat posed to notions of race by those who are neither black nor white: the 'yellow' hybrids (or 'mutts', to use the self-deprecating term favoured by Obama in his first post-election press conference), who include Jews, Asians and mixed-race people. The term yellow is used tellingly to describe the protagonists of all three novels. In *Mona* the epithet is used when the narrator observes that Mona's teenage anxieties about her body (which she relates to her ethnicity) will be displaced, in later years, by a recognition that she is 'yellow and beautiful' (p. 76). Partly a parody of the 'black is beautiful' slogan adopted by many African Americans in the

1960s, the equivalent moment in *The Time of Our Singing* comes when Jonah marches round his apartment 'brandishing a dark tan golf-gloved fist over his head, shouting "Mulatto Power! Mulatto Power!"' (p. 379). In both cases, the joke works by drawing attention to the disparity between the militant self-assertiveness of the Black Power Movement and the relatively low profile enjoyed by Chinese-Americans and people of mixed race. Whereas Jen treats the predicament of Chinese-Americans primarily in comic terms, reflecting their successful integration into American society, Powers' representation of the mixed-race Strom boys in *The Time of Our Singing* is essentially tragic. The awkwardness of this last formulation illustrates the point well: there is no collective term for those of mixed race because, as David Hollinger points out, there is no official recognition in America of the category of mixed race as a distinct ethno-racial group. Instead of any affirmative label to embrace, there is only 'mixed race' (with its unfortunate implicit reinstatement of the discredited, essentialist, pseudo-scientific idea of clearly differentiated races), 'biracial' (which has the same problems and also excludes those, like Tiger Woods, with a heritage deriving from more than two ethno-racial groups) or old pejorative labels such as mulatto, half-caste or yellow.

The last of these terms briefly drives a wedge between Joseph and Teresa, when Joseph discovers in her record collection a recording by the jazz singer and bandleader Cab Calloway of a song called 'Yaller', the lyrics for which are quoted in the novel:

> Black folk, white folk, I'm learning a lot,
> You know what I am, I know what I'm not,
> Ain't even black, I ain't even white,
> I ain't like the day and I ain't like the night.
> Feeling mean, so in-between, I'm just a High Yaller . . .
>   (p. 447)

In a later verse, the song refers to a 'no-'count yellow man': the implication is that the 'yaller', as he is simply called in the chorus of the song, is not a mixture of white and black, but rather inhabits a no-man's-land where he doesn't 'count', belonging to neither of the recognised racial categories. The self-contempt that offends

Joseph is the result of the speaker feeling not simply 'in-between' conventional definitions of race, but inferior to both whites and blacks – he is not 'even' one or the other. Like the 'little yellow / Bastard boy' of Langston Hughes' poem 'Mulatto' (1927), the protagonist of the Calloway song feels that his 'yellowness' illegitimises and disenfranchises him.

In *The Human Stain* the term 'yellow' is used twice to describe Silk: once by Zuckerman early in the novel, before he has revealed the truth about Silk's ethnicity, when he characterises him as 'the small-nosed Jewish type with the facial heft in the jaw, one of those crimped-haired Jews of a light yellowish skin pigmentation who possess something of the ambiguous aura of the pale blacks who are sometimes taken for white' (pp. 16–17); and again by Les Farley, when he whips himself into a jealous rage, imagining Faunia fellating the 'high-and-mighty Jew professor, his yellow Jew face contorted with pleasure' (p. 71). In both cases the epithet is used as a marker of Jewishness, but one that is associated with other 'in-between' ethnicities. In the first case, Zuckerman's analogy between Jews with 'light yellowish skin' and 'pale blacks who are sometimes taken for white' has dramatic irony for the (re-)reader aware that Silk is in fact a pale black passing as a yellow Jew; in the second, Farley's anti-Semitic bile is implicitly linked to his inveterate hatred of the yellow-skinned Asian-Americans who remind him of the Vietnamese enemy. Of course, the yellow star that Jews were forced to wear as markers of their difference in Nazi-occupied Europe lies, unarticulated but implied, behind these references.

In *Typical American* the narrator reports that when Mona was born she was 'so vigorous and wriggly that she managed to get herself dropped' (p. 119). This can be read as a metaphor for Mona's elusive, slippery ethnicity. Like Coleman Silk and the Strom brothers, Mona tries to wriggle out of the straitjacket of race with which American society tends to restrain its so-called ethnics; like them, she finds that, paradoxically, the further you travel from your origins, the closer you come to your initial point of departure. Like one of the Einsteinian curves in time that captivate David, their trajectories loop back onto themselves. Mona, the determined dissenter, comes to 'realize how wholly she fit the word *female*' and 'how partly she fit other words' (pp. 109–10). Silk, who resolves to escape from 'the tyranny of the we' (108), is confined, in the final chapter of *The Human Stain*, to the conventional narrative of the black man whose 'art was being a white man' (p. 345), stifled by 'the stranglehold of history' (p. 336). Jonah, who dedicates his life to defining himself by the tenor of his music rather than the tone of his skin, dies the morning after telling his brother about his crazed attempt, in the midst of a race riot, to paint everyone with a 'safe marker' that would leave everyone 'medium brown' (p. 618). By focusing on protagonists who disrupt the conventional boundaries between the races, all three novels challenge the validity of the concept of race itself; but at the same time their struggle to transgress racial norms and create new ethnicities for themselves are invariably contained and compromised by the old, indelible markers of race and by the limitations of language itself. As Freedman puts it:

> We stand . . . at . . . a moment when the old terms for thinking about race and ethnicity are inadequate, but no new lexicon has emerged to replace them – who uses the term *multiculturalism* any more, even as the dominant culture becomes, well, multicultural?' (p. 197)

Freedman's assumption that the dominant culture is becoming multicultural errs, as ever, on the side of optimism, but it is true that the particular political agenda associated with the term multiculturalism, with which all three novels engage, is beginning to seem somewhat anachronistic, not least because, as Hollinger has pointed out, the very terms it used to recalibrate ethno-racial identity tended paradoxically to retrench racist stereotypes.[35] Even Hollinger himself, subtle and nuanced though his discussion is, cannot escape this paradox: as soon as you start to discuss race, you implicitly legitimise the notion that there is such a thing. Moreover, militant anti-racists, such as Ruth in *The Time of Our Singing*, are often as reliant on traditional concepts of race and as inflexible in their categorisation of race as the racists they denounce. If Jen, Roth and Powers cannot avoid the tainted discourse of race altogether, they nonetheless excavate its flawed foundations, exploring its limits and exposing its limitations. They also express a profound ambivalence towards the project of multiculturalism, offering a critique of the tendentious identity politics with which it has become associated, but at the same time remaining sceptical about the cosmopolitan vision of 'post-ethnic America', which liberal critics of the project, such as Hollinger and Freedman, advocate.

- The legacy that slavery has left race relations can still be felt in every dimension of life in the US. Public opinion often divides along racial lines, notwithstanding the election of Barack Obama, which would not have been achieved without the mobilisation of the African-American vote.
- Though Jews only make up a small percentage of the American population, they occupy a central position in the symbolic imagination of both blacks and whites in America, because they fit into neither and both camps. The ambiguity of the term 'Jewish', which conflates racial, religious, ethnic and cultural characteristics, together with the complex history of black–Jewish relations, makes Jewishness a useful prism through which to refract contemporary racial politics in the US.
- The novels chosen for discussion in this chapter use Jewishness and other liminal, 'yellow' identities, such as Chinese-American and mixed race, to dramatise the paradox at the heart of all discourses about race.
- The very terms multiculturalists use in an attempt to recalibrate ethno-racial identity tend, paradoxically, to retrench racist stereotypes. The novelists chosen for discussion in this chapter are unable to avoid the tainted discourse of race altogether, but they do explore its limits and expose its limitations. These novels are sceptical about the liberal/cosmopolitan vision of 'post-ethnic' America which some critics advocate.

NOTES

1. For a discussion of the difficulties involved in defining Jewishness, see David Brauner, *Post-war Jewish Fiction: Ambivalence, Self-Explanation, and Transatlantic Connections* (Basingstoke: Palgrave Macmillan, 2001), p. x. For an excellent

analysis of postwar black–Jewish relations in the US, see Eric Sundquist, *Strangers in the Land: Blacks, Jews, Post-Holocaust America* (Cambridge, MA: Harvard University Press, 2005), *passim*.

2. Jonathan Freedman, *Klezmer America: Jewishness, Ethnicity, Modernity* (New York: Columbia University Press, 2008), p. 195. All subsequent references in the text are to this edition.

3. Erika T. Lin, 'Mona on the Phone: The Performative Body and Racial Identity in *Mona in the Promised Land*,' *MELUS*, 28:2 (Summer 2003), p. 55 (44–57).

4. Andrew Furman, 'Immigrant Dreams and Civic Promises: (Con-)Testing Identity in Early Jewish American Literature and Gish Jen's *Mona in the Promised Land*,' *MELUS*, 25:1 (Spring 2000), p. 214 (209–26).

5. Gish Jen, *Typical American* (London: Granta, 1991), p. 7. All subsequent references in the text are to this edition.

6. Gish Jen, 'Interview with Yuko Matsukawa', *MELUS*, 18:4 (Summer 1993), p. 120 (111–20).

7. Gish Jen, *Mona in the Promised Land* (London: Granta, 1998), p. 137. All subsequent references in the text are to this edition.

8. Sundquist, *Strangers in the Land*, p. 17.

9. Begoña Simal González,. 'The (Re)Birth of Mona Changowitz: Rituals and Ceremonies of Cultural Conversion and Self-making in *Mona in the Promised Land*', *MELUS*, 26:2 (Summer 2001), p. 230 (225–43).

10. Michelle Byers, 'Material Bodies and Performative Identities: Mona, Neil and the Promised Land', *Philip Roth Studies* 2:2 (Fall 2006), p. 117 (102–20).

11. Philip Roth, *The Human Stain* (London: Jonathan Cape, 2000), p. 88. All subsequent references in the text are to this edition.

12. After Monica Lewinsky, the White House intern with whom Clinton had an affair, which he initially repeatedly denied before eventually confessing to.

13. Freedman argues that Roth's novel aligns with a number of 'sentimental melodramas' of passing, in film, which achieved popularity in the US of the late 1940s and 1950s, notably *Lost Boundaries* (1949), *Pinky* (1949) and *Imitation of Life* (1959). For Faisst, on the other hand, Coleman's 'choice of

white Jewishness enables Roth to evade the trap of predictable melodrama so often inherent in the novel of passing'. See Julia Faisst, 'Delusionary Thinking, Whether White or Black or in Between': Fictions of Race in Philip Roth's *The Human Stain*, *Philip Roth Studies* 2:2 (Fall 2006), p. 123 (121–37).

14. Freedman sees Ernestine as 'Roth's surrogate', a 'one-dimensional' embodiment of 'the hectoring didacticism one finds elsewhere in Roth' (p. 172). This seems to me to be a misrepresentation of both Roth and Ernestine.

15. Ross Posnock, *Philip Roth's Rude Truth: The Art of Immaturity* (Princeton, NJ: Princeton University Press, 2006), pp. 281–2.

16. See David Brauner, *Philip Roth* (Manchester: Manchester University Press, 2007), p. 94.

17. Janet Wolff, 'The Impolite Boarder: Diasporist Art and Its Critical Response', in James Aulich and John Lynch (eds.), *Critical Kitaj: Essays on the work of R. B. Kitaj* (Manchester: Manchester University Press, 2000), pp. 33, 32 (29–43).

18. Ibid., p. 33. In the first of these, the words 'The Critic Kills' appear on the canvas (the words 'Critic' and 'Kills' sloping diagonally downwards on a black background); the second depicts Kitaj and fellow artists shooting at a grotesque creature representing the critic in the pose of the firing squad in Edouard Manet's famous painting *Execution of Maximilian*.

19. Ibid., p. 33.

20. Debra Shostak, *Philip Roth: Countertexts, Counterlives* (Columbia: University of South Carolina Press, 2004), p. 154.

21. James Aulich and John Lynch, 'Introduction', in James Aulich and John Lynch (eds.), *Critical Kitaj: Essays on the work of R. B. Kitaj* (Manchester: Manchester University Press, 2000), p. 10 (1–28).

22. Richard Morphet, 'The Art of R. B. Kitaj: To Thine Own Self be True', in Richard Morphet, ed., *R. B. Kitaj: A Retrospective* (London: Tate Gallery Publications, 1994), p. 33 (9–34).

23. Amy Hungerford, *The Holocaust of Texts: Genocide, Literature, and Personification* (Chicago: The University of Chicago Press, 2003), pp. 143–4. See also Shostak, *Philip Roth*, pp. 238–40; Posnock, *Philip Roth's Rude Truth*, pp. 205–6.

24. This may well be an allusion to Frantz Fanon's influential *Black*

Skin, White Masks (1952) in which the French anthropologist provocatively argues that 'The black man wants to be white'. Fanon, *Black Skin, White Masks* (New York: Grove, 1967), p. 9.

25. Richard Powers, *The Time of Our Singing* (London: St. Martin's Press, 2002), p. 3. All subsequent references in the text are to this edition.

26. As late as 1924 this principle was still being enshrined in law: in that year the state of Virginia passed an 'Act for the Preservation of Racial Integrity', which stated that only people with 'no trace whatsoever of any blood other than Caucasian' could be classified as white.

27. There are several allusions to the notion of invisibility as a metaphor for blackness which Ellison developed in his novel *Invisible Man* (1953). For example, when Joseph describes the neighbourhood in New York that the Stroms move to, he claims that '[w]e were as close to invisible there as we could get, on a street that teetered right on the color line' (p. 166); when Delia sets off for Marian Anderson's concert she concentrates on '[m]aking herself small, invisible' (p. 38) and when she joins the large crowd gathering to hear the singer 'she feels the best kind of invisible' (p. 39).

28. See Sundquist, *Strangers in the Land, passim.*

29. This is the title of the first chapter of *Strangers in the Land.* As Sundquist makes clear, this formulation was used in many different contexts, by both blacks and Jews, as a way of highlighting common ground (the implication being that blacks in America were suffering from the kind of discrimination to which Jews had historically often been subjected) and at the same time emphasising the divergence between the two groups, the implication being that in America blacks fulfil the role of scapegoated, stigmatised minority, so freeing Jews from this burden.

30. To paraphrase the title of Karen Brodkin's influential book *How Jews Became Whitefolks and What that Says About Race in America* (Piscataway, NJ: Rutgers University Press, 1998).

31. Dershowitz, writing in 1992, claimed that it is 'harder even today for a qualified Jew to get certain jobs and to gain admission to

some universities than it is for an equally qualified non-Jew' and a cursory glance at contemporary American white supremacist websites is sufficient to reveal that anti-Semitic rhetoric remains as central to their creed as other kinds of racism'. Alan M. Dershowitz, *Chutzpah* (New York: Simon & Schuster, 1992), p. 8.

32. Freedman also argues that there is, in the history of American constructions of race, both a 'seeping . . . of associations' (p. 271) between the Asian and the Jew and, following Paul Gilroy, between Jews and Africans (p. 23).

33. Simon Jenkins, 'All the Clichés about Colour Obscure the Real Challenges Awaiting Obama' ('Comment and Debate'), *Guardian*, 7 November 2008, p. 43.

34. Jesse Jackson, interview, 'Election Night' (BBC 1), 5 November 2008. Jackson's tearful acclaim for Obama's victory also seemed rather disingenuous, given his earlier complaints that Obama was not 'black enough' and 'behaved like a white man'.

35. Hollinger points out that what he refers to as the 'ethno-racial pentagon' – the 'officially sanctioned system of demographic classification' that consists of the categories 'African-American', 'Asian-American', 'Euro-American', 'Native American' and 'Latin-American' – 'replicates precisely the crude, colloquial categories, black, yellow, white, red, and brown'. David A. Hollinger, *Postethnic America: Beyond Multiculturalism*, rev. edn. (New York: Basic Books, 2005), p. 8.

CHAPTER 4

Contemporary American Fiction Goes to Hollywood: Genre in the Texts and Films of *Cold Mountain*, *Brokeback Mountain* and *No Country for Old Men*

The novelist Anthony Burgess once wryly observed that '[e]very best-selling novel has to be turned into a film, the assumption being that the book itself whets an appetite for the true fulfilment – the verbal shadow turned into light, the word made flesh'.[1] In recent years numerous bestselling American novels have indeed been made into films. Of the twelve fictions at the centre of this book, half have been adapted for the screen (in addition to the three discussed in this chapter, they are *American Psycho*, *A Thousand Acres* and *The Human Stain*). Since Burgess's statement, however, a new phenomenon has arisen: many high-grossing films are made into books, either as published screenplays or as a 'novelisation' of the filmic narrative. The assumption implicit in Burgess's statement – that there is a philistine preference for films and a concomitant undervaluing of novels – has been complicated by the emergence of a large body of film criticism legitimising the medium as an art-form. Much of this criticism takes issue with what it argues is an entrenched intellectual prejudice that novels are inherently superior to films. More specifically, there has been a concerted effort on the part of some film theorists to overturn a set of criteria for judging cinematic adaptations of fiction which they see as enshrining a generic hierarchy that places novels above films. Representative of this revisionist approach is this from Brian McFarlane's *Novel to Film: An Introduction to the Theory of Adaptation* (1996):

> Fidelity criticism depends on a notion of the text as having . . . a single, correct 'meaning' which the film-maker has either adhered to or in some sense violated or tampered with . . . the critic who quibbles at failures of fidelity is really saying no more than: 'This reading of the original does not tally with mine in these and these ways.' (p. 9)

As is often the case with revisionist criticism, what began as a necessary corrective to an irrational position – the belief that the more strictly a film adaptation adheres to the text on which it is based, the better it is – has itself evolved into a position at least as irrational – the belief that there is no such thing as fidelity. Whether what McFarlane calls 'failures of fidelity' are in themselves a significant measure of the relative success of an adaptation is a matter of opinion; to claim that the degree of fidelity to a text is simply a matter of opinion, however, is nonsense. McFarlane is conflating two very different things: interpretation and revision. The distinction can be clarified by considering the well-known film adaptation of Truman Capote's novella *Breakfast at Tiffany's*. In Capote's story, published in 1958, it is implied, though never explicitly stated, that Holly Golightly is a prostitute; in Blake Edwards' 1961 film adaptation the nature of her transactions with men is glossed over. This is a matter of emphasis, of interpretation. On the other hand, Capote's story ends with Holly leaving her Manhattan apartment for Brazil, whereas Edwards ends his film with Holly staying in New York and embarking on a romance with Paul Varjak (who in Capote's story is an unnamed narrator). This is not a case of Edwards reinterpreting Capote; rather, he materially alters the *facts* of the original, replacing one dénouement with another, radically different one.

McFarlane also claims that 'Whatever claims of fidelity and

authenticity are made by film-makers, what these essentially amount to are the effacement of the memory derived from reading the novel by another experience – an audio-visual-verbal one – which will seem, as little as possible, to jar with that collective memory' (p. 21). Again, this is misleading on a number of grounds. First, McFarlane assumes that those who see a film adaptation of a novel will have read that novel prior to seeing the film. Second, again he elides two terms – fidelity and authenticity – treating them as though they are synonymous. The problematic nature of McFarlane's formulation is nicely illustrated by two horror films released in the 1990s. The titles of Francis Ford Coppola's *Bram Stoker's Dracula* (1992) and Kenneth Branagh's *Mary Shelley's Frankenstein* (1994) are an implicit acknowledgement that in these cases the original texts have effectively been eclipsed by a series of films, so that what McFarlane calls the 'collective memory' of the audience is far more likely to be based on earlier film versions than on knowledge of the original texts. They also constitute a claim to authenticity, the implication being that these films represent an authorised version of the stories, restoring Stoker's and Shelley's narratives to a position of prominence from which innumerable apocryphal variations had displaced them. The virtues and flaws of such a project are debatable, but what is most notable is the way in which Coppola and Branagh, like McFarlane, apparently equate fidelity with authenticity. In fact, fidelity is a relative term which refers to the relationship between an original text and an adaptation of that text, whereas authenticity refers to the integrity of an individual work. An original work may be less authentic than an adaptation, but it cannot be less faithful. Authenticity, ultimately, is a purely subjective term, whereas fidelity – taken to mean the extent to which an adaptation diverges, factually, from the narrative of the original text – has an objectively verifiable meaning.

In the discussion of *Cold Mountain*, *Brokeback Mountain* and *No Country for Old Men* that follows, I do not wish to reinstate the old hierarchy of value that automatically privileges literature and disparages celluloid or suggest that the more closely a film adaptation adheres to the original literary text the more valuable it is. However, I do want to insist on the validity of fidelity as a concept, a term that describes one aspect of the relationship between an adaptation and the text it adapts. Rather than apportioning blame or credit to a director for his or her decisions to diverge from the text that is being adapted, I analyse the consequences of those decisions for any interpretation of the films, in particular the generic ramifications of these changes.[2] I also recognise the chronological primacy of the literary texts by discussing them in their own right before turning to their second life as a film. Finally, I consider the generic implications of the film treatments of each of the texts.

Cold Mountain, 'Brokeback Mountain' and *No Country for Old Men* gesture towards a number of popular literary genres, including the war novel, the romance and the thriller, but they are all also variations of the Western, a genre beloved more by filmmakers and filmgoers than by authors and readers. Whereas Frazier, Proulx and McCarthy invoke the conventions of the Western in order to subvert them, the cinematographic possibilities offered by the landscapes described in the texts prove powerfully seductive to Anthony Minghella, Ang Lee and Joel and Ethan Coen (the respective directors of the three films), so that their films conform, to varying degrees, to the elegiac tradition of the classic Western movies in which the sublime grandeur of the American scenery implicitly redeems the violence enacted in it.

CHARLES FRAZIER, *COLD MOUNTAIN*

Cold Mountain (1997) is that rare phenomenon: a novel that received wide critical acclaim and became a bestseller. The Sceptre paperback edition features excerpts from twenty-three reviews, all of them effusive in their praise. It won the National Book Award, the National Book Critics' Circle Award and the Pulitzer Prize for Fiction; it also made Frazier's fortune, leading to a widely publicised $8.5 million advance for his next book, in addition to the considerable royalties from its own sales. Later, it was made into a high-profile Hollywood film, directed by Anthony Minghella (who also wrote the screenplay) and starring Jude Law, Nicole Kidman and Renée Zellweger. Released in 2003, the film was nominated for seven Academy Awards, Zellweger winning the Best Supporting Actress Oscar for her performance as Ruby.

On the face of it, the success of both the book and film is hardly surprising. The narrative has all the elements one might expect to find in a bestselling novel and a Hollywood blockbuster: a romance between a rugged, taciturn man (referred to throughout only by his surname, Inman) and a refined, aloof woman (referred to by her first name, Ada), set against the epic backdrop of the American Civil War and in the beautiful rural landscape of North Carolina; a sadistic villain (Teague), who is eventually killed by the hero; and an alcoholic, negligent father (Stobrod), who is redeemed by the power of music and reconciled with his daughter (Ruby), who teaches the heroine how to farm her land and is in turn taught by her about literature. In a short piece published in *Salon*, in which he discusses the origins of the novel, Frazier does nothing to deter the romantic reader, describing it as 'a form of elegy' for a 'lost world' inhabited by people with 'a hint of deep earth spirituality' leading 'a very old way of life that had nurtured human beings for millennia'.[3] Most of the critics who have written on the novel have also placed it squarely in the romantic tradition, whether enthusiastically or dismissively. For McCarron and Knoke, '*Cold Mountain* ultimately transforms itself into a novel of peace and triumph in the best romantic literary tradition';[4] Piacentino argues that the novel 'promotes the sense of the values conducive to harmonic home life';[5] and Heddendorf similarly sees the novel as performing a redemptive function, offering the hope that 'a saner, quieter world is never lost for good . . . only temporarily misplaced'.[6] On the other side of the argument, Crawford claims that 'the novel's underlying sentimentality limits its value as historical fiction', exposing 'the romanticized foundation on which *Cold Mountain* is built'.[7]

In fact, any reader beginning *Cold Mountain* expecting to find a conventional romance is likely to end it (if he or she gets that far) frustrated and disillusioned. An early warning that this is not a sentimental book comes with the first of two epigraphs, taken from one of Charles Darwin's journals: 'It is difficult to believe in the dreadful but quiet war of organic beings, going on in the peaceful woods, & smiling fields.'[8] Frazier's novel exploits the tension between the 'peaceful woods' through which Inman travels on his long journey home to Cold Mountain after he has deserted from the Confederate forces, and the 'dreadful . . . war' that continues all around him and that repeatedly draws him back into its orbit, even as he struggles to escape from its horrors. The novel pointedly juxtaposes Inman's romantic, indeed Romantic, view of the North Carolina landscape – particularly of Cold Mountain itself – with the brutal violence not just of the combatants on the battlefield but also those living the 'old way of life' which Frazier celebrated in his *Salon* piece. More boldly, the narrative repeatedly appears to hold out the possibility of redemption, only to puncture such hopes pitilessly.

As the opening of the novel emphasises, Inman himself is nostalgic for a traditional way of life which he sees as threatened by the war. Lying in a hospital bed, surrounded by soldiers dying and 'broken', Inman first reflects on how 'he had seen the metal face of the age and had been so stunned by it that when he thought into the future, all he could vision was a world from which everything he counted important had been banished or had willingly fled' and then recalls how a history teacher had spoken of 'grand wars fought in ancient England' (p. 2). On one level, the movement from Inman's experience of the horrors of modern warfare ('the metal face of the age') to the memory of the glorification of war he was exposed to as a boy seems familiar to anyone who has read First World War poetry. Whereas Wilfred Owen's experience in the trenches allows him to see that 'Dulce et decorum est pro patria mori' ('It is sweet and honourable to die for your country') is an 'old lie', Inman's inability to foresee a future worth fighting for bespeaks not simply of disillusionment with the ideals fostered by the leaders of the secessionist army, but is a recognition that he himself belongs to an anachronistic world, an 'old way of life' doomed to extinction. Even after his reunion with Ada towards the end of the novel, Inman's vision of a prospective life together, extending into old age ('he and Ada bent, grey as ash . . . in some metallic future world, the dominant features of which he could not even imagine') is clouded by anxiety about a new era that is at once amorphous and defined, in an echo of the earlier passage, by the properties connoted by metal: bright, cold, unyielding, manufactured (p. 413).

Inman spends much of the novel paradoxically mourning a past that has not yet become historical and dreading a future that he fears he will not live to see: he self-consciously casts himself as an outcast, not merely by virtue of his desertion of the army but temperamentally, existentially, metaphysically. Early in his journey, he performs a strange ritual, 'daub[ing] on the breast of his jacket two concentric circles with a dot at the center' so that he is 'marked as the butt of the celestial realm, a night traveller, a fugitive, an outlier' (p. 67). As he does so, he thinks, 'this journey will be the axle of my life' (p. 67). Frazier has noted on many occasions the debt that Inman's story owes to Homer's account of Odysseus' arduous return home in *The Odyssey*, but here Inman more closely resembles the figure of Cain, on whom God sets a mark that both stigmatises and protects him.[9]

Whereas Cain, the first murderer, is exiled by God and condemned to live a rootless existence isolated from the company of other men, Inman shuns others not only out of necessity (as a deserter he is in danger of being captured) but by choice, as 'he had come to see himself as another kind of creature altogether from what he had been', whose 'lot' was 'to bear the penalty of the unredeemed, that tenderness be forevermore denied him and his life be marked down a dark mistake' (p. 299). This passage reveals a mixture of self-contempt and self-aggrandisement that is typical of Inman. On the one hand, he sees his life as a 'dark mistake' that ought not to blight others; on the other, the formulation that Frazier uses to describe his stoical acceptance of the burden of his sin ('to bear the penalty of the unredeemed') seems to allude to Christ's self-sacrifice. Moreover, Inman's desire to set himself apart from the ordinary run of men is motivated at least as much by fear of being corrupted by them – 'He wished not to be smirched with the mess of other people' (p. 119) – as by fear of corrupting them. Although he allows himself at certain points in the narrative to hope for a life with Ada on his return, more persistent is a fantasy of living, like an eremite, in absolute seclusion: 'He thought of getting home and building him a cabin on Cold Mountain so high that not a soul but the nighthawks passing across the clouds in autumn could hear his sad cry' (p. 80).[10]

Inman nourishes this vision of pastoral seclusion throughout the novel by observing two private rituals: opening at random and reading from a battered copy of the third volume of *Travels through North and South Carolina etc.* (1791) by the eighteenth-century American naturalist William Bartram, which he picks up by chance while recuperating in hospital; and reciting various features and landmarks of Cold Mountain to himself like a mantra.[11] Cynical about human nature, Inman nonetheless reveres these objects – the book and the mountain – as the repositories of a mystical wisdom. Most critics seem to accept at face value, and to assume that Frazier endorses, Inman's fetishisation of Bartram and Cold Mountain, but in fact the novel exposes the naivety of his beliefs. On the first night of their brief reunion, Inman confides to Ada his 'view that the book stood nigh to holiness and was of such richness that one might dip into it at random and read only one sentence and yet be sure of finding instruction and delight' (p. 402) and then attempts to demonstrate this by reading from a passage at which the book falls open. However, to his intense embarrassment, the sentence that he embarks upon turns out to be a eulogy to the charms of a group of 'young, innocent, Cherokee virgins . . . disclosing their beauties to the fluttering breeze and bathing their limbs in the cool fleeting streams' (p. 403) whom Bartram voyeuristically observes from the vantage point of a mountain summit. Having hoped to create a spiritual intimacy that might lead to a physical one, Inman has sheepishly to retreat, the narrator commenting drily: 'What he wanted to do was recline on the hemlock bed with Ada beside him and hold her close . . . But what Inman did was scroll up the book' (p. 403). The ironic disjunction between Inman's reliance on Bartram as a source of spiritual wisdom and moral guidance and the earthly desires displayed in the passage he reads to Ada is symptomatic of a more general incongruity between Inman's romantic view of Cold Mountain and the brutal reality.

This is illustrated with particular poignancy by two episodes towards the end of the novel. The first occurs when Inman is woken one morning by a black bear with her cub. He is reluctant to shoot the bear, but when he tries to move away the bear charges at him. Inman dodges and the bear hurtles over a mountain ledge that was obscured by the early morning mist. At this point Inman turns his attention to the cub, quickly realising that it 'would wither and die without a mother' (p. 341).

> To his credit, Inman could imagine reaching up and grabbing
> the cub . . . he might raise it to be a part-time bear, and when
> full grown it might stop by his hermit cabin at Cold Mountain
> now and again for company. Bring its wife and children so
> that in years to come Inman could have an animal family if
> no other . . .
> What Inman did, though, was all he could do. He . . . shot
> the cub in the head and watched it pause as its grip on the tree
> failed and it fell to the ground. (p. 342)

Inman's bucolic vision of a solitary life in harmony with nature on
Cold Mountain is abruptly undermined by the exigencies of the
situation. His sympathy for the plight of the cub gives way to his
pragmatism: rather than adopt the cub, he shoots it. Anticipating
the episode with the Bartram reading, Frazier's narrator draws
attention here to the disparity between aspiration and action,
using the same formula: 'What Inman did . . .'. The phrase 'To
his credit', which the narrator uses several times in the novel,
expresses approval while at the same time implying a lofty detachment from Inman. The rejection of the sentimental notion of
raising the cub as a companion is significant because it implicitly
casts doubt on the other details of Inman's idyllic vision: his plan
of living in splendid isolation in a hermit cabin on Cold Mountain.
When he finally reaches Cold Mountain it proves to be not the
refuge that he had hoped for, but a perilous place where the local
Home Guard, led by the unscrupulous Teague, are hunting for
'outliers' (Confederate deserters).

After finally consummating their relationship, Ada and Inman
part the following morning, Inman insisting that he should escort
Ruby's injured father, Stobrod (who miraculously survives an
execution ordered by Teague), home separately, in case they run
into the Home Guard. Sure enough, Inman soon finds himself
confronted by Teague and his gang. He manages to dispatch three
of them but is shot dead by the last surviving member, a 'boy'
whose lightning reflexes have been signalled in an earlier episode.
Although Inman has his gun trained on the boy and warns him to
put his gun down, the boy's hand moves 'quicker than you could
see' and Inman is fatally wounded. Ada turns back and runs towards

the sound of the gunshot, where she discovers Inman dying. The
final paragraph of the main narrative describes the scene as it might
have appeared to a witness from the sort of vantage point enjoyed
by Bartram when he observed the Cherokee virgins:

> An observer situated up the brow of the ridge would have
> [seen] . . . A wooded glade, secluded from the generality of
> mankind. A pair of lovers . . . touching each other with great
> intimacy . . . A scene of such quiet and peace that the observer
> could avouch to it later in such a way as might lead those
> of glad temperaments to imagine some conceivable history
> where long decades of happy union stretched before the two
> of them. (p. 432)

Terry Gifford comments of this passage:

> The reader does not know for sure that Inman is actually
> dying. Indeed, it is not really clear that he has been shot. I
> know of no reader who has not had to re-read [this passage]
> . . . This pastoral tableau is actually an image of 'Et in Arcadia
> Ego': even at the Arcadian narrative climax of the coming
> together of Inman and Ada, death is present – arbitrary,
> unexpected and ultimately unavoidable.[12]

Gifford is quite right that the scene draws on the pastoral convention, manifested most famously in paintings by Giovanni
Francesco Barbieri (known as Guercino) and Nicolas Poussin,
of the *memento mori* appearing in the midst of an otherwise
idyllic scene ('A wooded glade, secluded from the generality of
mankind'). However, it is absolutely clear that Inman has been
shot. Any attentive reader will also realise that Inman will not
survive, given the qualifications with which the narrator hedges his
hypothetical observer's report and the potential response to it: 'the
observer *could* avouch to it later in such a way as *might* lead those
of glad temperaments to *imagine some conceivable* history where
long decades of happy union stretched before the two of them' (p.
432).[13] In fact, to speculate as freely as Gifford does for a moment,
I would guess that for many readers Inman's death at this juncture

seems neither 'arbitrary' nor 'unexpected' but predictable and, in terms of the internal logic of the narrative, inevitable.

That Inman and Ada do not have 'long decades of happy union stretched before the two of them' is intimated almost from the start, both in psychological terms (the way in which Inman constructs himself as a doomed loner seems to preclude any possibility of domestic bliss with Ada) and in terms of the historical circumstances that Frazier works hard to establish (which make Inman's survival as a hunted outlier unlikely and the prospects of a happy marriage with Ada unimaginable). If the fate of the other outliers whom Inman encounters ('Inman had seen so many men shot in recent years that it seemed as normal to be shot as not') and his own conviction that he is 'ruined' beyond repair – rendered unfit for the intimacies of family life – have not alerted readers to the likely dénouement of the novel, then the manner of the lovers' long-awaited reunion ought to (pp. 398–9). Here, as elsewhere, Frazier begins by sketching a conventional, even stereotypical, romantic scenario:

> Ada would step out the door onto the porch without knowing he was coming, just going about her doings. She would be dressed in her fine clothes. She would see him and know him in every feature. She would rush across the yard and through the gate in a flurry of petticoats, and before the gate had even clapped shut they would be holding each other in the roadway. (p. 381)

Instead of this familiar staple of romantic literature, what we actually get is two figures approaching each other warily in the middle of a snowstorm, their guns trained on each other. When they get a little closer, Inman recognises 'Ada's fine face atop some strange trousered figure, like a mannish boy', while Ada 'examined him and did not know him' (p. 390). Instead of running to meet each other, 'They stood wary, about the number of paces specified for duelists. Not clasping heart to heart as Inman had imagined, but armed against each other, weapons glinting hard light into the space between them' (p. 390).

Here Inman reflects explicitly on the painful contrast between what he had envisaged would happen when he saw Ada again ('clasping heart to heart') and what actually transpires for they seem more like duellists than lovers, facing each other with loaded guns. Each detail of this moment, the moment to which the whole novel has been building up, is deliberately anti-climactic and unromantic: whereas Inman had imagined Ada 'dressed in her fine clothes', oblivious to his approach, she is actually dressed 'like a mannish boy', alert to his every move. Whereas Inman anticipates that she will immediately 'know him in every feature', she does not recognise him even when he addresses her by name. And once she realises who he is there is no passionate embrace, no declaration of love, but rather Ada's brisk instruction: 'You come with me' (p. 392).

In the light of this inauspicious beginning, the lovers' subsequent collaboration on the construction of 'an imaginary marriage, the years passing happy and peaceful' (p. 420) seems more like an implicit recognition that such a marriage can only exist in the realms of the imagination than a confident anticipation of the fulfilment of their hopes. Similarly, Inman's death, which McCarron and Knoke hail as a 'sacrifice . . . for the worthiest of human, apolitical causes' (p. 274), seems more like definitive proof of the destructive power of the Civil War than a vindication of Inman's attempt to defy it. In fact, McCarron and Knoke's insistence on finding consolation in Inman's death – 'However tragic this scene may first appear to be, the tone here is upbeat' (p. 281) – seems to anticipate Minghella's film more than reflecting the reality of Frazier's novel.

Frazier's novel presented Minghella – himself a distinguished playwright as well as the director of a number of critically acclaimed films, notably *Truly, Madly, Deeply* (1990) and *The English Patient* (1998) – with many opportunities but also some significant problems. On the one hand, the novel readily lends itself to adaptation for the screen because it has many memorable characters – from the opportunistic, adulterous and nearly murderous, yet charming minister, Veasey, who becomes Inman's travelling companion for some time before being executed by the Home Guard, to Sarah, the Confederate widow whose life Inman saves from Federal troops, to the Goat Woman, who saves Inman when he is at the point of collapse and nurses him back to health, to Stobrod, whose shameless selfishness is partly redeemed by a mysterious gift for music, to Strobod's daughter, Ruby, whose pragmatism, doggedness and unflagging optimism rescue Ada from despair and her farm from ruin – and many dramatic set-pieces, from the so-called 'Battle of the Crater' at Petersburg, to Ruby wringing the neck of the rooster that has been terrorising Ada, to the drugging and attempted seduction of Inman by a man and his wife who make a living by waylaying deserters and giving them up to the Home Guard, to the final showdown between Inman and Teague on Cold Mountain. On the other hand, as Martin Crawford points out, the book tells us 'literally . . . nothing of Inman's social roots: he seems to have no family, no community, or cultural affiliations'.[14] Furthermore, Ada and Inman's courtship is perfunctory and their correspondence during their four years' separation minimal. Most seriously for a Hollywood film, their life together after Inman's return is over barely before it has begun.

Minghella deals with the first of these issues by filling in some of the blanks: in the film Inman tells Monroe (Ada's father) that his mother died giving birth to him and that his father, now also dead, had been a teacher. Whereas in the book Inman is first introduced to Ada after one of her father's services, in the film they meet for the first time during a scene in which Inman is shown helping other local men build the chapel in which Monroe is to preach. This episode does not occur in the book (Monroe and Ada find a chapel when they first arrive),[15] but it serves several useful functions for Minghella. First, it establishes that sense of a community of which Inman is a part whose absence from the novel Crawford notes. Second, it allows Ada to watch and then approach Inman on the pretext of offering him one of the drinks that she is carrying on a tray (in the book it is Inman who approaches Ada, having come to church with the express intention of seeing her). Finally, it alludes to a famous scene from another film, Peter Weir's *Witness* (1985), in which Harrison Ford, playing a cop named John Book, who has joined an Amish community in order to protect a young boy who has witnessed a murder, helps the Amish men raise the roof of a new barn, while Kelly McGillis, playing Rachel Lapp, the widowed mother of the boy, looks on. This visual reference, with its implicit analogy between the romance that flourishes between Book and

Lapp, and that which will develop between Inman and Ada, places *Cold Mountain* in a tradition of what we might call hybrid romance movies: whereas *Witness* is a cross between a thriller and a romance, *Cold Mountain* combines the genres of war film and romance.

Minghella inserts a number of scenes which consolidate both the sense of Inman's place in the community and of his developing relationship with Ada, but he also radically alters the dynamics of their relationship in other ways. Whereas in the novel their correspondence is 'irregular' (p. 236), in the film she claims to have sent over a hundred letters, excerpts from which are read in voice-over at intervals during the course of the film. In the film, she also gives Inman his two most prized possessions – the Bartram book and a photograph of herself – and sends him off to war with the conventional promise 'I'll be waiting for you', words which the narrator of the novel explicitly insists that she neither utters, nor regrets not uttering:

> A number of things about the morning bothered her . . . Not among them was . . . that she had left unsaid the things many thousands of women . . . said as men left, all of which boiled down to the sentiment that they would await the man's return forever. (p. 244)

Although the primary meaning of 'sentiment' here is an expression of belief, it also has the secondary meaning of an exaggerated, melodramatic emotion, lent weight by the dismissive tone with which Ada refers to the trite formulation and her conscious refusal to indulge in it.

This is one of several instances where Minghella not only departs from Frazier's novel but directly contradicts it, presumably because of the impulse to satisfy the very romantic expectations that Frazier has subverted. This tendency is particularly evident in his treatment of the relationship between Ruby and her father. In the film Ruby reproaches Stobrod saying, 'You beat me, you abandoned me', whereas in the novel she makes a point of telling Ada that, for all his faults, Stobrod 'never laid a hand to her in anger' (p. 330). In the film Ruby cries when she is informed of her father's 'death' and then again when she discovers that he is still alive, saying 'Don't you die on me again'; in the novel she remains impassive on both occasions.

These changes tend to smooth the rough edges of the novel so that it slips more easily into the conventional romance template. Arguably, the defining moment in the film from this point of view is Minghella's handling of Inman's death. In Frazier's novel, Inman, having killed the rest of Teague's gang, finds himself facing the youngest of them, a boy whose pathetic appearance – 'a little wormy blond thing' – belies his brutality (p. 431). Inman manages to unseat him from his horse and has him in his sights, but because 'he looked as if his first shave lay still ahead of him, and Inman hoped not to have to shoot a boy', he hesitates fatally, giving the boy the chance to shoot first (p. 429). In the film, however, the two shoot each other at the same time, the boy (more of a young man in the film) immediately falling and Inman remaining upright for several seconds, so that viewers might think he is unhurt, before coughing up blood. This is partly a visual analogue of Gifford's reading of the scene, in which he claims that 'it is not really clear that he [Inman] has been shot', but if this is a matter of interpretation, the fate of Inman's adversary is not. Whereas in Frazier's novel he literally gets away with murder, in the film he is killed, thereby mitigating any sense of injustice and heightening Inman's heroism. Similarly, while there are no parting words spoken by the lovers in the novel, in the film Inman gets the chance to deliver a self-vindicating epitaph, saying 'I came back'. This is a reference to a letter from Ada which he receives in hospital, which in the novel consists simply of the line 'Come back to me is my request', but which in the film becomes part of a more expansive text, spoken as a voice-over by Nicole Kidman. Finally, another crucial divergence between the novel and film is the last view each gives us of the lovers. As we have seen, Frazier imagines how an observer looking down from a height might misinterpret Inman and Ada's embrace as a romantic tryst rather than the dying moments of a wounded man. Minghella follows the novel in that he films the end of the scene from a bird's-eye view, but he does not retain the ironic misprision of the novel because in the film the snow on which the lovers crouch is vividly stained with Inman's blood, making the context of the lovers' embrace unambiguous.

Overall, then, the film is a powerful work in its own right and its cinematography accurately reflects the lyricism of Frazier's prose (even if the locations used were in Hungary rather than America). However, it repeatedly rejects the subtleties, ambiguities and lacunae of the novel, revising Frazier's narrative so that it conforms to generic cinematic conventions. Although Frazier's narrator offers tantalising glimpses of rehabilitation, reconciliation and redemption, he invariably withdraws them abruptly, refusing the easy consolations of romance. There is an ostensibly inconsequential moment in the novel that nicely encapsulates this refusal to lapse into sentimentality when Ruby pours some cider for her father and he 'touche[s] the back of her hand with a forefinger' (p. 326). At first Ada, watching, 'thought it a tender gesture' but then she realises that 'it was but to urge the pouring of an extra measure' (p. 326). If this is an implied warning to readers of a romantic disposition, it is one that has been unheeded not just by Minghella but by critics such as McCarron and Knoke, for whom the novel 'transform[s] horror into heroism and mindless violence into moral victory' (p. 274). Heroism is arguably in the eye of the beholder, but it seems to me that Inman is more of an anti-hero than a hero, and he certainly commits much of the violence in the novel, albeit usually in self-defence. *Cold Mountain* ends not with Inman's death but with an Epilogue in which it emerges that Ada has had a daughter by him and is living with Ruby, Stobrod, Ruby's husband, Georgia, and their three sons. Nonetheless, Frazier is at pains even here to emphasise that life is not idyllic but 'demanding as always' (p. 436). In the final paragraph, Ada is telling the children the story of Baucis and Philemon, in which 'the old lovers after long years together in peace and harmony had turned to oak and linden' (p. 436). This final note is characteristically bittersweet, since the eternal union of the mythological lovers implicitly contrasts with the brief time Ada has enjoyed with Inman. If Inman is an anti-hero, *Cold Mountain* is perhaps an anti-romance; Frazier often invokes the imagery and rhetoric of romance, but he does so to emphasise how far removed from this idyll is the amoral world in which the novel's action unfolds. Minghella's reinterpretation, on the other hand, locates the narrative firmly in the cinematic tradition of the Civil War romance of which *Gone with the Wind* (1939) is the most famous example.

ANNIE PROULX, 'BROKEBACK MOUNTAIN'

Annie Proulx's short story 'Brokeback Mountain' was first published in *The New Yorker* in 1997. Later it became the final story in a collection – *Close Range: Wyoming Stories* – before reaching a mass audience in Ang Lee's film version (2005), which won three Academy Awards, including Best Director. To coincide with the release of the film, *Wyoming Stories* was reissued with the title *Close Range: Brokeback Mountain and Other Stories* (2006). Proulx had achieved literary fame in 1993, when her second novel, *The Shipping News*, like Frazier's *Cold Mountain* four years later, was awarded both of America's most prestigious literary prizes, the National Book Award and the Pulitzer Prize, as well as becoming a bestseller. *The Shipping News* was made into a Hollywood film in 2001, directed by Lasse Hallstrom and starring Kevin Spacey and Julianne Moore, but unlike *Brokeback Mountain* received mixed reviews and was not a box office success.

Originally 'conceived . . . as one of a set of stories' that were to deal with 'offbeat and difficult love situations', Proulx seems to have placed 'Brokeback Mountain' at the end of her *Close Range* collection rather uneasily, feeling that 'it stands out rather like a sore thumb in comparison to the rest of the work'.[16] 'Brokeback Mountain' tells the story of two young men, Ennis del Mar and Jack Twist, both estranged from their families, who are hired to look after a flock of sheep one summer in Wyoming on 'Brokeback Mountain'. The two discover an intense sexual attraction that survives their subsequent marriages and fatherhood (Ennis marries a grocery store worker, Alma, with whom he has two daughters, and Jack marries Lureen, a farming machinery company heiress, with whom he has a son). Over the course of twenty years, the men contrive to meet periodically for trips to 'Brokeback Mountain', where they try to relive their youthful idyll, Jack hoping for a more fulfilling relationship, Ennis resigned to fitting their furtive trysts in when they can. After a final meeting at which these tensions come to a head, Ennis hears of Jack's death (which might have been either a freak accident or a homophobic murder) and visits Jack's parents to offer to scatter their son's ashes on 'Brokeback Mountain' according to his wishes. He is rebuffed by Jack's father, but Jack's mother invites Ennis to see Jack's room, where he finds an old shirt, which he thought he had lost during their summer of shared shepherding, concealed underneath one of Jack's shirts. Ennis leaves with both shirts and when he gets home hangs them up in his wardrobe, underneath a postcard of 'Brokeback Mountain', uttering the words 'Jack, I swear – '. The story ends with a description of the dreams that Ennis begins to have in which Jack reappears as his youthful self, leaving Ennis alternating between 'grief' and 'joy'.[17] These ambivalent emotions, and the way in which they defy articulation – symbolised by the elliptical, ambiguous sentence fragment ('Jack, I swear –') that constitutes Ennis's final speech in the story – encapsulate nicely the preceding narrative. With laconic detachment, Proulx's narrator draws attention to the ambiguity and irony of Ennis's last words, observing that 'Jack had never asked him to swear anything and was himself not the swearing kind' (p. 317). Whether Ennis intended to make a vow to his deceased lover or to utter a more profane oath, his inability to complete his thought is entirely characteristic and provides an apt epitaph to a relationship that is, paradoxically, both abortive and unending, inchoate and mature, superficial and profound.

From the outset, the transactions between the men demonstrate both a mutual understanding and a failure of communication. After their first sexual encounter, which is itself wordless, the narrator comments that 'without saying anything about it both knew how it would go for the rest of the summer' (p. 291), implying that they will continue to have sexual relations for the duration of their stint as shepherds. He goes on to state that '[t]hey never talked about the sex, let it happen . . . but saying not a goddamn word except once Ennis said, "I'm not no queer,' and Jack jumped in with 'Me neither. A one-shot thing. Nobody's business but ours' (p. 291). Their collaboration in the transparent fiction that their relationship is an anomaly (a 'one-shot thing') which does not reflect their sexual orientation ('"I'm not no queer" . . . "Me neither"'), is undermined by their reluctance to talk about what they are doing, by Jack's instinctive conviction that the nature of their relationship must remain secret ('Nobody's business but ours') and by the double negative ('not no queer') which implicitly contradicts Ennis's intended denial of his homosexuality. The mixture of exhilaration and shame that characterises this first phase of their relationship is manifested particularly painfully in an episode on their last day together on the mountain, the details of which are withheld until much later in the story.

During their parting conversation, which ends with words whose noncommittal, inexpressive quality ('Well, see you around, I guess') anticipates those spoken by Inman and Ada in *Cold Mountain*, Ennis averts his gaze at one point 'from Jack's jaw, bruised blue from the hard punch Ennis had thrown him on the last day' (p. 293). No further explanation is forthcoming here, but towards the end of the story, when Ennis finds Jack's 'old shirt from Brokeback days' (p. 315) enfolding his, the context for this incident is belatedly provided:

> The dried blood on the sleeve was his own blood, a gushing nosebleed on the last afternoon on the mountain when Jack, in their contortionistic grappling and wrestling, had slammed Ennis's nose hard with his knee. He had staunched the blood which was everywhere, all over both of them, but the staunching hadn't held because Ennis had suddenly swung from the deck and laid the ministering angel out in the wild columbine, wings folded. (pp. 315–16)

The symbolism of the lovers' commingled blood, the product of both their mutual sexual attraction and their mutual resentment (Ennis's injury is sustained as a result of their passion, Jack's as a result of Ennis's outburst), and the metaphor of Jack as an angel spreadeagled on the earth, reinforces the paradoxical nature of their relationship. The fact that Jack's keepsake contains the evidence of both Ennis's love for and hatred of him (the dried blood), and that he has to steal it in the first place, demonstrates poignantly both the strength and the fragility of their bond. The inability of the lovers to discuss the feelings which lead to this violent assault corresponds of course to their inability to discuss the feelings that lead them into a sexual relationship, but arguably the latter also causes the former: what really provokes Ennis's blow seems to be not the initial accidental blow to his nose from Jack's knee, but rather the tenderness with which he ministers to him afterwards. It is Ennis who adopts the active role in the men's lovemaking and when Jack tries to nurse his wound his masculinity is threatened. In this sense, the incident establishes a pattern: whenever Jack demonstrates loving feelings outside the context of sexuality, Ennis feels uneasy. In fact, it is Jack's suggestion, at their final meeting, that they might have 'had a good life together' had Ennis been willing to commit himself to a long-term relationship that precipitates a stream of long-repressed recriminations:

> Like vast clouds of steam from thermal springs in winter the years of things unsaid and now unsayable – admissions, declarations, shames, guilts, fears – rose around them. (p. 309)

Again, there is a paradox here, since many of these 'now unsayable' things have just been said in what is the longest speech in the book, in which Jack reproaches Ennis for the 'damn few times we been together in twenty years' (p. 309). At the same time, the implication is that many other things have been left unsaid and that Jack's outburst has left 'nothing resolved' (p. 310).

One of the most striking characteristics of Proulx's story is how much is left unarticulated, not just by the protagonists, but by the narrator, who is both a chronicler of their reticence and complicit in it. This narrative reticence manifests itself in the elliptical conversations between the lovers and in the way that the prose often conveys information implicitly rather than explicitly. To give one example: during the lovemaking between Ennis and his wife, we are told that 'he rolled her over, did quickly what she hated' (p. 294), and afterwards, that Alma thinks bitterly (without voicing her thoughts): 'what you like to do don't make too many babies' (p. 302). The reader is left to infer that Ennis prefers to sodomise his wife rather than have vaginal sex, and further to infer that this is due to his homosexuality. These lacunae in the narrative must have posed problems for, but also liberated, Ang Lee.

If *Cold Mountain* seems to lend itself naturally to screen adaptation, 'Brokeback Mountain' seems, at first sight, rather unpromising film material. First, there is little in the way of incident: the story is less than forty pages long whereas Frazier's novel runs to more than 400 pages and the most dramatic episode in the narrative

– Jack's death – is reported at second-hand. Second, whereas the love between the protagonists of *Cold Mountain* is based on the classical model of *The Odyssey*, the affair between Ennis and Jack remains taboo territory for a mainstream Hollywood film. Finally, the ending of the story is rather downbeat: Ennis is alone and Jack dead, possibly murdered. On the other hand, Proulx's story has in common with Frazier's a spectacular location – a mountain that is both a physical space and a metaphysical concept, a symbol of an irrecoverable, prelapsarian past and an unattainable utopian future.

In an interview with Rebecca Murray, Lee spoke of his conviction that 'Brokeback Mountain' should become 'a character in the movie' because of its symbolic importance to the story. He went on to explain that it represents 'a very existential idea . . . an illusion of love' to which they 'keep wanting to go back' even though 'they really didn't understand to begin with when they are inside of it'.[18] In the opening section of the film in particular, Lee manages to imbue the mountain used in the film (which in reality is in Alberta, Canada, rather than Wyoming) with a combination of majesty and austerity which makes it an ideal setting for the coming together of Ennis and Jack (the natural beauty of the landscape inspiring romance, its harshness providing more prosaic reasons – the need for mutual warmth and protection – for their intimacy). He also gives it a prominence that ensures it becomes more than simply a scenic background and becomes in fact the 'character' in its own right that Lee envisaged (p. 1), which he does not only to provide a visual analogue to the descriptions of the mountain in Proulx's story but also as a means of locating the film in the tradition of the Hollywood Western. In the interview with Murray, Lee confesses to having a weakness for this genre, adding that 'the American West really attracts me because it's romantic' (p. 1). The panoramic shots of the mountainous landscape, and of the men herding the sheep through it, allude to many classic Westerns in which the West itself occupies a transcendent, mythical role, dwarfing the actors literally and metaphorically. Finally, the time devoted to showing the men working, eating and sleeping on the mountain serves another crucial function: to enlarge the context for the story that follows.

In the Murray interview, Lee explained that he had to shoot 'additional scenes' for the film 'because we don't have internal depiction, which she did most brilliantly' (p. 2). What is striking about the opening of Proulx's story, however, is how little 'internal depiction' precedes the first sexual encounter. Just as the sex itself is initiated with no foreplay ('Ennis . . . wanted none of it when Jack seized his left hand and brought it to his erect cock . . . got to his knees, unbuckled his belt, shoved his pants down, hauled Jack onto all fours and . . . entered him'), so the scene itself springs abruptly on readers with no prior knowledge of the plot. The narrator does describe a process of bonding in which the two men drink together, exchanging confidences, but the only real indication, before they consummate their relationship, of the trajectory that their story will follow comes in the opening, italicised section of the story, in which Ennis 'is suffused with a sense of pleasure because Jack Twist was in his dream' (p. 283). In structural terms, this section functions as an epilogue to the main narrative, but Proulx's decision to invert the chronology by placing it at the beginning of the story poses a mystery for the reader which the copulation resolves. In the film, however, Lee shifts this passage to the end of the narrative, thus restoring to the story the linearity that Proulx disrupts. Because of this, there is a greater need to prepare the audience, emotionally, for the moment when the men become lovers, as well as a practical need to prolong the prologue to their union so that the narrative can make the transition of scale from what Proulx called 'a little canoe' (her story) to 'an ocean liner' (the film).[19] So Brokeback Mountain, the place, fills the screen not only literally, connecting Lee's film with a specific generic tradition, but also figuratively, filling in some of the narrative gaps from Proulx's story and filling up screen time so that the first climactic moment of the narrative doesn't come prematurely.

In general, Lee is very faithful to Proulx's story – much more so than Minghella is to Frazier's – but the changes he does make tend, like Minghella's, to forfeit some of the subtleties of the original. A good example of this is his treatment of the episode described above in which Jack and Ennis injure each other on the final day of their mountain vigil. Whereas in the story the narrator withholds the revelation of how the men sustained their cuts and bruises until near the end of the story, Lee smoothes out this temporal wrinkle (as he does with the prologue/epilogue), inserting a scene in which the audience witnesses the lovers' fight at the time of its occurrence. More importantly, Lee alters the nature of the event. In Proulx, as we have seen, Ennis strikes Jack after he tries to make amends, having accidentally kneed Ennis in the nose in the course of their lovemaking; in Lee's adaptation, Jack repeatedly lassos Ennis, finally tripping him up, before Ennis loses his temper and floors him with a punch. By dramatising this scene directly, rather than Ennis recalling it at the moment of discovering his bloodstained shirt in Jack's wardrobe, and by introducing the heavy-handed symbolism of the lasso, Lee focuses on Ennis's fear of – and anger at – being defined by his feelings for Jack, in a way that is undeniably effective and affecting cinematically but that distorts the dynamics of Proulx's story. The inclusion of other scenes dealing with Ennis that have no basis in Proulx's story – notably several detailing the progress and eventual dissolution of his post-divorce involvement with a woman who picks him up at a bar and dealing with his relationship with his daughter, who at one point asks him if she can live with him ('You know I ain't set up for that', Ennis observes, cryptically) and invites him to her wedding near the end of the film (Ennis initially declines, before finally agreeing to attend) – emphasise his emotional isolation and repression. Those pertaining to Jack, on the other hand – such as a Thanksgiving dinner at which he faces down his bullying father-in-law in a quarrel concerning Jack's son, a scene in which Jack is apparently propositioned by the husband of his wife's friend, and a brief vignette in which Jack is shown picking up a young boy prostitute in Mexico – suggest that he has been more successful in coming to terms with his sexuality.

Several of these episodes are developed from hints or asides in Proulx's story and none is inconsistent with it, but at the same time their cumulative effect is to paint both characters in broader, heavier strokes than is the case in Proulx's story: understated distinctions between the two men in the story become bold contrasts in the film. Even when Lee takes great pains to preserve the ambiguities of his source, he comes up against the incommensurability of film and fiction. This is particularly evident in the way in which Ennis learns about Jack's death. In Proulx's story the first reference to his death is when the narrator announces, with typical abruptness, that 'Ennis didn't know about the accident for months until his postcard to Jack . . . came back stamped DECEASED' (p. 311). When Ennis questions Jack's widow about the circumstances of her husband's death, she informs him that an exploding tyre had 'knocked him unconscious on his back' and that he had 'drowned in his own blood' (p. 311). Ennis instinctively rejects this account, deciding that 'they got him with the tire iron' (p. 311). After listening a little more to Lureen, he retreats from this position, so that 'he didn't know which way it was, the tire iron or a real accident, blood choking down Jack's throat and nobody to turn him over' (p. 312). Later, when Jack's father tells him that Jack had begun talking about moving in with 'some ranch neighbour a his from down in Texas', he decides that 'it had been the tire iron' (p. 314). In Lee's visual version of this narrative uncertainty, Ennis's conversation with Lureen is overlaid with images of Jack being beaten to death by a group of indistinctly seen men. This cleverly captures Ennis's paranoid vision of an undefined homophobic mob – 'they' – ever-ready to recreate the murder of two gay men whose disfigured bodies he had seen as a child, while maintaining the possibility that this is indeed what happened (it is not clear whether these images are purely the product of Ennis's imagination or whether they are invested with objective narrative authority). However, what Lee cannot recreate is the series of subtle shifts traced by Proulx's narrative, which first describes Jack's death unequivocally as an accident, then provides details of that accident, then offers an alternative scenario, then half-retracts that alternative, before finally apparently reinstating it as the definitive account: 'So now he *knew* it had been the tire iron' (p. 314, my emphasis) – except, of course, that this final word on the matter is really no such thing, since it only poses more questions. Ennis cannot *know* the truth any more than readers of the story can. Do we trust Ennis's judgement or do we accept Lureen's account? Furthermore, does Lureen believe her own story, or is it a convenient fiction concocted to hide from others the truth about Jack's sexuality, which has been exposed by the manner of his death? Or is it perhaps a story told to her by others to protect her from the truth?

Brokeback Mountain is a fine film, but it cannot pose such questions in the same open-ended way that 'Brokeback Mountain' does, because film as a medium must commit itself to realising a finite set of narrative possibilities, whereas a prose narrative can preserve, as potentially equally viable, an infinite range of scenarios. Thoughtful though his direction is, Lee cannot suggest, as Proulx does with the phrase 'blood choking down his throat and no one to turn him over' (p. 312), that even as he imagines him enduring a violent death, Ennis eroticises Jack, his regret that he could not 'turn him over' to save him implicitly invoking those occasions when he used to 'turn him over' prior to penetrating him. That this seems to place Ennis in queasy apposition to Jack's (possible) murderers also recalls the moment, during their final meeting, when Ennis, enraged by Jack's confession that he travels to Mexico (with the implicit suggestion that the purpose of these visits is to pick up male prostitutes), warns him that 'all them things I don't know could get you killed if I should come to know them' (p. 309). Although Ennis characteristically uses a euphemism ('all them things') to refer to Jack's sexual escapades, and a passive construction ('could get you killed') so as to avoid taking responsibility for his threat, his meaning is clear enough. Paradoxically, then, Ennis is both Jack's potential saviour and his potential killer.

It is not the case that Lee's film is simply an impoverished version of Proulx's story. In some respects, it is richer and more fully realised as a narrative. For example, it gives greater prominence to the women in the story and makes clear that they, as much as the two male protagonists, are victims of the inability of Jack and Ennis to live with each other or without each other. In this sense, Lee's film represents a departure from the phallocentric tradition of the Western, which, as Jay Hoberman puts it, 'has always been the most idyllically homosocial of modes – and often one concerned with the programmatic exclusion of women'.[20] Yet in its greater inclusiveness, the film also dilutes some of the solipsistic intensity of Jack and Ennis's relationship, rendering it, in Hoberman's words, a 'universal romance' acceptable to a mainstream cinema audience.

CORMAC MCCARTHY, *NO COUNTRY FOR OLD MEN*

No Country for Old Men (2005) is Cormac McCarthy's tenth novel.
Until recently his reputation as one of the most important living
American novelists rested primarily on the 'Border Trilogy',
consisting of *Blood Meridian* (1985), *All the Pretty Horses* (1992)
and *The Crossing* (1994). The first of these was placed third in a
2006 list of the best American fiction published over the previous
quarter-century, compiled by *The New York Times* on the basis of
a survey of contemporary authors; the second won the National
Book Award. However, his last two novels have brought McCarthy
to the attention of a wider audience: *The Road* (2007) was awarded
the Pulitzer Prize for Fiction and became a bestseller, in spite of
its bleak subject matter (it is set in a post-apocalyptic world). In
the same year that *The Road* was published, a film adaptation of
No Country for Old Men won four Academy Awards, including
Best Picture and Best Director for Joel and Ethan Coen and Best
Supporting Actor for Javier Bardem.

No Country for Old Men deals with the manifold repercussions
of a botched drug deal. While on a hunting expedition, Llewellyn
Moss, a welder and Vietnam veteran, accidentally discovers a scene
of carnage: abandoned trucks, dead bodies, a large stash of heroin
and a satchel containing $4.2 million in cash. His decision to make
off with the money ensures that the other two protagonists of
the novel – Bell, the local sheriff, on the point of retirement, and
Chigurh, a psychopathic killer and freelance hit-man – are soon on
his trail. The novel gestures towards a number of popular genres:
a reviewer in *The Times* (quoted on the back of the 2007 Picador
paperback) described it as 'a western thriller with a racy plot and
punchy dialogue, perfect for a lazy Sunday' (n.p.). Yet its distinctive, stylised prose and its persistent engagement with profound
existential and moral questions, a number of which are alluded
to in its title, make it a work that resists conventional generic
categorisation.

The country and the old men to which it refers are never explicitly identified but several possibilities are offered by the italicised
first-person narrative sections that open each of the chapters. These
passages – Sheriff Bell's meditations on his life and work – are one

of the things that distinguishes McCarthy's novel from conventional 'western thrillers'. Although they overlap with the main narrative insofar as Bell's unsuccessful pursuit of Moss and Chigurh feeds into his reflections, for the most part these sections enjoy a tangential relationship with the action, providing a counterpoint to or an oblique commentary on it.

One of the central questions posed by these sections, and by the novel as a whole, is of the extent to which Bell's decision to retire, taken before the opening of the novel, is an admission of defeat, a confirmation that he is an old man unsuited to surviving in what has become increasingly inhospitable terrain. Certainly, much of what Bell says serves to encourage this identification of himself as one of the 'old men' of the title. He is unabashedly nostalgic about a bygone era of law enforcement when '*old-time sheriffs wouldnt*[21] *even carry a firearm*' and exhibited an '*old time concern . . . for their people*'.[22] Conversely, he is dismayed by what he sees as evidence of a deterioration of moral values in contemporary society, demonstrated in particular by the lurid stories he reads in the newspapers: of two boys from opposite ends of the country who meet by chance and embark on a killing spree, of '*a woman put her baby in a trash compactor*' (p. 40), of a couple of Californian serial killers, who '*would rent out rooms to old people and then kill em and bury em in the yard and cash their social security checks*' (p. 124). The fact that it is 'old people' who are the victims in this last example of depravity reinforces the sense of a chasm that has opened up between Bell's generation and its successors, an absolute divide between young and old, in which you are defined not just by your age but by your attitudes to the modern world. In this binary scheme, Bell's identity as an old man is confirmed not just by his conviction that '*the world is goin to hell in a handbasket*', but by the responses of those who dissent from this view: '*people will just sort of smile and tell me I'm gettin old*' (p. 196).

There is a danger at times of Bell becoming a caricature of a teeth-sucking reactionary. When he pours scorn on the views of a woman ('*the wife of somebody or other*', as he dismissively refers to her) who tells him that she is worried about the '*right wing*' (p. 196) direction the country is taking, or when he confesses that he sometimes feels like '*them old people*' who '*wouldnt of believed*' that one day *'there would be people on the streets of our Texan towns with green hair and bones in their noses speakin a language they couldnt even understand'* (p. 295), Bell may seem not simply old-fashioned but neo-conservative. On the other hand, his use of the third-person plural when referring to the older generation incredulous at the appearance and demeanour of the younger ('them *old people*') suggests that Bell does not affiliate himself with them. This implied distance between Bell and an undefined old(er) generation is reinforced later, when he notes that *'the old people . . . just look crazy . . . like they woke up and they dont know how they got where they're at'* (p. 304). If Bell is disconcerted about the changes he has witnessed over his lifetime, he is not disoriented in the manner of these 'old people'. He is in fact as far removed from them as he is from the youngsters with the green hair.

Bell's ambivalence towards 'old people' is perhaps most conspicuous in the long conversation he has with his uncle Ellis, an elderly, wheelchair-bound man living alone in a dilapidated house that smells of 'old bacon-grease and stale woodsmoke . . . [with] a faint tang of urine' (p. 263). During their discussion of family history, the two men touch on the fate of Ellis's older brother, Harold, who died 'somewhere in a ditch' (p. 268) at the age of seventeen, a casualty of the First World War, and his uncle, Mac, who was 'shot down on his own porch' (p. 269) by a group of Native Americans, before Bell confesses to Ellis something that he has never revealed to anyone else: that the medal he was awarded for service during the Second World War was the result of an incident in which he abandoned his position, not knowing whether any of the other members of his platoon were still alive. One of the things that haunts Bell is the conviction that his father, Jack, would never have 'cut and run' (p. 276) had he found himself in Bell's predicament. However, Ellis points out that 'he lived in different times. Had Jack of been born fifty years later he might of had a different view of things' (p. 279).

This episode complicates the image of Bell as an old man. In the context of the visit to Ellis, a decrepit man who is referred to throughout the chapter by the third-person narrator as 'the old man', and who provides a connection to much earlier conflicts (the 'Indian Wars' and the First World War) than the one in which his nephew fought, Bell's professed alienation from contemporary society appears less profound. Bell himself seems to acknowledge this when he concedes that 'I'm not the man of an older time they say I am . . . I'm a man of this time' (p. 279). Whereas Ellis seems a relic of an older period of American history and has withdrawn altogether from the modern world, living the life of a recluse and deliberately discarding the only piece of modern technology he had (he tells Bell that he has 'throwed . . . out' his television) (p. 272), Bell reads the newspapers every day. Although elsewhere Bell reflects that when he recalls his father, Jack, '*I've been older now than he ever was for almost twenty years so in a sense Im lookin back at a younger man*' (p. 308), as Ellis points out he will always be an older man in historical terms. Both Jack and Ellis are 'old men' in a sense that Bell, for all his distrust of the present and fear for the future, is not: they are both part of a past from which Bell is excluded.

If Bell's encounter with Ellis demonstrates the difficulty of identifying the referents of the 'old men' of the novel's title, it appears at the same time to clarify its use of the word 'country'. Ellis's account of the death of his uncle prompts him to reflect on the harsh history of America:

> This country was hard on people . . . How come people dont feel like this country has got a lot to answer for? They dont. You can say that the country is just the country, it dont actively do nothin. But that dont mean much. I seen a man shoot his pickup truck with a shotgun one time. He must of thought it done somethin. This country will kill you in a heartbeat and still people love it. You understand what I'm sayin? (p. 271)

Paradoxically, Ellis characterises America (which, however, he never names) both as an autonomous agent of destruction that 'will kill you in a heartbeat' and, in the implicit analogy with the pickup truck, as an inanimate object. Alive to the absurdity of the man directing his anger at a truck, Ellis nonetheless finds it even more irrational that 'people' 'love' a country that is so 'hard' on them. For Ellis, 'the country' is essentially separate from – even antagonistic towards – its inhabitants: a hostile, malevolent force that 'has . . . a lot to answer for', a land for the fit and young – not old men.

However, Ellis's construction of 'the country' is no more definitive than Bell's self-fashioning as an old man, is in fact only one of a number of competing designations. Another potential meaning of the term is 'countryside' – the harsh landscape of the Texas–Mexico border in which Llewellyn Moss stumbles on the bloody aftermath of the drugs deal. In fact, Bell explicitly considers the relationship between this country and the larger country that contains it when he returns, late in the novel, to the site of the shoot-out:

> *I went back out there one more time. I walked over that ground and there was very little sign that anything had ever took place there . . . I still keep thinkin maybe it is somethin about the country . . . it just seemed to me that this country has got a strange kind of history and a damned bloody one too.* (p. 284)

This bloody history extends beyond the borders of America, of course, as Bell is reminded by his colleague, Wendell, on his first visit to the crime scene:

> It must of sounded like Vietnam out here.
> Vietnam, the Sheriff said. (p. 75)

It is not clear from this typically clipped exchange whether Bell's repetition of 'Vietnam' constitutes an endorsement of Wendell's simile, a dismissal of it or a noncommittal meditation on its relative virtues. What becomes increasingly apparent as the novel proceeds, however, is that the bloody episode in American history for which the word Vietnam has become a metonym lies behind much of its action. When Moss is lying low, trying to evade his pursuers in the floodplain of the Rio Grande, the narrator observes that 'He'd had this feeling before. In another country. He never thought he'd have it again' (p. 30). Although the country is pointedly not named, the clear implication is that Moss is a Vietnam veteran and this is confirmed when Carson Wells, a hit-man hired by one of the parties involved in the drug deal to retrieve the money that Moss steals, tracks Moss down to a hospital on the Mexican side of the border, where he is recuperating from shotgun wounds inflicted by Chigurh. Wells warns Moss that he won't escape from Chigurh unless he cooperates with him, but Moss is unreceptive, so Wells tries to establish some common ground:

> Were you in Nam?
> Yeah. I was in Nam.
> So was I.
> So what does that make me? Your buddy? (p. 156)

Although Moss peremptorily rejects the idea that their service in Vietnam implies any kinship between them, his very acceptance of Well's terminology (he echoes his use of the abbreviation 'Nam' just as Bell had echoed Wendell's 'Vietnam' earlier in the novel) and his candid confession that Wells's conjecture is correct, suggests that there is a sort of shared experience that unites all veterans of the conflict. This idea is reinforced by the fact that when Chigurh kills Wells shortly after the latter's conversation with Moss, the narrator tells us that one of the final images to drain away from Well's consciousness is that of '[t]he body of a child dead in a roadside ravine in another country' (p. 178). The use of the phrase 'another country' echoes the moment earlier in the novel when Moss recalls his experiences in Vietnam. Taken cumulatively, these references suggest that the 'country' of the novel's title may refer not just to America but also to that other country with whose fate its own became so embroiled in the 1960s and 1970s, particularly given the tendency of Vietnam veterans to refer to their tours of duty as time spent 'in country'.[23]

Towards the end of the novel, Bell visits Moss's father to let him know the facts about his son's death. Initially, Bell describes him '*as bit oldern me. Ten years maybe*' (p. 293), but subsequently revises his opinion: '*then I thought he looked a lot older. His eyes looked old*' (p. 294). Painfully taciturn at first, Moss Sr eventually volunteers the information that Moss had been a sniper in Vietnam and then begins to reflect on the impact of the Vietnam conflict on American society:

A lot of them boys that come back, they're still havin problems.
I thought it was because they didn't have the country behind em.
But I think it might be worse than that even. The country they did
have was in pieces . . . People will tell you it was Vietnam brought
this country to its knees. But I never believed that. It was already
in bad shape. Vietnam was just the icin on the cake. (p. 294)

Like Ellis and Bell earlier in the novel, Moss's father refers to
America as the 'country' and appears to exclude himself from
it. When he says that *'they didn't have the country behind em'*, he
implicitly distances himself from this position and it is clear from
all that he says that he views domestic opposition to the war as
symptomatic of a larger malaise. That the three old men of the
novel all talk about America as though it was another country –
something from which they are alienated and over which they
have no control – might seem to bear out the contention that it is
'no country for old men'. On the other hand, there is something
paradoxical about their position: they are all American citizens and
their views are obviously shared by many, perhaps primarily but
certainly not exclusively of their generation and gender, so they are
very much part of the country that they invoke as absolutely other.
Their sense of alienation is perhaps more a symptom of their age –
and of their (very American) conviction that their nation is always
defined by the new – than an accurate reflection of their social or
political marginality. As Loretta, Bell's wife, puts it: 'past a certain
age I dont guess there is any such thing as good change' (p. 301).

Certainly, Bell's disillusionment with America is largely derived
from his sense that 'new' usually means 'worse'. One of the newspaper stories that Bell cites as empirical evidence of the decline
in moral standards in America is a comparison of the results of a
survey of American schoolchildren from the 1930s and 1970s: the
worst problems identified by the earlier generation were *'things*
like talkin in class and runnin in the hallways', whereas the later
generation identify *'Rape, arson, murder'* (p. 196) as their biggest
concerns. What Bell does not take into account, of course, is that,
although the survey demonstrates a radical change in the *percep-*
tions of the children, it does not in itself provide proof that, for
example, more rapes took place among American schoolchildren

of the 1970s than in the 1930s. For Bell, however, the responses of the schoolchildren confirm his instinctive sense that the problems of modern American society are unprecedented. When he and Wendell – another of the old men of the novel, who tells Bell that he too is soon 'goin to quit' (p. 46) – discover the body of a driver whom Chigurh has killed with the unconventional weapon that he carries everywhere with him (an oxygen tank connected by a hose to a stun-gun used in slaughter-houses), Wendell says: 'I just have this feelin we're looking at somethin we really aint never even seen before' (p. 46), a sentiment with which Bell concurs and which anticipates his response when he surveys the scene of the derailed drug deal: 'I aint sure we've seen these people before. Their kind' (p. 79). This in turn echoes something that Bell says at the very outset of the novel.

The novel begins with Bell's recollections of visiting a nineteen-year-old murderer, on the eve of his execution, whom he had arrested and testified against. Taken aback by the boy's lack of remorse and frank confession that '*he had been plannin to kill somebody for about as long as he could remember*', the sheriff recalls '*wonderin if maybe he was some new kind*' (p. 3). Bell's characteristi-cally elliptical diction introduces ambiguity to this passage (does he mean a new kind of offender, a new kind of murderer, a new kind of person altogether?), but what is clear is that this young man stands in symbolic opposition to the 'old men' invoked by the title of the novel and that he is the harbinger of a new breed of humanity, or masculinity, whose inhumanity far exceeds his own: '*he wasn't nothin compared to what was comin down the pike*' (p. 4), as Bell puts it.

What is coming down the pike turns out, literally and meta-phorically, to be Anton Chigurh: literally, because the novel moves straight from this invocation of cold-blooded homicide to a description of the first of the numerous casually violent murders committed by Chigurh that punctuate the narrative; and meta-phorically, because Chigurh is as much a symbolic embodiment of malevolence as he is an individual criminal ('what' is in this sense a more appropriate pronoun for him than the 'who' that grammar demands). This impression is underlined by Bell's final pronouncement on him: '*When you encounter certain things in the world, the evidence for certain things, you realize that you have come upon somethin that you may very well not be equal to and I think that this is one of them things'* (p. 299). In a sense, Bell's use of 'thing' to refer to Chigurh here is euphemistic: it is easier to attribute the appalling crimes that he has committed to an abstraction than to a human being. However, it is also consistent with the way in which McCarthy's narrator and the Coen brothers, in their film adaptation, present the character.

Chigurh is a shadowy figure in a number of ways: his motivations are obscure; he appears, reappears and finally disappears from the narrative abruptly and without explanation. He is also essentially context-less: he apparently has no friends, no family, no community, no employer, no history (the only thing we discover about his past is that he once worked with Carson Wells). Even his physical appearance defies definition. When Bell asks one of the two boys – witnesses to a collision in which Chigurh is seriously injured as he drives away from the scene of one of his innumerable murders – what he looked like, he is told: '[M]edium height. Medium build . . . He looked like anybody' (p. 292).

In part, Chigurh's supernatural aura is self-fashioned: he likes to represent himself as an impersonal agent of fate rather than a human being with personal motives for his actions. Twice in the novel he allows the toss of a coin to determine the fate of his potential victims: the first time the proprietor of a filling station escapes by calling 'heads' correctly; the second time Carla Jean Moss (widow of Llewelyn Moss) calls 'heads' but the coin has landed on 'tails' and Chigurh shoots her. On both occasions, he refers enigmatically (and presumably with a self-conscious pun alluding to the dual function of the coin) to an 'accounting' (pp. 57, 259) of which he seems to see himself as the instrument. He tells Carla Jean that he 'model[s] himself after God' (p. 256) and that '[m]ost people dont believe that there can be such a person [as himself]' (p. 260).

However, if Chigurh mythologises himself, other characters in the novel collude in this enterprise. Bell refers to him both as *'a true and living prophet of destruction'* (p. 4) and as *'pretty much a ghost'* (p. 299). When he does confer on him the status of an ordinary creature of flesh and blood, he does so in the manner of someone trying to convince himself of something that he doesn't really believe:

'*Now I aim to quit and a good part of it is knowin that I wont be called on to hunt this man. I reckon he's a man*' (p. 282). The only person in the novel who has had any personal acquaintance with Chigurh, his erstwhile colleague Carson Wells, dismisses his employer's description of 'The invincible Mr Chigurh' (p. 140), insisting that he is 'a psychopathic killer', of whom there are 'plenty . . . around' (p. 141). Yet, when pressed, Wells concedes that Chigurh is 'a peculiar man' with 'principles . . . that transcend money or drugs or anything like that' (p. 153). In fact, it is Chigurh's peculiarity that posed the greatest problem for the Coen brothers in their translation of McCarthy's novel to the screen.

Although Javier Bardem won an Oscar in the Best Supporting Actor rather than Best Actor category, his performance as Chigurh dominates the film, just as his features, superimposed over the skyline like a vengeful deity, loom large in the poster used to advertise the film and on the cover of the Picador paperback released to coincide with it. This image cleverly captures both the apparent omniscience of Chigurh (his eyes look down from the sky at the figure of Moss fleeing with the bag of drug money) and his elusiveness (his nose and eyes are clearly visible, but his other features blur into the background) – qualities that characterise Chigurh in the novel and that the film strives to replicate. In spite of Bardem's chilling performance and the best efforts of the Coen brothers, however, Chigurh becomes more human (and hence less mysterious) in the film. This is partly the inevitable consequence of the process of adapting fiction for the cinema in which a faceless and bodiless character, imagined differently by each reader, is represented by, and becomes identified with, a particular actor. This disjunction between book and film is exacerbated in the case of Chigurh, however, because of the narrator's reticence (as noted before) when it comes to describing his appearance. In this respect, McCarthy adopts the strategy recommended by Henry James in his Preface to *The Turn of the Screw* published in the New York edition of his complete works in 1908–9: 'Make the reader *think* the evil, make him think it for himself, and you are released from all weak specifications.'[24] This was not an option for the Coens; they had to cast someone in the role of Chigurh and, in doing so, embody the evil that in the book is incorporeal.

There are also a number of changes that the film makes which serve further to demystify Chigurh. In the book, for example, Chigurh first appears in the deputy's office of his own volition: the deputy tells Lamar, his superior, that he '[j]ust walked in the door' (p. 5). In the film, we are shown the deputy driving a handcuffed Chigurh back to the station in a police car, though the circumstances of his arrest remain obscure. In the film, when Chigurh kills the (unnamed) businessman who had hired Wells to kill him, there are no witnesses and he manages to shoot the businessman even though he is armed and waiting for him. In the film, he takes the man by surprise and kills him in the presence of another man. When this bystander asks Chigurh if he intends to kill him too, Chigurh replies: 'That depends. Do you see me?' and then leaves him unharmed. Finally, in the book, when Chigurh goes to kill Moss's widow, Carla Jean, and tells her to 'call' the coin that he tosses to determine whether or not he will kill her, although she initially demurs, saying 'God would not want me to do that' (p. 258), she gives in and guesses, incorrectly, that the coin has landed on 'heads'. In the film, however, she simply refuses to 'call' the toss. These are minor changes, but in each case they diminish Chigurh's power. Because we first see him having been arrested, it is not clear in the film, as it is in the book, that he has deliberately allowed himself to be apprehended. Allowing someone to witness him murdering the businessman, yet live, makes the film Chigurh more merciful – and fallible – than the Chigurh of the book and the fact that the businessman is entirely unprepared for Chigurh's entrance makes the ease with which Chigurh carries out his execution easier to account for than in the book. The fact that that he cannot compel Carla Jean in the film to cooperate with his coin-tossing ritual makes her seem more heroic than she does in the book, and Chigurh less omnipotent.

If in the film Chigurh is more psychopathic killer than irresistible force of nature, he is at the same time more prominent in the film than the book. I have already commented on the perversity of the decision to confer on Bardem the award for 'Best Supporting Actor' (as opposed to 'Best Actor'), but to a reader of the novel his inclusion in the former category makes more sense. I began this discussion of *No Country for Old Men* by noting that the book has three protagonists: Chigurh, Bell and Moss. However, these three don't enjoy strictly equal status in the book. Bell arguably has a greater claim than the other two to be the hero of the novel, both because he occupies the moral high ground and because he shares narrating duties with an unnamed third-person narrator. Then again, he is usually at the periphery of the action, lagging behind Moss and Chigurh. In contrast Moss is, until his abrupt death more than two-thirds of the way into the book, very much at the centre of the action and conforms in many ways to the profile of the conventional hero. It is his moral dilemmas (whether or not to take the money in the first instance, whether or not to return to the floodplain later to take water to the man whose request for it he had initially ignored) that involve the reader most urgently, and it is his decisions (to take the money and to return with the water later) that sets the chain of events with which the rest of the novel is concerned in motion.

The manner in which Moss's death is dealt with, however, undermines his case to be regarded as the central figure in the novel. Rather than directly relating the circumstances of his demise, the third-person narrator reports them third-hand, through the account of the local sheriff, a friend of Bell's, who in turn is reporting the account of an unnamed witness. In fact, it becomes clear that the male fatality of the shooting that Bell hears about is Moss only when Bell, acting on a hunch, goes to the morgue and identifies him. Like the death of George Osborne in *Vanity Fair* (who had, until that point, seemed likely to be the hero, albeit a rather unsympathetic one), reported with calculated casualness at the end of a long description of the British triumph at Waterloo, the bathos of Moss's death might be read as an ironic judgement on his complacent belief in his ability to determine his own fate.[25] When Chigurh warns him that he cannot save himself and gives him the opportunity to spare Carla Jean if he agrees to give him the money, Moss tells him: 'I'm goin to bring you somethin all right . . . I've decided to make you a special project of mine' (pp. 184–5).

Again, however, the film subtly alters the narrative of the book by allowing Bell (and the viewer) to see the dead bodies of Moss and a woman staying at the same hotel moments after they have been killed, rather than hearing about their deaths from another law enforcement officer, as he does in the book (and not in fact knowing that they are the victims of the incident that is described until Bell's visit to the morgue).[26] Although Moss's death is likely still to seem shocking and premature to the viewer of the film who has perhaps assumed (or hoped) that Moss might be given a happy ending and allowed to escape with the drug money, it is nonetheless given greater dramatic prominence than in the book.

However, the most important difference, in narrative terms, between the book and film is the strong presence in the former and relative absence in the latter of Bell's voice. Bell is ostensibly ill-suited to the narrative duties with which McCarthy entrusts him. At times he can seem like a grumpy old man, garrulous with gripes about the decline of American values but perversely reticent about his private life. His narrative is defined as much by its omissions – *'We lost a girl but I won't talk about that'* (p. 90); *'I won't talk about the war neither'* (p. 195); *'I have not said much about my father and I know I have not done him justice'* (p, 308) – as by its disclosures; he often tells us that he has thought deeply about something or other but does not always divulge these thoughts. Yet in spite – or perhaps because – of these flaws, Bell is an endearing figure, the moral centre of an otherwise chillingly amoral world. The humanity of his voice provides a necessary counterpoint to the appalling inhumanity of Chigurh's actions – a counterpoint that, in spite of the incorporation of some of his comments in the dialogue, and others in the voice-over that opens the film, is not as vividly articulated in the Coens' film.

The Bell of the film is also represented as more of an anachronism than is the case in the book. Whereas the first line of Cormac McCarthy's novel, *'I sent one boy to the gas chamber at Huntsville'* (p. 3), immediately confronts readers with the brutality of the world in which Sheriff Bell operates and with the moral compromises that this world has forced him to make, the opening line of the Coens' film, spoken in voice-over by Tommy Lee Jones, playing the part of Bell, *'I was sheriff of this county when I was twenty-five'* (which in the book appears at the start of Chapter 4, p. 90), places more emphasis on the nostalgic side of Bell's retrospection. He is, from the outset, more unequivocally the old man of the title in the film than in the book. Old man or not, there is something genuinely heroic about Bell's (doomed) attempts to arrest Chigurh and protect Moss. Bell is in this sense an old-style sheriff, a stoical hero in the mould of many sheriffs of Western novels and films, a lone upholder of justice in a lawless world. Yet he is also radically different from the kind of square-jawed saviours of communities played by John Wayne. The revelation of his abandonment (by his own account) of his platoon during the Second World War and his prudent refusal to confront Chigurh alone when he gets the chance (both episodes omitted from the film) are the actions of a man whose bravery, considerable though it is, never trumps his instinct for self-preservation.

CONCLUSION

The fiction of McCarthy, Frazier and Proulx is, in most respects, more generically subversive than the film versions of their narratives by Minghella, Lee and the Coen brothers. As their titles suggest (invoking the mountain and the country as metonyms for the semi-mythical landscape of the West), the stories *Cold Mountain*, 'Brokeback Mountain' and *No Country for Old Men* are all, in a sense, versions of that old Hollywood staple, the Western. Whereas in their published versions these stories deconstruct the genre, becoming in effect anti-Westerns, in their film adaptations they conform more closely to the conventions established by the great Westerns of the Hollywood tradition. Indeed, one of the attractions for the directors of the films was clearly to make their mark in this tradition. All three had track records that made them eminently well-qualified to take on this task: Minghella and Lee had both achieved critical and commercial success for previous adaptations of contemporary North American fiction (Minghella won the Best Director Oscar for his version of the Canadian author Michael Ondaatje's novel *The English Patient* (1996) and Lee's film of American novelist Rick Moody's *The Ice Storm* (1997), although initially given only a limited release, became a big hit when released on DVD and received excellent reviews), while the Coens had received critical acclaim and acquired a cult following for their darkly humorous treatment of the crime thriller genre in films such as *Fargo* (1996) and *The Big Lebowski* (1998). So it should be no surprise that the films *Cold Mountain*, *Brokeback Mountain* and *No Country for Old Men* are all accomplished works which garnered a total of twenty-three Academy Award nominations.

They are all, however, formally less challenging than the texts they are adapting. In a highly critical review of Lee's film, Gary Indiana accused him of 'overt pandering to Rousseauian notions of the American West and its insularity, the toughness and self-sufficiency of its tight-lipped, xenophobic denizens, its rituals of faith and patriotism . . . its quasi-mystical connection to harvest, soil, livestock, and weather', while J. Hoberman, Indiana's colleague at the *Village Voice*, sardonically described the opening section of the film as 'a boy's-life Eden, camping out in a tent under the stars'.[27] Indiana and Hoberman are rather ungenerous, I think, to what is a very moving film distinguished by an extraordinary performance by the late Heath Ledger, but they are right to identify a romanticising of the landscape – and, by implication, of the relationship between the two men who become an integral part of it – in Lee's film that is not there in Proulx's story. Faithful though Lee is to the spirit of Proulx's story, he cannot resist celebrating the landscape in a manner reminiscent of the great epic Western films. Minghella's *Cold Mountain* also employs lyrical cinematography as one of a series of strategies that ensure that his film satisfies the romantic expectations of its audience in ways that Frazier's book conspicuously refuses to. Finally, the Coen brothers' *No Country for Old Men*, though it no more partakes of the pastoral than McCarthy's novel, nonetheless smoothes some of its rough edges, making Chigurh less mysterious, Moss less central and Bell less complex than they are in the original.

There is a moment in Frazier's *Cold Mountain* in which the narrator describes the super-sensitivity to her environment enjoyed by Ruby, and Ada's desire to emulate it:

> Ada did not yet have those answers [to questions about the workings of nature], but she could feel them coming, and Ruby was her principal text. During the daily rounds of work,

Ada had soon noted that Ruby's lore included many imprac-
ticalities beyond the raising of crops. The names of useless
beings – both animal and vegetable – and the custom of their
lives apparently occupied much of Ruby's thinking, for she
was constantly pointing out the little creatures that occupy
the nooks of the world. Her mind marked every mantis in a
stand of ragweed, the corn borers in the little tents they folded
out of milkweed leaves, striped and spotted salamanders with
their friendly smiling faces under rocks in the creek. Ruby
noted little hairy liverish poisonous-looking plants and fungi
growing on the damp bark of dying trees, all the larvae and
bugs and worms that live alone inside a case of sticks or grits
or leaves. Each life with a story behind it. Every little gesture
nature made to suggest a mind marking its own life as its own
caught Ruby's interest. (p. 132)

This passage – which might be read as an implicit apologia for the
expansiveness of the realist novel – perfectly demonstrates the distinction between the aesthetics of fiction and film. Whereas Frazier
is happy, like Ruby herself, to dwell on details that are not germane
to the narrative of his novel – to spend time on that which is apparently 'useless' and 'impractical', on the premise that even the most
inconsequential life has 'a story behind it' – Minghella could not
afford to film Ruby observing 'all the larvae and bugs and worms'
at work, even if he had been able to do so. Just as Ruby becomes
Ada's 'principal text' (a telling metaphor here) – her authority on
the 'lore' and laws of nature – so the text of *Cold Mountain* can
function in this way for its readers. Minghella's film, on the other
hand, must maintain the momentum of its storyline, in which
nature always plays a symbolic role.

In a BBC *Omnibus* programme devoted to Proulx, she revealed
that as part of her research for her books she paints watercolours of
the landscapes in which they are set in order to try to capture 'an
intense absorption of everything that's going on: the sound of the
wind, the movement of the clouds, the temperature of the air, foot-
prints in the dust, what vehicles people drive and what's in those
vehicles besides the people themselves'.[28] Compare this desire to
register all the vibrations of the natural world with Lee's ingenuous

confession that 'the American West really attracts me because it's romantic' and you have, in microcosm, the difference between the film and text of 'Brokeback Mountain'.

Although it is a novel with a bewildering body count, *No Country for Old Men* is also punctuated by moments of quiet contemplation. At the start of the novel Bell confesses that he '*thought about it* [what he might have said to the boy whose execution he attended] *a good deal*' (p. 4); towards the end, he returns to the scene of the gunfight where Moss found the briefcase full of money and '*stood out there a long time and . . . thought about things*' (p. 284). When Moss first encounters the carnage in the desert, he 'stood there thinking' for some time (p. 15); after his first encounter with Chigurh, having checked into a new hotel room, he 'sat on the bed thinking things over' (p. 107); less than a page later, McCarthy reiterates that he 'thought about a lot of things' (p. 108). The Coen brothers use an image first of Moss, then of Bell, staring at a blank television screen in Bell's trailer in order to represent these moments of contemplation, but of course the camera cannot linger long on such moments. Consequently, the film of *No Country for Old Men*, in spite of its art-house touches and in common with many of the previous crime-gone-wrong narratives in which the Coens have specialised, resembles mainstream thrillers closely enough to keep happy an audience used to relentless action.

There has always been a close relationship between Hollywood and American novelists: the latter have provided a rich source of material for the studios and the former have provided work for the latter, as adapters of their own work and as writers of other screenplays. At the same time, authors whose work has been made into films have tended to be ambivalent about the results: even when they approve of the adaptation, they may find other aspects of their involvement with the film industry difficult to accept (Proulx's account of her experience of Oscar night, 'Blood on the Red Carpet', is a good example of the disillusionment that sometimes sets in).[29] In this context, there is nothing new about the relationship between contemporary American fiction and Hollywood. What is different about the world in which Proulx, Frazier and McCarthy are working, however, from that inhabited by F. Scott Fitzgerald and William Faulkner, to take two of the most famous examples of American novelists who became part of the film industry, is the way in which films and books are marketed.

It has always been the case, and remains so, that viewers of films based on books they know and like are often disappointed by them, a disappointment that may be no more than the inevitable recognition that the director's vision is different from their own. This, indeed, is the consequence of any film adaptation of any fiction, however faithful and/or successful it may be: it produces one fixed, unchanging version of a story, whereas each time that story is read, it is realised differently, in an imaginative space accessible only to the reader. For this reason, a film also alters the way in which a book is re-read, displacing subjective, individual responses with a common memory.

Given the difference in scale between the audiences who see big box office films and those who buy literary novels, however, it is more likely that a viewer of a Hollywood adaptation of a novel or short story today will read the book *after*, and as a direct result of, seeing the film, than the other way round. Sales of books that have been made into Hollywood films invariably receive a huge boost when the film is released, an eventuality for which its publishers prepare by producing new editions with an image from the film on the front cover. In this way, the book also serves as promotional material for the film, and vice versa: a symbiotic marketing relationship is created in which not only is the film an adaptation or version of the book but the book is a 'tie-in' – that is to say, another piece of merchandise – for the film. If their marketing relationship is reciprocal, however, their impact on each other's status is not: whereas a film can gain credibility from a literary work, the critical reputation of a book is rarely enhanced by a film adaptation. For this reason, many writers of contemporary American fiction continue to enjoy an ambivalent relationship with the film industry: grateful for the increased exposure and revenue that film adaptations can bring them, but concerned that their status as serious novelists may be compromised by the association.

The degree of involvement of a writer in the film-making process varies considerably – from those who sell the rights to their stories but take no interest in, and may even disown, the adaptations that ensue, to those who write the screenplays and/or act as on-set advisers for the film versions of their fictions – but in any case writers used to virtual autonomy (allowing for some editorial interventions) never exercise the same authority over films they do in their stories. On the other hand, there is no doubt that the sophisticated use of mise-en-scène, editing and new technologies, as well as other cinematic techniques, in contemporary film has influenced many modern novelists and short-story writers, so that the concessions made by authors to the other participants in the film-making process must be measured against the debts – artistic and financial – that they owe to directors, actors, cinematographers and others. Any adaptation from a text to celluloid will invariably entail the omission of certain details and amplification, or invention, of others, but a film may also 'read' a book in ways that written criticism cannot and may self-reflexively interrogate the very process of adaptation that it enacts, as in the Spike Jonze/Charlie Kaufman film *Adaptation* (2001), which brilliantly deconstructs Susan Orlean's *The Orchid Thief* (1999) and its own interpretation of it.

- Without reinstating the old hierarchy of value which automatically privileges literature and disparages celluloid, it is important to recognise the chronological primacy of the novels by discussing them in their own right, before turning attention to their second lives as films. The decisions that directors and scriptwriters take when altering the details of the source novels have generic ramifications. Film adaptations alter the way in which a book is re-read, displacing subjective, individual responses with a common memory.
- Frazier invokes the imagery and rhetoric of romance to emphasise how far removed from this idyll is the amoral world in which the novel's action unfolds. By contrast, Minghella's reinterpretation of the novel locates the narrative firmly in the cinematic tradition of the civil war romance, omitting certain episodes and adding others that change materially the substance and spirit of the novel.
- Lee's *Brokeback Mountain* sometimes struggles to do justice to the narrative subtleties of Proulx's story. It dilutes some of the solipsistic intensity of Jack and Ennis's relationship and

conforms to the elegiac tradition of the movie Western through its lyrical cinematography, rendering it acceptable to a mainstream audience familiar with the conventions of the genre. On the other hand, the greater prominence it gives to the female characters of the story, as much as the nature of the relationship between the male protagonists, makes it an unorthodox Western, one that is in some respects richer and more fully realised as a narrative than Proulx's story.

• In narrative terms, the most important differences between the book and the film of *No Country for Old Men* are their respective representations of Chigurh and Bell. A metaphysical menace in McCarthy's novel, Chigurh becomes, in the Coens' version, a more conventional kind of villain; Bell is a stronger presence in the former than the latter, partly because of the difficulty of incorporating his narrating voice into the film. In many ways Bell is in the mould of the sheriff heroes of the classic film Westerns and it is generically significant that the film omits details which complicate his characterisation in the novel.

NOTES

1. Anthony Burgess, quoted in Brian McFarlane, *Novel to Film: An Introduction to the Theory of Adaptation* (Oxford: Clarendon, 1996), p. 7. All subsequent references in the text are to this edition.

2. In the cases of *Cold Mountain* and *No Country for Old Men*, the directors are also the authors of the screenplays, whereas in *Brokeback Mountain* the screenplay was written not by the director, Ang Lee, but by Larry McMurtry and Diana Ossana (novelists themselves). While recognising the collaborative nature of the film-making process, in the discussion that follows for the sake of clarity I attribute to the three directors the role of 'author' of their respective films.

3. Charles Frazier, 'Cold Mountain Diary' (*Salon*, 1997), http://www.salon.com/july 1997/colddiary970709.html, p. 2.

4. Bill McCarron and Paul Knoke, 'Images of War and Peace: Parallelism and Antithesis in the Beginning and Ending of *Cold*

Mountain', *Mississippi Quarterly* 52:2 (1997), p. 273 (273–85). I wish here to acknowledge a debt to my colleague Pat Righelato, who generously shared with me the materials, including this article, that she had assembled when teaching Frazier's novel.

5. Ed Piacentino, 'Searching for Home: Cross-Racial Bonding in Charles Frazier's *Cold Mountain*', *Mississippi Quarterly* 55:1 (2001–2), p. 116 (97–116).

6. David Heddendorf, 'Closing the Distance to Cold Mountain'. *Southern Review* 36:1 (2000), p. 195 (188–95).

7. Martin Crawford, '*Cold Mountain* Fictions: Appalachian Half-Truths', *Appalachian Journal* 30: 2–3 (2003), pp. 182, 184 (182–95).

8. Charles Frazier, *Cold Mountain* (London: Sceptre, 1998), n.p. All subsequent references in the text are to this edition.

9. Later in the novel, Inman uses the epithet 'Ishmaelite' (after Abraham's son, who is exiled with his mother, Hagar, after the birth of Issac) to describe himself (p. 120).

10. There is, of course, also an obvious secular model for Inman's ambition to live as a recluse in the wilderness of the Appalachians: Thoreau's *Walden*, published just seven years before the start of the Civil War and a decade before Inman's desertion after being wounded at the battle of Petersburg.

11. 'Years on years they worked their way through the high meadows and mountain drainages, horse-packing into the Big Horns, Medicine Bows, south end of the Gallatins, Absarokas, Granites, Owl Creeks, the Bridger-Teton Range, the Freezeouts and the Shirleys, Ferrises and the Rattlesnakes, Salt River Range, into the Wind Rivers over and over again, the Sierra Madres, Gros Ventres, the Washakies, Laramies, but never returning to Brokeback' (p. 304).

12. Terry Gifford, 'Terrain, Character and Text: Is *Cold Mountain* by Charles Frazier a Post-Pastoral Novel?' *Mississippi Quarterly* 55:1 (2001–2), p. 94 (87–96).

13. Gifford has clearly not read the novel very attentively, as is apparent from his bizarre assertion that the epilogue to the novel 'suggests that . . . Ruby has had children with the boy who shot [Inman]' (ibid., p. 95). In fact, the father of Ruby's children is not Inman's murderer but another boy, nicknamed Georgia,

who takes refuge at Black Cove after the Home Guard shoot his companions and fellow outliers, Stobrod and Pangle.

14. Crawford, 'Cold Mountain Fictions', p. 189.

15. After a long day travelling, Monroe and Ada are trying to find Cold Mountain in the darkness, beginning to despair, when they suddenly 'came to a dark chapel on a hill above the road and a river' (p. 51). Monroe takes this as a providential sign for his ministry.

16. John Detrixhe, 'An interview with Annie Proulx', http://www.bookslut.com/features/2005_12_007310.php, p. 1.

17. Annie Proulx, *Close Range: Brokeback Mountain and Other Stories* (London: Harper, 2006), pp. 317, 318. All subsequent references in the text are to this edition.

18. Rebecca Murray, 'Director Ang Lee Talks about *Brokeback Mountain*', http://www.movies.about.com/od/brokebackmount ain/a/brokeback120605 (2005), p. 1.

19. Dextrihe interview, p. 1.

20. J. Hoberman, 'Blazing Saddles', *The Village Voice*, 22 November 2005, http://www.villagevoice.com/20005-11-22/film/blazing-saddles/, p. 2.

21. All spelling and punctuation omissions are reproduced as in the original.

22. Cormac McCarthy, *No Country for Old Men* (Basingstoke: Picador, 2007), pp. 63, 64. All subsequent references in the text are to this edition.

23. A phrase used by the contemporary American author Bobbie Ann Mason as the title of her novel, published in 1985, dealing with the legacy of the war on a Kentucky family.

24. Henry James, 'The Turn of the Screw', in *The Ghost Stories of Henry James*, ed. Martin Scofield (Ware: Wordsworth, 2001), p. 8.

25. 'No more firing was heard at Brussels . . . Darkness came down on the field and city: and Amelia was praying for George, who was lying on his face, dead, with a bullet through his heart.' William Thackeray, *Vanity Fair* (Oxford: Oxford's World Classics, 1983), p. 406.

26. The treatment of the woman is another point of divergence between book and film. In the book, she is a teenage drifter

whom Moss befriends and who becomes his Platonic companion during the days before their deaths, whereas in the film she is a woman whom he meets just moments before they are both shot.

27. Gary Indiana, 'West of Eden', *Village Voice*, 22 November 2005, http://www.villagevoice.com/20005-11-22/film/west-of-eden/, p. 2; Hoberman, 'Blazing Saddles', p. 1.

28. Annie Proulx, quotd in Julie Scanlon, 'Why Do We Still Want To Believe? The Case of Annie Proulx', *Journal of Narrative Theory* 38: 1 (2008), p. 93 (86-110).

29. Annie Proulx, 'Blood on the Red Carpet', *The Guardian* 11 March 2006, http://www.guardian.co.uk/books/2006/mar/11/awardsandprizes.oscars.2006/.

Conclusion

Any study of contemporary fiction represents a gamble: some of the investments critics make in the reputation of their chosen authors pay dividends while others depreciate over time. In the introduction to his *Contemporary American Fiction* (2000), Kenneth Millard notes that he includes for discussion only two of the forty or so writers chosen by Tony Tanner for his definitive (at the time) study of contemporary American fiction, *City of Words: American Fiction 1950–1970* (1971).[1] Between Millard's thirty authors, the eight profiled in Alan Bilton's *An Introduction to Contemporary American Fiction* (2002) and the twelve whom I discuss, there is more continuity, with Auster, DeLillo, McCarthy and Proulx featuring in all three books, but there are also a number of figures whom Millard and Bilton discuss who already seem destined for obscurity, and several of my authors whom they overlooked.[2] Any book of this sort makes an implicit case for the inclusion of certain writers in, and exclusion of others from, the canon, and making judgements on the worth of writers before their careers are over is invariably fraught with difficulties, particularly in the field of contemporary American fiction, in which new contenders for the title of Great American Novelist appear almost weekly and often disappear virtually overnight.

During the final stages of my work on this book, an excerpt from Elaine Showalter's book *A Jury of her Peers: American Women Writers from Anne Bradstreet to Annie Proulx* (2009) appeared in

The Guardian, in which she nominated nine American authors whom she argued should be included in any canon of contemporary American literature: Proulx, Jane Smiley, Gish Jen, Toni Morrison, Joyce Carol Oates, Jayne Anne Phillips, Bobbie Ann Mason, Anne Tyler and Marilynne Robinson.[3] This article followed hard on the heels of an essay by Stephen Amidon in *The Sunday Times*, written following John Updike's death, in which the reviewer speculated on whether any contemporary American novelists might, like Updike, make 'the front page of the *New York Times*' when they die. Confining himself to writers in 'mid-career', Amidon proposed six contenders: Jonathan Franzen, Michael Chabon, Jhumpa Lahiri, Dave Eggers, Jeffrey Eugenides and Jonathan Lethem.[4]

These pieces bring into sharp relief the perils of writing about a field as fluid and diverse as contemporary American fiction. The first questions that occurred to me were: Why does Showalter not include Lorrie Moore, Amy Hempel or Alison Lurie in her list? And why does Amidon omit Jonathan Safran Foer and Richard Powers? These, in turn, led to a larger question: what criteria should be used when constructing a canon of contemporary American fiction? Showalter, writing polemically about the neglect of women writers in the American canon, points out that many of the 'outstanding contemporary American writers' have impeccable 'intellectual credentials', boasting an impressive array of PhDs, MAs and MFAs' (p. 2). But is formal education necessarily a reliable indicator of likely prowess as a writer of fiction? Amidon seems more impressed by the public image and marketability of his authors than by the aesthetic merits of their work: he remarks on Chabon's 'photogenic' looks, on Lahiri's 'ability to connect with a new readership, coupled with her broad appeal to traditional book buyers' and on Eggers' creation of the 'web-savvy press', McSweeney's, which has published work by Chabon, David Foster Wallace, George Saunders, Joyce Carol Oates and Stephen King, among others (pp. 10, 11). Certainly, contemporary authors are increasingly visible, literally (both Showalter's and Amidon's articles were accompanied by photographs of each of the writers they were championing) and figuratively (through the increasingly sophisticated marketing strategies employed by publishers).

The uneasy relationship between the values informing Showalter's and Amidon's canons – crudely put, between high art and commerce – was perfectly illustrated by the furore that surrounded Oprah Winfrey's endorsement of Jonathan Franzen's *The Corrections* (2001) as one of her Book Club choices. Although initially happy enough to cooperate with the process that this involves (recording an interview with Winfrey), at some point Franzen seems to have had second thoughts, expressing anxiety about the appearance of Winfrey's Book Club logo on the cover of his book. Winfrey responded by refusing to broadcast the interview and withdrawing her invitation to Franzen to appear on her show. *The Corrections* went on to become a bestseller and won the National Book Award, so the Winfrey affair did Franzen no harm, but did highlight the compromises that writers of so-called serious fiction routinely make in order to reach a wider public. The proliferation, over the past two decades, of book clubs (in large part, it must be said, as a result of Oprah Winfrey's), book festivals,[5] book readings, book tours and book prizes have raised the profile of many authors such as Franzen, who might otherwise have only reached a very specialised, limited audience. It has transformed what used to be a largely private, virtual relationship between solitary readers and the authors of the books they read into a more public transaction, in which the writers themselves become brands that can benefit from formal celebrity endorsements such as Winfrey's, or from more informal recommendations on personal websites, blogs or Twitter. The phenomenon of the book tie-in to a film, which I discuss in Chapter 4, has also contributed to this commodification of the author.

In its own modest way, a book such as this also contributes to this process, for better or worse. Consequently, the timing of Showalter's and Amidon's interventions in the ongoing debate over the identities of the most eminent writers of contemporary American fiction naturally made me reflect on the decisions I made about which writers to include and which to exclude from this book. Of Showalter's nine writers, only three (Proulx, Smiley and Jen) feature here; only Eugenides, from Amidon's selections, makes it into this study. Of course, unless you follow the approach of Kathryn Hume's *American Dream, American Nightmare* (2000), in which she decides to celebrate what she calls 'the carnival of bustling diversity' of American fiction by discussing, albeit briefly, nearly 100 novels, there are bound to be notable omissions in any study of contemporary American fiction.[6] Rather than attempting to produce a comprehensive survey of the field, I have chosen my texts with a mixture of pragmatism and enthusiasm, which is to say I have grouped together texts I believe are worthwhile in themselves but which also shed light on each other and on a common set of ideas. It would be foolish, for example, to pretend that Powers is a better novelist than Morrison (though I would suggest that the former is underrated and the latter overrated), but in the context of my chapter on race and ethnicity I felt that *The Time of Our Singing* would be a more interesting text to juxtapose with *Mona in the Promised Land* and *The Human Stain* than any of Morrison's novels. Ultimately, all aesthetic judgements are subjective, but I am happy to stick my neck out and predict that, with the probable exception of Frazier (whose *Cold Mountain* looks like a one-off) and possible exception of Bret Easton Ellis (whose troubling *American Psycho* is bound always to overshadow his other books, not necessarily for the right reasons), all the other authors whom I write about here will continue to be read and studied for many years to come. If this book helps bring them to a wider audience, and to demonstrate some of the possibilities that their work offers for study, then it will have served its purpose.

NOTES

1. Kenneth Millard, *Contemporary American Fiction* (Oxford: Oxford University Press, 2000), p. 3.
2. Among Millard's subjects, John Dufresne, Donald Antrim, Po Bronson and Leonard Gardner look like one-hit wonders, while Bilton's inclusion of Rolando Hinojosa was either brave or perverse, depending on your point of view. Neither Millard nor Bilton discusses the work of Carol Shields, Richard Powers, Charles Frazier or Jeffrey Eugenides.
3. Elaine Showalter, 'The Female Frontier', *Guardian* ('Review'), 9 May 2009, pp. 2–4.

4. 'Who Will Fly the Flag for the Great American Novel Now?' *The Sunday Times* ('Culture'), pp. 10–11.

5. Perhaps most notably the annual National Book Festival in Washington, DC, sponsored by the Library of Congress and initiated by Laura Bush in 2001, which attracts over 100,000 people.

6. Kathryn Hume, *American Dream, American Nightmare: Fiction since 1960* (Champaign, IL: University of Illinois Press, 2000), p. 1.

Student Resources

ELECTRONIC RESOURCES

Because of copyright restrictions, there are no legally available digitised editions of contemporary American fiction.

General

American Literature on the Web
http://www.nagasaki-gaigo.ac.jp/ishikawa/amlit/#contents
The *American Literature on the Web* site is maintained by Akihito Ishikawa, Department of English, Nagasaki University of Foreign Studies, Japan. This set of American literature resource pages is mainly a collection of links to sites on the Internet, especially those dealing with American literature and its social and cultural contexts. It includes homepages and documents on over 300 authors, including some contemporary American novelists.

PAL: Perspectives in American Literature – A Research and Reference Guide
http://www.csustan.edu/english/reuben/pal/TABLE.html
On the history of American fiction, with a section devoted to the late twentieth century and postmodernism, offering information on a huge number of writers, including McCarthy, Jen and Roth, giving a list of works and a selected bibliography. There is

also an appendix which offers bibliographies on 'minorities and women's studies', such as Asian–American studies, Gay and Lesbian studies and Jewish-American studies.

British Association for American Studies
http://www.baas.ac.uk/resources/resources.asp
The British Association for American Studies provides several valuable resources for its members and others. It produces a number of its own publications, and in partnership with other organisations such as Cambridge University Press, Edinburgh University Press and Microform Academic Publishers helps in the publication of others. It has developed an invaluable database of American newspaper holding in UK institutions and there are links to this database and to several other useful resources on their website.

The Eccles Centre for American Studies
http://www.bl.uk/ecclescentre
Based at the British Library, which houses the foremost collection of American books, manuscripts, journals, newspapers and sound recordings outside of the United States, the Centre has two broad aims: to promote the Library's North American materials and to support American Studies in schools and universities. Most of its online resources are pre-twentieth century but the Centre does have some materials, particularly bibliographical guides, relating to contemporary American fiction and it also sponsors lectures and exhibitions pertaining to the field.

Individual Authors

Auster, Paul
Paul Auster: The Definitive Website
http://www.stuartpilkington.co.uk/paulauster/body.htm
A site which includes information on Auster's essays, biographical works, fiction and films.

DeLillo, Don
The Don DeLillo Society

http://www.k-state.edu/english/nelp/delillo/
A bibliography of works by DeLillo and literary criticism about
him, including an annual bibliography.
Don DeLillo's America
http://perival.com/delillo/delillo.html
A website about DeLillo, including a bibliography, biography,
pages devoted to novels, stories, plays, literary criticism, reviews,
interviews, links, events, news and more. Site established in
February 1996.

The Cormac McCarthy Society
http://www.cormacmccarthy.com/
Includes a list of works, a biography and links to some resources.

Powers, Richard
Richard Powers: American Novelist
http://www.richardpowers.net/index.htm
Among other resources, it includes a biography and lists works,
reviews, academic articles on Powers.

Roth, Philip
The Philip Roth Society
http://orgs.tamu-commerce.edu/rothsoc/society.htm
Founded in 2002, the Philip Roth Society is devoted to the study
and the appreciation of the writings of Roth. Its site includes
an extensive list of bibliographical resources, including bibliographies, book-length studies and monographs, special issues
of journals, journal articles, chapters on Roth from books of
criticism, dissertations and interviews.

ALTERNATIVE PRIMARY TEXTS FOR CHAPTER TOPICS

Chapter 1: Irony and Paradox

Eggers, Dave. *A Heartbreaking Work of Staggering Genius* (2000)
Franzen, Jonathan. *The Corrections* (2001)
Moore, Lorrie. *The Collected Stories of Lorrie Moore* (2008)

Chapter 2: Gender and Sexuality

Hempel, Amy. *The Collected Stories of Amy Hempel* (2006)
Janowitz, Tama. *The Male Cross-Dresser Support Group* (1992)
Robinson, Marilynne. *Housekeeping* (1980)

Chapter 3: Race, Ethnicity and Hybridity

Everett, Percival. *Erasure* (2001)
Senna, Danzy. *From Caucasia with Love* (1998)
Whitehead, Colson. *The Intuitionist* (2000)

Chapter 4: Genre in Film Adaptations of Contemporary American Fiction

Chabon, Michael. *The Wonder Boys* (1995); film version (dir. Curtis Hanson), released in 2000.
Eugenides, Jeffrey. *The Virgin Suicides* (1993); film version (dir. Sofia Coppola), released in 1999.
Foer, Jonathan Safran. *Everything is Illuminated* (2002); film version (dir. Liev Schreiber), released in 2005.

QUESTIONS FOR DISCUSSION

Chapter 1: 'The space reserved for irony': Irony and Paradox in Don DeLillo's *White Noise*, Paul Auster's *City of Glass* and Bret Easton Ellis's *American Psycho*

General

Do contemporary American writers fear or celebrate postmodern loss of meaning and values?

To what extent do contemporary American writers rely on their readers' sense of irony to inform readings of their work?

How do contemporary American writers, writing at the end of the twentieth century, show interest in ideas of apocalypse?

How conservative are the moral values of contemporary American writers?

Do contemporary American writers make it both imperative and impossible to infer an authorial perspective which diverges from their narrators'?

DeLillo, *White Noise*

Does DeLillo have his cake and eat it in *White Noise*, in the sense that he makes use of the same values he parodies?

How serious is the novel in suggesting that shopping and advertising have spiritual value?

What is the significance of white noise as a metaphor?

How does DeLillo use irony and black humour to unsettle the reader?

How does DeLillo's tone balance satire and encomium?

How is the narrative shaped by DeLillo's use of popular genres (e.g. the campus novel, the conspiracy novel, the *noir* novel)

Auster, *City of Glass*

How does Auster's use of style and structure communicate complexity and ambiguity?

Is less more in *City of Glass*? How effective is Auster's minimalist prose style?

How and why does Auster use recurring motifs of detachment, reticence and failed communication?

What is the effect of using characters who impersonate and replicate each other?

How does Auster use irony to unsettle the reader?

What role does digression play in *City of Glass*?

Ellis, *American Psycho*

Does *American Psycho* reinscribe or contest the hedonistic, consumerist values of Bateman's world?

James Annesley claims that 'Ellis orientates his text around an obviously moral position'. Do you see a clear divergence between Bateman's values and opinions and Ellis's?

What do Bateman's eulogies to pop music add to the meanings of the novel?

Is the misogyny some might see in Bateman's torture and mutilation of women mitigated in some way by the fact that women are not his only victims?

Is conformity something which is seen as desirable in *American Psycho*?

Is *American Psycho* a good title for Ellis's novel?

Chapter 2: Silence, Secrecy and Sexuality: 'Alternate Histories' in Jane Smiley's *A Thousand Acres*, Carol Shields' *The Stone Diaries* and Jeffrey Eugenides' *Middlesex*

General

How does the theme of silence inflect the presentation of female sexuality and gender identity in contemporary American novels?

How do contemporary American writers negotiate between public and private politics in their novels?

How do themes of secrecy and revelation emerge in these novels? What are the implications for gender politics of these themes?

What formal opportunities does female narrative perspective offer contemporary American novelists?

Smiley, *A Thousand Acres*

What are the implications of Smiley's decision to give the narrative perspective to one of the 'villains' of Shakespeare's play?

How is the narrative shaped by the tension between secrets and revelation?

'Smiley's representation of the events directly preceding the storm is one of the most effective (and affecting) episodes in the novel, because it echoes, but also amplifies and distorts Shakespeare's scene.' Do you agree?

How is sisterly love and support complicated and ultimately undermined?

In what ways does Smiley complicate the gender politics of the novel? Why?

Do you see the ending of the novel as life-affirming or as bleak as Shakespeare's play?

Shields, *The Stone Diaries*

How is the narrative shaped by shifts of perspective and the use of letters and lists?

How important is humour, and how is it used?

Does Shields 'lack a tragic register'? What elements of tragedy shape the novel?

Do you agree that the novel offers an implied feminist critique of the male authority and authorship with which history is traditionally invested?

What are the implications for gender politics of making the protagonist an 'ordinary' woman, living a life among characters who are 'basically good'?

Daisy is the narrator and protagonist of the novel, but is also strangely absent from it. How and why?

Eugenides, *Middlesex*

Do you see Cal as male or female, or both? Does it matter?

How does Eugenides enter the debate about whether nature or nurture is definitively important in the formation of sexuality and gender identity? Do you share Cal's scathing attitude to Dr Luce?

How is the novel shaped by a tension between a public, masculinist discourse and a covert, private feminist discourse?

How is the narrative shaped by the movement between Cal's family history, personal development and historical events?

How does Eugenides use dramatic irony in the novel?

How does Greek myth inflect Cal's narrative?

Chapter 3: 'Nes and Yo': Race, Ethnicity and Hybridity in Gish Jen's *Mona in the Promised Land*, Philip Roth's *The Human Stain* and Richard Powers' *The Time of Our Singing*

General

Does the ethnicity of the authors of these novels matter?

Is it possible to write about race without being racist?

To what extent are the protagonists of these novels able to redefine themselves racially, and to what extent are they unable to do so? How does language itself complicate their attempts to redefine themselves?

What are the advantages and limitations of 'yellow' and 'hybrid' as racial categories in these novels?

How do contemporary American writers interrogate and deconstruct the antithesis of black and white as a way of understanding modern race relations?

Jen, Mona in the Promised Land

How does Jen use comedy to interrogate racial categories and tensions between races?

In what ways does the characterisation of Mona allow Jen to explore anxieties about ethnic and racial hybridity?

What is the significance of the concept of 'the promised land'?

How is the narrative shaped by the relationship between Mona's feminine identity and racial identity?

At the end of the novel, Mona describes herself as 'not wasp, and not black, and not as Jewish as Jewish can be; and not from Chinatown, either.' Is this a positive resolution for her story?

Roth, The Human Stain

How does Roth complicate the issues surrounding Coleman's fall, to create sympathy for him and to force us to think about the way that multiculturalism can become a tool of intolerance?

In what ways does Roth use historical events (notably 'Monicagate') to add meaning to his narrative?

How important is it that Coleman 'passes' not as a white man, but as a Jew?

Which meanings attach to notions of purification, purity, corruption and stain?

How does Zuckerman's narration affect our understanding of the novel?

Powers, *The Time of Our Singing*

How does Powers manipulate narrative perspective and with what effect?

What is the nature of the relationship between Jonah and Joseph and how does its development from the single entity their mother calls 'Jojo' to the separate men they become as the novel progresses reflect the themes and values of the novel?

What symbolic resonances do music and colour accrue as the novel develops?

David argues that 'Race is only real if you freeze time, if you invent a zero point for your tribe'. What other meanings does the concept of time offer in the novel? Is race merely an abstract concept, as he implies?

How does Powers negotiate the tensions between blacks and Jews?

Is the ending of the novel hopeful?

Chapter 4: Contemporary American Fiction Goes to Hollywood: Genre in the Texts and Films of *Cold Mountain, Brokeback Mountain* and *No Country for Old Men*

General

What are the advantages and disadvantages of using fidelity as a criterion for criticism of film adaptations of novels?

How should filmmakers deal with such problems as narrative ellipses, elisions and ambiguities when adapting a novel for a

film? Is there a justification for changing basics of character and/
or plot to suit the exigencies of film narrative?

What advantages and opportunities does place setting offer the
filmmakers of *Cold Mountain, Brokeback Mountain* and *No
Country for Old Men*?

Frazier, *Cold Mountain*

In what ways does Frazer reaffirm and/or subvert the conventions
of romance in *Cold Mountain*?

How does Frazier use mythic archetypes (e.g. Odysseus, Cain) in
his presentation of Inman? Is he a hero or an anti-hero?

What symbolic meanings attach to the landscapes of *Cold
Mountain*?

Is Inman's death arbitrary and unexpected or predictable and, in
terms of the logic of the narrative, inevitable?

In what ways does Minghella satisfy the romantic expectations
which the source novel subverts?

Proulx, *Brokeback Mountain*

How does Proulx present the strength and fragility of the relationship between Ennis and Jack?

How does Proulx use lacunae and reticence in her writing style?

How are the dynamics of Proulx's story distorted when it is transformed from her 'little canoe' (the story) to Lee's 'ocean liner'
(the film)?

What does Lee's film offer the viewer that the story does not?

McCarthy, *No Country for Old Men*

In what ways does McCarthy evoke a sense of American national
identity in his novel?

Is Chigurh best understood as a 'force of nature' or as a character with plausible motivations? Does this vary from novel to
film?

How is heroism represented? Is there a hero in the novel or the
film?

How do Bell's narrative sections relate to the main plot of the novel? How does the film compensate for the loss of these sections?

GUIDE TO FURTHER READING

Rather than a list of all works cited, this is a guide to key secondary reading for each topic and text.

INTRODUCTION

Contemporary American Fiction and 9/11

Alex Houen, *Terrorism and Modern Literature from Joseph Conrad to Ciaran Carson* (Oxford: Oxford University Press, 2002)

Catherine Morley, 'Writing in the Wake of 9/11', in Martin Halliwell and Catherine Morley, eds., *American Thought and Culture in the 21st Century* (Edinburgh: Edinburgh University Press, 2008)

Per Serritslev Petersen, '9/11 and the Apocalyptic Enemy Within: Terrorist Scenarios in Postmodern American Fiction and Film', http://www.hum.au.dk/engelsk/naes2004/download_paper.html?ID

Transatlanticism and Globalisation

James Annesley, *Fictions of Globalization: Consumption, the Market and the Contemporary American Novel* (New York: Continuum, 2006).

David Brauner, *Post-War Jewish Fiction: Ambivalence, Self-Explanation and Transatlantic Connections* (Basingstoke: Palgrave Macmillan, 2001).

Paul Giles, *Virtual Americas: Transnational Fictions and the Transatlantic Imaginary* (Durham, NC: Duke University Press, 2002).

Paul Gilroy, *The Black Atlantic: Modernity and Double Consciousness* (London: Verso, 1993).

Heidi Macpherson, *Transatlantic Women's Literature* (Edinburgh: Edinburgh University Press, 2009).

Catherine Morley, *The Quest for Epic in Contemporary American Fiction* (New York: Routledge, 2009).

Judie Newman, *Fictions of America: Narratives of Global Empire* (New York: Routledge, 2009).

Irony

Wayne Booth, *Rhetoric of Irony* (Chicago: University of Chicago Press, 1974).

Linda Hutcheon, *Irony's Edge: Theory and Politics of Irony* (New York: Routledge, 1994).

Richard Rorty, *Contingency, Irony, and Solidarity* (Cambridge: Cambridge University Press, 1993).

Gender and Sexuality

Ann Brooks, *Postfeminisms: Feminism, Cultural Theory and Cultural Forms* (New York: Routledge, 1997).

Judith Butler, *Gender Trouble: Feminism and the Subversion of Identity* (New York: Routlege, 1990).

Stephanie Genz and Benjamin Brabon, eds., *Postfeminism: Cultural Texts and Theories* (Edinburgh: Edinburgh University Press, 2009).

Race and Ethnicity

David S. Goldstein and Audrey B. Thacker, eds., *Complicating Constructions: Race, Ethnicity, and Hybridity in American Texts* (London : University of Washington Press, 2007).

David A. Hollinger, *Postethnic America: Beyond Multiculturalism*, rev. edn. (New York: Basic Books, 2005)

Werner Sollors, *Beyond Ethnicity: Consent and Descent in American Culture* (Oxford: Oxford University Press, 1986).

Film Adaptation

Gary R. Bortolotti and Linda Hutcheon, 'On the Origin of Adaptations: Rethinking Fidelity Discourse and "Success" – Biologically', *New Literary History* 38 (2007), 443–58.

Thomas Leitch, 'Twelve Fallacies in Contemporary Adaptation Theory', *Criticism*, 45:2 (Spring 2003), 149–71.

Brian McFarlane, *Novel to Film: An Introduction to the Theory of Adaptation* (Oxford: Clarendon, 1996).

CHAPTER 1: IRONY AND PARADOX IN *WHITE NOISE, CITY OF GLASS, AMERICAN PSYCHO*

DeLillo, *White Noise*

Peter Boxall, *Don DeLillo: The Possibility of Fiction* (London: Routledge, 2006)

David Cowart, *Don DeLillo: The Physics of Language*, rev edn. (Athens, GA: University of Georgia Press, 2002)

John N. Duvall, *The Cambridge Companion to Don DeLillo* (Cambridge: Cambridge University Press, 2008).

Frank Lentricchia, ed., *New Essays on White Noise* (Cambridge: Cambridge University Press, 1991).

Leonard Orr, *Don DeLillo's White Noise: A Reader's Guide* (New York: Continuum, 2000)

Auster, *City of Glass*

Dennis Barone, ed., *Beyond the Red Notebook: Essays on Paul Auster* (Philadelphia: University of Philadelphia Press, 1995).

Pascalle-Anne Brault, 'Translating the Impossible Debt: Paul Auster's *City of Glass*', *Critique: Studies in Contemporary Fiction* 39:3 (Spring 1998), 228–38.

Mark Brown, *Paul Auster* (Manchester: Manchester University Press, 2007).

Brendan Martin, *Paul Auster's Postmodernity* (London: Routledge, 2008).

Aliki Varvogli, *The World that is the Book: Paul Auster's Fiction* (Liverpool: Liverpool University Press, 2001).

Ellis, *American Psycho*

James Annesley, *Blank Fictions: Consumerism, Culture and the Contemporary American Novel* (London: Pluto, 1998).
Ruth Heyler, 'Parodied to Death: The Postmodern Gothic of *American Psycho*', *Modern Fiction Studies* 46:3 (Fall 2000), 725–46.
Julian Murphet, *Bret Easton Ellis's* American Psycho: *A Reader's Guide* (London: Continuum, 2002).
D. W. Price, 'Bakhtinian Prosaic, Grotesque Realism and the Question of the Carnivalesque in Bret Easton Ellis' *American Psycho*', *Southern Humanities Review* 32:4 (Fall 1998), 321–46.
Elizabeth Young, 'The Beast in the Jungle, the Figure in the Carpet', in Elizabeth Young and Graham Caveney, *Shopping in Space: Essays on American 'Blank Generation' Fiction* (London: Serpent's Tail, 1992), 85–122.

CHAPTER 2: GENDER AND SEXUALITY IN *A THOUSAND ACRES, THE STONE DIARIES* AND *MIDDLESEX*

Smiley, *A Thousand Acres*

Susan Farrell, *Jane Smiley's A Thousand Acres* (New York: Continuum, 2001).
Tim Keppel, 'Goneril's Version: *A Thousand Acres* and *King Lear*', *South Dakota Review*, 33:2 (Summer 1995), 105–17.
Marianne Novy, ed., *Transforming Shakespeare: Contemporary Women's Re-Visions in Literature and Performance* (New York: St. Martin's Press, 1999).
Martha Tuck Rozett, *Talking Back to Shakespeare* (Newark, DE: University of Delaware, 1994).
Susan Strehle, 'The Daughter's Subversion in Jane Smiley's *A*

Thousand Acres', *Critique: Studies in Contemporary Fiction* 41:3 (Spring 2000), 211–26.

Shields, *The Stone Diaries*

Neil Besner, ed., *Carol Shields: the Arts of a Writing Life* (Winnipeg: Prairie Fire, 2003).

Edward Eden and Dee Goertz, eds., *Carol Shields, Narrative Hunger and the Possibilities of Fiction* (Toronto: University of Toronto Press, 2003).

Coral Ann Howells, *Contemporary Canadian Women's Fiction: Refiguring Identities* (Basingstoke: Palgrave Macmillan, 2003).

Alex Ramon, *Liminal Spaces: the Double Art of Carol Shields* (Cambridge: Cambridge Scholars, 2008)

Abby Werlock, *Carol Shields's The Stone Diaries* (New York: Continuum, 2001)

Eugenides, *Middlesex*

Francisco Collado-Rodríguez, 'Of Self and Country: U.S. Politics, Cultural Hybridity, and Ambivalent Identity in Jeffrey Eugenides's *Middlesex*', *International Fiction Review* 33:1–2 (2006), 71–83.

Daniel Mendelsohn, 'Mighty Hermaphrodite' (review of *Middlesex*), *New York Review of Books* 7, November 2002.

Debra Shostak, '"Theory Uncompromised by Practicality": Hybridity in Jeffrey Eugenides' *Middlesex*', *Contemporary Literature* 49:3 (Fall 2008), 383–412.

Zachary Sifuentes, 'Strange Anatomy, Strange Sexuality: The Queer Body in Jeffrey Eugenides' *Middlesex*', in Richard Fantina, ed., *Straight Writ Queer: Non-Normative Expressions of Heterosexuality in Literature* (Jefferson, NC: McFarland, 2006), 145–57.

James Wood, 'Unions' (review of *Middlesex*), *New Republic*, 7 October 2002, 31–4.

CHAPTER 3: RACE, ETHNICITY AND HYBRIDITY IN
MONA IN THE PROMISED LAND, *THE HUMAN STAIN*
AND *THE TIME OF OUR SINGING*

Jen, *Mona in the Promised Land*

Michelle Byers, 'Material Bodies and Performative Identities: Mona, Neil and the Promised Land', *Philip Roth Studies* 2:2 (Fall 2006), 102–20.

Jonathan Freedman, *Klezmer America: Jewishness, Ethnicity, Modernity* (New York: Columbia University Press, 2008).

Andrew Furman, 'Immigrant Dreams and Civic Premises: (Con-) Testing Identity in Early Jewish American Literature and Gish Jen's *Mona in the Promised Land*', *MELUS* 25:1 (Spring 2000), 209–26.

Begona Simal Gonzalez, 'The (Re)Birth of Mona Changowitz: Rituals and Ceremonies in Cultural Conversion and Self-making in *Mona in the Promised Land*', *MELUS* 26:2 (Summer 2001), 225–41.

Erika T. Lin, 'Mona on the Phone: The Performative Body and Racial Identity in *Mona in the Promised Land*', *MELUS* 28:2 (Summer 2003), 47–57.

Roth, *The Human Stain*

Julia Faisst, '"Delusionary Thinking, Whether White or Black or in Between": Fictions of Race in Philip Roth's *The Human Stain*', *Philip Roth Studies* 2:2 (Fall 2006), 121–37.

Dean J. Franco, 'Being Black, Being Jewish, and Knowing the Difference: Philip Roth's *The Human Stain*; Or, It Depends on What the Meaning of "Clinton" Is', *Studies in American Jewish Literature* 23 (2004), 88–103.

Jennifer Glaser, 'The Jew in the Canon: Reading Race and Literary History in Philip Roth's The Human Stain', *The Modern Language Association* 123:5 (October 2008), 1465–78.

Timothy Parrish, 'Becoming Black: Zuckerman's Bifurcating Self in *The Human Stain*', in Derek Parker Royal, ed., *Philip Roth: New Perspectives on an American Author* (Westport, CT: Praeger, 2005), 209–24.

David Tenenbaum, 'Race, Class, and Shame in the Fiction of Philip Roth', *Shofar: An Interdisciplinary Journal of Jewish Studies*, 24:4 (Summer 2006), 34–49.

Powers, *The Time of Our Singing*

Jabari Asim, 'The Music of Chance' (review of *The Time of Our Singing*), *Washington Post*, 9 February 2003, http://www.washingtonpost.com/ac2/wp-dyn/A26806-2003Feb4.

Sven Birkets, 'Harmonic Convergence' (review of *The Time of Our Singing*), *The New Yorker*, 13 January 2003, http://www.newyorker.com/archive/2003/01/13/030113crbo-books1?.

Rosellen Brown, 'A Clash of Cultures' (review of *The Time of Our Singing*), *The New Leader*, November/December 2002, 40–1.

Nicholas Lezard, 'The Voice of America' (review of *The Time of Our Singing*), *The Guardian*, 7 February 2004, www.guardian.co.uk/books/2004/feb/07/featuresreviews.guardianreview17/.

Daniel Mendelsohn, 'A Dance to the Music of Time' (review of *The Time of Our Singing*), *The New York Times*, 26 January 2003, http://www.nytimes.com/2003/01/26/books/a-dance-to-the-music-of-time.html.

GENRE IN THE TEXTS AND FILMS OF *COLD MOUNTAIN*, *BROKEBACK MOUNTAIN* AND *NO COUNTRY FOR OLD MEN*

Frazier, *Cold Mountain*

Martin Crawford, '*Cold Mountain* Fictions: Appalachian Half-Truths', *Appalachian Journal* 30:2–3 (2003), 182–95.

Terry Gifford, 'Terrain, Character and Text: Is *Cold Mountain* by Charles Frazier a Post-Pastoral Novel?' *Mississippi Quarterly* 55:1 (2001–2), 87–96.

Martin Heddendorf, 'Closing the Distance to *Cold Mountain*', *Southern Review* 36:1 (2000), 188–95.

Bill McCarron and Paul Knoke, 'Images of War and Peace: Parallelism and Antithesis in the Beginning and Ending of *Cold Mountain*', *Mississippi Quarterly* 52:2 (1999), 273–85.

Ed Piacentino, 'Searching for Home: Cross-Racial Bonding in Charles Frazier's *Cold Mountain*', *Mississippi Quarterly* 55:1 (2001–2), 97–116.

Proulx, 'Brokeback Mountain'

Richard Block, '"I'm nothin. I'm nowhere": Echoes of Queer Messianism in *Brokeback Mountain*', *The New Centennial Review*, 9:1 (Spring 2009), 253–78.

William Leung, 'So Queer and Yet So Straight: Ang Lee's *The Wedding Banquet* and *Brokeback Mountain*', *Journal of Film and Video* 60:1 (Spring 2008), 23–39.

Martin Mühlheim, 'Between Wild West and Pastoral Peace: Genre, Nature and the Politics of Ambivalence in Annie Proulx's *Brokeback Mountain*', in Bernadette H. Hyner and Precious Stearns, eds., *Forces of Nature: Natural(-izing) Gender and Gender(-izing) Nature in the Discourses of Western Culture* (Newcastle upon Tyne: Cambridge Scholars, 2009), 210–41.

Christopher Pullen, 'Brokeback Mountain as Progressive Narrative and Cinematic Vision: Landscape, Emotion and the Denial of Domesticity', in Alex Hunt, ed., *The Geographical Imagination of Annie Proulx: Rethinking Regionalism*. (Lanham, MD: Lexington Books, 2009), 155–67.

Christopher Sharrett, 'The Achievements of *Brokeback Mountain*', *Film International* 7:1 [37] (2009): 16–27.

McCarthy, *No Country for Old Men*

Lydia R. Cooper, 'He's a Psychological Killer, But So What? Folklore and Morality in Cormac McCarthy's *No Country for Old Men*', *Papers on Language and Literature: A Journal for Scholars and Critics of Language and Literature*, 45:1 (Winter 2009), 37–59.

Richard Gilmore, '*No Country for Old Men*: The Coens' Tragic Western', in Mark T. Conard, ed., *The Philosophy of the Coen Brothers* (Lexington, KY: University Press of Kentucky, 2009), 55–8.

Douglas McFarland, '*Remove from folderNo Country for Old Men as Moral Philosophy*', in Mark T. Conard, ed., *The Philosophy of the Coen Brothers* (Lexington, KY: University Press of Kentucky, 2009), 163–75.

Joyce Carol Oates, 'The Treasure of Comanche County' (review of *No Country for Old Men*), *New York Review of Books* 52:16, 20 October 2005, http://www.nybooks.com/authors/25.

Annie Proulx, 'Gunning for Trouble' (review of *No Country for Old Men*), *The Guardian* (29 October 2005), http://www.guardian.co.uk/books/2005/oct/29/featuresreviews.guardianreview16.

CONCLUSION

Contemporary American Fiction and the Canon

Alan Bilton, *An Introduction to Contemporary American Fiction* (Edinburgh: Edinburgh University Press, 2002).

Kathryn Hume, *American Dream, American Nightmare: Fiction Since 1960* (Champaign, IL: University of Illinois Press, 2000).

Kenneth Millard, *Contemporary American Fiction since 1970: An Introduction to American Fiction since 1970* (Oxford: Oxford University Press, 2000)

Index